Issues in Religion and Theology

6

Creation in the Old Testament

Issues in Religion and Theology

SERIES EDITORS

DOUGLAS KNIGHT
Vanderbilt University
The Divinity School

ROBERT MORGAN
University of Oxford

ADVISORY EDITORIAL BOARD

GEORGE MACRAE sj
Harvard University
The Divinity School

SALLIE MCFAGUE
Vanderbilt University
The Divinity School

WAYNE MEEKS
Yale University

JOHN ROGERSON
University of Sheffield

MICHAEL PYE
University of Marburg

STEPHEN SYKES
University of Durham

Titles in the series include:

Issues in Religion and Theology 6

Creation
in the Old Testament

Edited with an Introduction by

BERNHARD W. ANDERSON

FORTRESS PRESS | SPCK
Philadelphia   London

First published in Great Britain 1984
SPCK
Holy Trinity Church
Marylebone Road
London NW1 4DU

First Published in the USA 1984
Fortress Press
2900 Queen Lane
Philadelphia
Pennsylvania 19129

Library of Congress Cataloging in Publication Data
Main entry under title:

Creation in the Old Testament.

  (Issues in religion and theology; 6)
  Bibliography: p.
  Includes index.
  Contents: The influence of Babylonian mythology upon the Biblical creation story / Herrmann Gunkel—The theological problem of the Old Testament doctrine of creation / Gerhard Von Rad—In the beginnning / Walther Eichrodt—[etc.]
    1. Creation—Biblical teaching—Addresses, essays, lectures. 2. Bible. O.T.—Criticism, interpretation, etc.—Addresses, essays, lectures. I. Anderson, Bernhard W. II. Series.
BS651.C693 1984   231.7′65   83–48910
ISBN 0–8006–1768–1

British Library Cataloguing in Publication Data

Creation in the Old Testament.—(Issues in
  religion and theology; 6)
  1. Creation
  I. Anderson, Bernhard W.
  233.11   BT695

  ISBN 0–281–04100–8

Filmset by Northumberland Press Ltd, Gateshead
Printed in Great Britain by Richard Clay (The Chaucer Press) Ltd,
Bungay, Suffolk

Contents

Contents

The Contributors

BERNHARD W. ANDERSON, Emeritus Professor of Old Testament Theology at Princeton Theological Seminary and Adjunct Professor of Old Testament at the School of Theology of Boston University, is the author of *Creation versus Chaos, Out of the Depths: The Psalms Speak for us Today*, and the widely acclaimed *Understanding the Old Testament* (known in Britain as *The Living World of the Old Testament*).

HERMANN GUNKEL (1862–1932), the "father of form criticism," taught at the Universities of Halle (1889–94) and Berlin (1894–1907). He was a founding editor of *Die Religion in Geschichte und Gegenwart*. His religio-historical point of view marks his classic works on Genesis, the Psalms, and Old Testament eschatology.

GERHARD VON RAD (1901–71) was Professor of Old Testament at the University of Heidelberg. There he wrote his classic work, *Old Testament Theology*, commentaries on Genesis and Deuteronomy, and *Wisdom in Israel*.

WALTHER EICHRODT (1890–1978) was Professor of Old Testament and History of Religion at the University of Basel. He is best known for his *Theology of the Old Testament*.

DENNIS J. McCARTHY, S. J. (1924–83) was of late Professor of Old Testament at the Pontifical Biblical Institute in Rome. He contributed to *The Jerome Biblical Commentary* and wrote *Old Testament Covenant: A Survey of Current Opinions*.

CLAUS WESTERMANN is Professor of Old Testament at the University of Heidelberg. His monumental commentary on Genesis is to be issued in English translation. Among his many works are *Creation, Handbook to the Old Testament, The Promises to the Fathers*, and *The Structure of the Book of Job*.

HANS HEINRICH SCHMID is Professor of Old Testament at the University of Zurich. Many of his articles have been collected in *Altorientalische Welt in der alttestamentlichen Theologie* (1974). His important monographs include *Wesen und Geschichte der Weisheit, Gerichtigkeit als Weltordnung*, and *Der sogenannte Jahwist*.

The Contributors

HANS-JÜRGEN HERMISSON is Professor of Old Testament at the University of Tübingen. Among his major works are *Sprache und Ritus im altisraelitischen Kult* and *Studien zur Israel: Spruchweisheit.*

GEORGE M. LANDES is Davenport Professor of Hebrew and Cognate Languages at Union Theological Seminary, New York. He has published several studies on the Hebrew language, archaeology, and the Book of Jonah.

Acknowledgements

Hermann Gunkel, "The Influence of Babylonian Mythology Upon the Biblical Creation Story" was first published in *Schöpfung und Chaos in Urzeit und Endzeit: Eine religionsgeschichtliche Untersuchung über Gen 1 und Ap Joh 12* (Göttingen: Vandenhoeck & Ruprecht, 1895) 3–120.

Gerhard von Rad, "The Theological Problem of the Old Testament Doctrine of Creation" was first published as "Das theologische Problem des alttestamentlichen Schöpfungsglaubens" in *Werden und Wesen des Alten Testaments* (BZAW 66; Berlin, 1936 [= *Gesammelte Studien zum Alten Testament* I: 136–47; TBü 8; Munich: Chr. Kaiser, 1958]). It appeared in English translation in *The Problem of the Hexateuch and Other Essays* (New York: McGraw-Hill; Edinburgh: Oliver & Boyd, 1966). This English translation is reprinted by permission of Chr. Kaiser. Copyright © 1958 by Chr. Kaiser.

Walther Eichrodt, "In the Beginning: A Contribution to the Interpretation of the First Word of the Bible" was first published in *Israel's Prophetic Heritage: Essays in honor of James Muilenburg* (ed. Bernhard W. Anderson and Walter Harrelson; New York: Harper & Brothers, 1962). The essay is reprinted by permission of Harper & Row, Publishers, Inc. Copyright © 1962 by Bernhard W. Anderson and Walter Harrelson.

Dennis J. McCarthy, S. J., "Creation Motifs in Ancient Hebrew Poetry" is a revised reprint from *Catholic Biblical Quarterly* 29 (1967) 393–406 by permission of the author and *CBQ*. Copyright © 1967 by Dennis J. McCarthy, S. J.

Claus Westermann, "Biblical Reflection on Creator-Creation" was first published in *Schöpfung* (Stuttgart: Kreuz, 1971). It appeared in English translation as the Introduction to *Creation*, 1–15 (London: SPCK; Philadelphia: Fortress Press, 1974) and is reprinted by permission of the publishers. Copyright © 1974 by SPCK and Fortress Press.

H. H. Schmid, "Creation, Righteousness, and Salvation: 'Creation Theology' as the Broad Horizon of Biblical Theology" was first published as "Schöpfung, Gerechtigkeit und Heil," in *ZTK* 70 (1973) 1–19 [= *Altorientalische Welt in der Alttestamentlichen Theologie*, 9–30 (Zurich: Theologischer Verlag, 1974)]. It is translated by permission of the author. Copyright © 1973 by H. H. Schmid.

Hans-Jürgen Hermisson, "Observations on Creation Theology in Wisdom" was first published in *Israelite Wisdom: Theological and Literary Essays in Honor of Samuel Terrien* (ed. J. G. Gammie, W. A. Brueggemann, W. L. Humphreys, J. M. Ward; Missoula, Mont.: Scholars Press, 1978). It is reprinted by permission of the Society of Biblical Literature and Scholars Press. Copyright © 1978 by Union Theological Seminary, New York.

George M. Landes, "Creation and Liberation" is reprinted from *Union Seminary Quarterly Review* 33/2 (1978) 78–99 by permission of the author and *USQR*. Copyright © 1978 by George M. Landes.

Bernhard W. Anderson, "Creation and Ecology" is reprinted by permission from *American Journal of Theology and Philosophy* 1 (1983) 14–30 by permission of the author and *AJTP*. Copyright © 1983 by Bernhard W. Anderson.

The editor and the publishers gratefully acknowledge the help of the translators: Charles A. Muenchow (ch. 1), and B. W. Anderson and Dan Johnson (ch. 5).

ix

Series Foreword

The Issues in Religion and Theology series intends to encompass a variety of topics within the general disciplines of religious and theological studies. Subjects are drawn from any of the component fields, such as biblical studies, systematic theology, ethics, history of Christian thought, and history of religion. The issues have all proved to be highly significant for their respective areas, and they are of similar interest to students, teachers, clergy, and general readers.

The series aims to address these issues by collecting and reproducing key studies, all previously published, which have contributed significantly to our present understandings. In each case, the volume editor introduces the discussion with an original essay which describes the subject and its treatment in religious and theological studies. To this editor has also fallen the responsibility of selecting items for inclusion – no easy task when one considers the vast number of possibilities. Together the essays are intended to present a balanced overview of the problem and various approaches to it. Each piece is important in the current debate, and any older publication included normally stands as a classical or seminal work which is still worth careful study. Readers unfamiliar with the issue should find that these discussions provide a good entrée, while more advanced students will appreciate having studies by some of the best specialists on the subject gathered together in one volume.

The editor has, of course, faced certain constraints: analyses too lengthy or too technical could not be included, except perhaps in excerpt form; the bibliography is not exhaustive; and the volumes in this series are being kept to a reasonable, uniform length. On the other hand, the editor is able to overcome the real problem of inaccessibility. Much of the best literature on a subject is often not readily available to readers, whether because it was first published in journals or books not widely circulated or because it was originally written in a language not read by all who would benefit from it. By bringing these and other studies together in this series, we hope to contribute to the general understanding of these key topics.

The series editors and the publishers wish to express their gratitude to the authors and their original publishers whose works are reprinted or translated here, often with corrections from living authors. We are also conscious of our debt to members of the editorial advisory board. They have shared our belief that the series will be useful on a wide scale, and they have therefore been prepared to spare much time and thought for the project.

DOUGLAS A. KNIGHT
ROBERT MORGAN

Abbreviations

AB	Anchor Bible
ADB	Allgemeine deutsche Biographie
AJTP	*American Journal of Theology and Philosophy*
ANEP	J. B. Pritchard (ed.), *Ancient Near East in Pictures*
ANET	J. B. Pritchard (ed.), *Ancient Near Eastern Texts* (1955², 1969³)
AOT	*Altorientalische Texte zum Alten Testament*
BASOR	*Bulletin of the American Schools of Oriental Research*
B.C.E.	Before the Common Era
BEvT	Beiträge zur evangelischen Theologie
BHT	Beiträge zur historischen Theologie
BibOr	Biblica et orientalia
BKAT	Biblischer Kommentar: Altes Testament
BJRL	*Bulletin of the John Rylands University Library of Manchester*
BR	*Biblical Research*
BWANT	Beiträge zur Wissenschaft vom Alten und Neuen Testament
BZAW	Beihefte zur *ZAW*
C&C	*Christianity and Crisis*
CAT	Commentaire de l'Ancien Testament
CBQ	*Catholic Biblical Quarterly*
C.E.	Common Era
CQR	*Church Quarterly Review*
DS	Denzinger-Schönmetzer, *Enchiridion symbolorum*
ET	English translation/English translator
FRLANT	Forschungen zur Religion und Literatur des Alten und Neuen Testaments
HAT	Handbuch zum Alten Testament
HTR	*Harvard Theological Review*
IDB	G. A. Buttrick (ed.), *Interpreter's Dictionary of the Bible*
Int	*Interpretation*
JAOS	*Journal of the American Oriental Society*
JB	Jerusalem Bible
JBL	*Journal of Biblical Literature*
JNES	*Journal of Near Eastern Studies*
JSS	*Journal of Semitic Studies*
KAT	Kommentar zum A.T.

KB	L. Koehler and W. Baumgartner, *Lexicon in Veteris Testamenti libros*
KEH	Kurzgefasstes exegetisches Handbuch
MDAI.K	Mitteilungen des deutschen archäologischen Instituts Abteilung Kairo
MT	Mélanges theologiques
NAB	New American Bible
NEB	New English Bible
NIV	New International Version
NRT	*La nouvelle revue théologique*
NT	New Testament
OBT	Overtures to Biblical Theology
OT	Old Testament
OTL	Old Testament Library
PRU	*Le Palais royal d'Ugarit*
RRel	*Review of Religion*
RSV	Revised Standard Version
SBT	Studies in Biblical Theology
TBü	Theologische Bücherei
TD	*Theology Digest*
TDOT	G. J. Botterweck and H. Ringgren (eds.), *Theological Dictionary of the Old Testament*
TGl	*Theologie und Glaube*
TT	*Theology Today*
USQR	*Union Seminary Quarterly Review*
VT	*Vetus Testamentum*
VTSup	Vetus Testamentum, Supplements
WdF	Wege der Forschung
WMANT	Wissenschaftliche Monographien zum Alten und Neuen Testament
WPKG	Wissenschaft und Praxis in Kirche und Gesellschaft
WuD	*Wort und Dienst*
ZA	*Zeitschrift für Assyriologie*
ZAW	*Zeitschrift für die alttestamentliche Wissenschaft*
ZBK	Züricher Bibelkommentare
ZTK	*Zeitschrift für Theologie und Kirche*

Introduction:
Mythopoeic and Theological Dimensions of
Biblical Creation Faith

BERNHARD W. ANDERSON

The exposition of biblical creation theology in the twentieth century has been profoundly affected by two dramatic publication events that occurred in the mid-nineteenth century, indeed within a few years of each other. The first event was the publication in 1859 of Charles R. Darwin's great work *The Origin of Species*. The reverberations of this event have continued into the twentieth century, as evident from the recent lawsuit (1982) over an Arkansas law permitting the teaching of "creationism" in public schools.[1] The second event was the discovery in 1853 of the library of Ashurbanipal, the last great king of the Assyrian empire, at the site of ancient Nineveh (Kuyunjik, near Mosul, Iraq). The impact of this early venture in archaeology was like a delayed time bomb. It was not until some twenty years later that George Smith, a young Assyriologist employed as an assistant in the British Museum, came to realize that the library contained documents that relate to the biblical primeval history, including a creation story which he published in 1876 under the title *The Chaldean Account of Genesis*. The report of the archaeological shot was heard around the world, owing to the enterprising journalism of *The Daily Telegraph*.[2] The reverberations of this event have also been felt during the twentieth century, thanks especially to the monumental book on *Creation and Chaos* by Hermann Gunkel, published in 1895 under the title *Schöpfung und Chaos in Urzeit und Endzeit*, a portion of which constitutes ch. 1 in this volume.[3]

Before these events the account of creation, as formulated classic-

1

ally in the Genesis creation story (1:1—2:3), was generally accepted as both "gospel truth" and sober fact. The challenge to the traditional belief came from two sides: from the modern scientific world view and from the history of religions. The history of biblical creation theology in the twentieth century may be regarded as a response to this pincers movement, whether in defensiveness, accommodation, or retrenchment.

After decades of discussion the controversy is far from being settled. The distinguished American theologian Langdon Gilkey, who composed a major work on creation theology (*Maker of Heaven and Earth*, 1959) and who was drawn into the Arkansas lawsuit as an "expert witness," has helped us to see that the fundamental issue is the relation between scientific truth and religious truth and their respective modes of apprehension. Reflecting on the Arkansas court case, he observes that there is not only a powerful religious fundamentalism entrenched in parts of the United States but also "there is another kind of fundamentalism manifested by scientists – including some on both sides of the issue argued in Little Rock."[4]

Perhaps the time has come when the issues may be seen in a clarifying light. Today many scientists are aware of the boundaries of natural science and are not inclined to hold that the scientific method is the only approach to truth. Moreover, the history of religions has opened up mythopoeic dimensions of Scripture that enhance our theological understanding. As already observed, it was the great scholar Hermann Gunkel who, after the sensational publicity had subsided, pursued the biblical implication of the archaeological discovery at the site of ancient Nineveh. His seminal book on *Creation and Chaos* carried a subtitle that characterized the study as "a history of religious investigation," extending from Genesis 1 to Revelation [Apocalypse of John] 12. He believed that the Babylonian creation account, with its characteristic theme of the *Chaoskampf*, the battle between the creator-god and the powers of chaos, was the source of the mythopoeic imagery found in Scripture.

When Gunkel looked at the Babylonian materials, he perceived only the tip of an iceberg. Since his time, the discovery of other materials, such as the Ugaritic mythological literature in the 1920s, has widened our horizons. No longer can we view the Bible solely from a Babylonian perspective, for the *Chaoskampf* is a more ubiquitous motif, indeed one that is not only ancient Near Eastern in the broad sense but one that touches the depths of a mythical apprehension of reality found in "archaic" societies, as Mircea Eliade and others have shown.[5] Nevertheless, Gunkel's book has proved to be a major breakthrough in theological understanding. For by inviting people to read biblical texts in the light of the mythopoeic language of the ancient world, it has introduced a linguistic revolution in our understanding of how biblical language – even cosmological language – functions in various circles of tradition and in particular biblical contexts.

The myth of the *Chaoskampf* is cosmological in the sense that it portrays the origin and ordering of the world in which people live and move and have their being. Yet the "truth" that is apprehended and expressed in mythopoeic language is of a different order than the speculative thought that has dominated Western civilization. This point was made in an important book that appeared in 1946 under the title *The Intellectual Adventure of Ancient Man*. In the introduction, written by H. and H. A. Frankfurt, we read:[6]

> Myth is a form of poetry which transcends poetry in that it proclaims a truth; a form of reasoning which transcends reasoning in that it wants to bring about the truth it proclaims; a form of action, of ritual behavior, which does not find its fulfillment in act but must proclaim and elaborate a poetic form of truth.

Insofar as biblical creation texts have been cast in, or influenced by, mythopoeic language, as Gunkel rightly demonstrated, the interpreter must take two matters seriously: First, due regard must be given to the poetic character of biblical language, and that demands a refusal to let traditional doctrinal or philosophical considerations dictate the way questions are raised. Second, due attention must be given to the way the biblical language functions in its given literary contexts or circles of tradition, and that requires refusing to "use" the Bible by appealing to isolated texts in support of positions arrived at on other grounds. When these two things – poetic form and literary function – guide interpretation, it can be seen that there are various theological dimensions to the biblical creation faith, though not all need be present at one time or in one text. The task of the biblical theologian is to differentiate these theological dimensions, to notice how one or another facet receives special attention in a particular circle or stream of tradition, and finally to perceive how they are all interrelated in the final canonical Scriptures.

I *Creation of a People*

Let us begin, insofar as possible, with the earliest, and undoubtedly the fundamental, stage of Israelite tradition: the period before the monarchy.

In past decades scholars carried on a lively debate on the question as to whether Yahweh was originally a creator deity.[7] The debate was touched off in 1924 when W. F. Albright, picking up suggestions made earlier by Paul Haupt, proposed that the divine name "Yahweh" originally was a causative verb form meaning "he causes to be," and that the formula in Exod. 3:14 means "he causes to be what comes into existence." Albright maintained that the divine name, whether invoked in the Mosaic period or in the period of the ancestors of Israel, was part of a litanic formula (such as *yahweh 'ašer yihweh* or *yahweh seba'ot*), in which the ancestral god was praised as creator of the cosmos. This discussion has been advanced by Frank M. Cross who argues forcefully, on the basis of epigraphic evidence and mythological parallels, that in the earliest tradition Israel's God was described as *dū yahwī saba'ôt*, the One "who creates the [heavenly] armies." The title of Israel's God, "the divine warrior and creator," Cross maintains, "was akin to epithets attributed to Canaanite high god *'El*, namely, 'Father of the gods,' 'creator of creatures.'"[8]

This is a strong counterargument to those who maintain, under the influence of Gerhard von Rad (see ch. 2 of this volume), that originally the faith of Israel was restricted to Yahweh's historical acts of liberation and that creation in a cosmic sense was peripheral if not absent altogether at first. The argument of Albright and his followers, however, though bringing a burst of light from extra-biblical sources, suffers under the limitation of the etymology of the Tetragrammaton. It is worth noting that the context of the cryptic etymological passage Exod. 3:14–15, a *hapax legomenon* in the OT, does not deal with cosmic issues at all; there Yahweh is introduced as the liberating God rather than as the creator.[9] So we may find ourselves on a bit firmer ground methodologically by following the lead of the late Dennis McCarthy and concentrating on references to Yahweh's "creative" actions in early poetic texts.[10] In these texts we may see how Yahweh (whatever the etymology) is identified.

Of all the examples of early Israelite poetry, clearly the Song of the Sea (Exod. 15:1–18) claims the primary attention of those who seek to explore Israel's earliest creation faith. The research of Frank M. Cross and David Noel Freedman has convincingly demonstrated that this poem comes from the premonarchic period of the tribal confederacy and that, in poetic style and literary structure, it exhibits a striking affinity with Canaanite (Ugaritic) literature. The movement of the poem corresponds to the mythical drama: the Divine Warrior faces adversaries (the power of chaos), moves triumphantly to the sacred mountain (temple), and there is acclaimed as divine King over the cosmos.[11]

Clearly this poem employs the cosmological language of the ancient creation myth, the *Chaoskampf*. To be sure, Sea (*Yam*) is not the adversary of the divine warrior but is only "a passive instrument in Yahweh's control" (Cross) in the combat against Pharaoh's hosts. And yet the language, as Umberto Cassuto pointed out in his commentary on Exodus, is redolent of the ancient chaos myth, hinting that the victory was "not only a mighty act of the Lord against Pharaoh and his host, but also an act of might against the sea, which was compelled to submit to His will." So the language was interpreted, Cassuto observes, in inner-biblical interpretation and in rabbinical exegesis.[12]

The question, however, is how this cosmological language actually functions in its poetic context. There is no suggestion here of creation in a cosmic sense; rather, the emphasis falls upon the coming to be of a people. At one point the poet praises Yahweh, who "faithfully led the people whom you redeemed" (Exod. 15:13a: the verb is *ga'al*). The poet proceeds to relate that the divine warrior inspired panic in the peoples in 15:16b: "While your people passed over, Yahweh, the people whom you have created." Here we follow the translation of Cross, who construes the verb *qana* to mean "create" (cf. Gen. 14:19–20, 22), as in Ugaritic texts where this verb displays "sexual overtones" (see McCarthy, ch. 4 of this volume) of procreation. In another ancient poem, the covenant lawsuit known as "The Song of Moses" (Deut. 32:1–43), the same verb is used, along with other creation verbs, to refer to the creation of the people in 32:6b (cf. Ps. 74:2): "Is not Yahweh your Father, who created you, who made you and established you?"

These early poems belong to the Mosaic covenant tradition, whose trajectory can be traced throughout the OT – and beyond. In this circle of tradition, represented for instance by the prophet Hosea, the people are reminded of the mystery of their existence, their creation out of chaos, so to speak. Once they were "no people" (cf. 1 Pet. 2:10); but they were formed to be a people through the action of Yahweh, their "Maker" (Hos. 8:14). They are dependent on Yahweh for their very existence, so much so that betrayal of their covenant loyalty is under the curse of *lô' 'ammî* ("not my people," Hos. 1:8). This view of creation is echoed in some of the psalms, as in the Old Hundredth (i.e., Ps. 100:3; cf. 95:6–7).

> Recognize that Yahweh is God!
> He made us, and to him we belong.
> His people we are, and the sheep of his pasture.

And the view receives its consummate expression in the poems of Second Isaiah. There Yahweh is extolled as "the Creator of Israel" (Isa. 43:15; cf. 43:1a), the one "who made you, who formed you from the womb" (44:2a), "the Holy One of Israel, and his Maker" (45:11). Overwhelmed by the wonder of Israel's existence and survival as a people, this poet often turns to the ancestral traditions that stress the divine blessing of creation and fertility, evident preeminently in procreation by Abraham and Sarah as in 51:1b–2a:

> Look to the rock from which you were cut,
> to the quarry from which you were mined.
> Look to Abraham, your father,
> and to Sarah who gave birth to you.

It is especially, however, the Exodus tradition that fires the prophet's imagination, prompting a poetic identification of the passage through the Sea of Reeds with the Divine Warrior's triumph over the powers of chaos (Isa. 51:9–11). In this respect, the prophet stands in a tradition that accords with Israel's earliest poetry wherein cosmological language functions to portray the creation (or re-creation) of a people. Creation and redemption belong together, as the obverse and reverse of the same theological coin.

In one context, however, where Second Isaiah speaks of the creation of Israel (Isa. 45:9–13), using the imagery of the potter fashioning clay and of parents giving birth to a child, the horizon expands to the creation of humanity. Yahweh, "the Holy One of Israel, the One who formed him" has disposition over the people ("my children"/"the work of my hands") precisely because "I made the earth, and created humankind upon it" (45:12a). The creation of people or humanity (*'ādām*) in the broadest sense is, of course, the subject of the Genesis creation account (Gen. 1:26–27) and especially of the Paradise Story (Gen. 2:4b—3:24) where again the image of the potter is found (2:7). Even the latter story, however, highlights the social dimension of creation, as Phyllis Trible has shown in her exquisite and incisive treatment of "A Love Story Gone Awry" in *God and the Rhetoric of Sexuality*. To be sure, human beings are bound to the soil, from which they are taken and to which they return (as scientific naturalism reminds us). But the narrator also portrays the transcendence that arises from the social nature of human beings: "Ein Mensch ist kein Mensch" ("A single human being is not human at all"), as the German proverb goes. In this story, whose full meaning is given by its function within the primeval history (see ch. 9 of this volume), creation is the coming to be of 'ādām – human being that is made for community in which life is given in relation to God and in relation to the other, the partner.

II *Creation and Order*

We turn now to a second dimension of Israel's creation faith: the divine creation and maintenance of order. If the first dimension, the creation of a people, belongs primarily in the Mosaic covenant tradition, this second one, which stresses the correspondence between the cosmic order and the social order, is peculiarly at home in the royal covenant tradition. Viewed in this theological perspective, the relationship between God and the social world is not grounded fundamentally in the events of the Mosaic age, though these are not excluded, but primarily in the election of the Davidic king and the choice of Zion as the divine dwelling place. This is the theme of Psalm 78.

In 1936 Gerhard von Rad penned "The Theological Problem of the Old Testament Doctrine of Creation," in which he set forth the thesis that the faith of Israel "is based on the notion of election [of a people] and therefore primarily concerned with [historical] redemption." In this seminal essay (ch. 2 of this volume) von Rad admitted that the doctrine of creation is indeed early: it "was known in Canaan in extremely early times, and played a large part in the cultus in the pre-Israelite period through mythical representations of the struggle against primeval chaos." Israel was able, he wrote, to absorb these mythical elements; "but because of the exclusive commitment of Israel's faith to historical salvation, the doctrine of creation was never able to attain to independent existence in its own right." The independence of creation from soteriology, in his view, came into Israelite faith through the influence of wisdom – "a highly rationalised mode of speculation concerning the divine economy in this world which we may regard as being of Egyptian origin."[13]

The sharp separation of creation from soteriology, of cosmology from history – a separation which von Rad later came to qualify[14] – may find some support in Israel's premonarchic poetry such as the Song of the Sea in which, as we have seen, creation is a soteriological event: the creation of a people. Von Rad's view, however, completely ignores the new theology espoused by Davidic theologians, a theology which coexisted with, and interacted with, the Mosaic covenant tradition during the period of the monarchy. The main axis of Davidic (royal) covenant theology was vertical (cosmic) rather than horizontal (historical). According to this circle of tradition, the security, health, and peace of society depend upon the cosmic, created order, whose saving benefits are mediated through the Davidic monarch. Creation in the sense of the maintenance of cosmic and social order was "the broad horizon" that Israel shared with peoples of the ancient Near East, as H. H. Schmid has shown in a forceful rejoinder to von Rad (ch. 6 of this volume).[15] In my judgment, however, this cosmic view of creation was probably introduced into the mainstream of Israelite life and thought by interpreters who stood in the royal covenant tradition. Hence the view was not alien to Israelite faith, or a late contribution of the wisdom school, but belonged essentially to worship in the temple of Zion.[16]

One of the chief witnesses to this theological perspective is Psalm 89, a combined hymn and lament based on the premise of Yahweh's promises of grace to David (2 Samuel 7). In the past some interpreters have supposed that the hymnic interlude dealing with Yahweh's power as creator (89:5–18) was a later addition to the psalm. But when the psalm is considered as a unity, it is evident that the cosmic dimension of creation corresponds to the mundane sphere and hence provides the basis for the stability of the Davidic throne and the order of society.[17] In the hymnic passage Yahweh is praised as the Incomparable One in the Heavenly Council – the Divine Warrior who "rules the raging of the sea" and is triumphant in the *Chaoskampf*.

> Thou dost rule the raging of the sea;
>> when its waves rise, thou stillest them.
> Thou didst crush Rahab like a carcass,
>> thou didst scatter thy enemies with thy mighty arm.
> The heavens are thine, the earth also is thine;
>> the world and all that is in it, thou hast founded them.
>
> Ps. 89:9–12, RSV

In this instance, the mythopoeic language does not portray the creation of a people, as in the Song of the Sea; indeed, the psalm is silent about the Exodus tradition, the so-called saving history (*Heilsgeschichte*). The language functions, rather, to place the Davidic kingdom in a vertical, cosmic dimension. The poet announces that "righteousness and justice are the foundation of [Yahweh's] celestial throne." The Davidic rule, therefore, is related to cosmic righteousness, just as the Egyptian throne is founded on the cosmic principle of *Maat* (truth, order, justice).[18] Moreover, just as Yahweh, the Divine Warrior, is victorious over the powers of chaos, so the earthly king, the representative of the deity, will be victorious over the mythical "floods."

> My faithfulness and loyalty will be with him,
>> and in my name his horn will be exalted.
> I will set his hand against the sea,
>> and his right hand against the floods.
>
> Ps. 89:24–25

A later phase of this royal covenant tradition is found in Psalm 74, a community lament which appeals to God (Yahweh) for help in a time of historical chaos, probably after the fall of Jerusalem and the exile of the people. Here the poet uses the parallel creation/redemption verbs (*qana* and *ga'al*) – not to refer to the Exodus, but to the founding of Zion.

> Remember your community which you created in ancient times,
>> the tribe of your inheritance that you redeemed,
> Mount Zion wherein you tabernacled.
>
> Ps. 74:2

The lament contains a hymnic interlude that extols Yahweh's power as creator. It begins:

> Yet you God (Yahweh) are my King from ancient times,
>> who accomplishes salvation in the center of the earth.
> You divided Sea by your might,
>> you shattered the heads of the dragons on the waters.
> You crushed the heads of Leviathan,
>> giving him as food for desert creatures [sharks? sailors?].
>
> Ps. 74:12–14

Here the mythopoeic language functions cosmologically, for the poet goes on to speak of the creation of springs and brooks, the alternation of day and night, the establishment of the heavenly bodies, the fixing of the boundaries of the earth, and the creation of the seasons (vv. 15–17). The center, or omphalos, of the earth (v. 12) refers to Mount Zion (v. 2b), where the divine King is sacramentally present ("tabernacles"). God's creative activity, which suppliants hope to reexperience in chaotic times, is the working of salvation in Zion – that is, the restoration of the order and stability that correspond to the cosmic creation. In this cosmic perspective, Israel's creation theology, like other ancient Near Eastern views, was liberation theology. To quote George Landes (ch. 8 of this volume), it was "a freeing of the ordered cosmos from the ever present menace of primordial chaos, so that especially human social and political structures might be prevented from disintegration, the bonds of cohesion, cooperation, and stability maintained and strengthened, and continuity, social unity and solidarity ensured."[19]

The theme of divine kingship that appears in Psalm 74 in a creation context is emphasized in a number of psalms that celebrate Yahweh's enthronement as king of the cosmos. These psalms (47, 91, 93–99) are oriented primarily in the vertical axis of the relation between the celestial and mundane realms. Accordingly, mythopoeic creation language functions to show that the order and stability of Zion are established and maintained by the cosmic King, who is victorious over all powers of chaos that threaten the divine rule. In Psalm 93, for instance, the cultic exclamation that "Yahweh is King" prompts the announcement that the world is "established"; and this statement is parallel to the affirmation that Yahweh's throne, both macro-cosmically (in the heavenly palace) and microcosmically (in the temple of Zion), is founded or established from of old. The "establishing of the earth," as Theodore H. Ludwig has shown, is language that was peculiarly at home in the Jerusalem cult and has to do especially with "the ordering of the world" as a human dwelling.[20] It is appropriate, then, that psalms of Yahweh's kingship employ language reminiscent of the Canaanite myth of Baal's victory over the "sea" or "floods." "Creation of the Baal type,"[21] to use Loren Fisher's expression, is reflected for instance in Psalm 93, especially vv. 3–4 (RSV; cf. 29:10):

> The floods have lifted up, O Yahweh,
>   the floods have lifted up their voice,
>   the floods lift up their roaring.
> Mightier than the thunders of many waters,
>   mightier than the waves of the sea,
>   Yahweh on high is mighty.

In these psalms of the Jerusalem cult we find, as in the case of early poems of the Mosaic tradition, that creation and redemption are intimately related. Indeed, as Ben Ollenburger remarks in his perceptive study of Zion theology, "the notion of Yahweh's kingship was closely associated with his function as creator and defender of Israel." "These two functions," he says, "were, in fact, two modes of the same activity."[22]

It must be added, however, that these psalms display a definite cosmological interest in the sense that the cosmic order is seen in relation to the social world, that is, "the heavens and the earth" are seen to be corresponding spheres. Even when poets speak of the "foundation" of the world, the linguistic horizon at times seems to recede beyond the maintenance of order and implies the origination of the cosmos. In Psalm 96, a hymn celebrating Yahweh's enthronement as celestial king, a poet exclaims (vv. 4–5):

> Yea, great is Yahweh, who is to be praised exceedingly!
> Indeed, all the gods of the peoples are idols,
>   but Yahweh made the heavens.

Here, as in another hymn to Yahweh's enthronement (Ps. 95:3–5), the issue is not just that the world is established on firm foundations but is that of "making" the cosmos: the heavens above and the habitable earth with its waters, dry land, and mountains. In contrast to the "gods of the peoples," which are phenomena of the world and hence "idols," Yahweh is the one who transcends the world and everything in it and is acclaimed as creator in a cosmic sense.

III *Creation and Creaturely Dependence*

The discussion of creation in the royal or Zion tradition brings us close to the Genesis creation story. Before turning to that classical account, however, let us consider Psalm 104, one of the most important and exquisite creation texts in the OT. There are numerous affinities between Genesis 1 and Psalm 104, such as linguistic parallels and similarity in the sequence of events of creation. In a seminal essay the great French scholar Paul Humbert argued that both texts originally served as librettos for a festival in the Jerusalem Temple.[23]

Psalm 104 is cast in the literary form of the hymn. It begins with an invocation addressed to the poet's *nefesh* or self (v. 1a); there follows a long ascription of praise to Yahweh (much of it in participial "who" clauses characteristic of hymnic ascriptions of praise) in seven strophes which parallel essentially the sequence of creative events in the Genesis story (vv. 1b–30); and it concludes with a refrain (vv. 31–35) which echoes the initial invocation, thereby rounding off the whole. It is important to notice what is lacking in this text. There is no reference to the creation of a people; in fact, Israel is not even mentioned. Moreover, there is no reference to the social order, or to the king who mediates the blessings of the cosmic order. To be sure, at the conclusion of the psalm the poet exclaims about the glorious majesty of the Creator before whom the earth trembles (vv. 31–32) and prays that those elements ("sinners," "the wicked") that are incongruous with the created order may be eradicated (v. 34). This "eschatological" note, if it be such, is predicated on the tension between the cosmic order and the mundane order. In general, however, the psalmist's interest is cosmological, and lacks the dimension of history or even *Heilsgeschichte* found in the Mosaic tradition.[24] It is noteworthy that this psalm, in contrast to the Genesis creation story (and Psalm 8), puts all creatures, including human beings, on a plane of equality in the wonderful order of God's creation (see Ps. 104:27–30). Here one does not find the "dualism" of humanity and nature or the Creator's grant of human dominion over the nonhuman creation – views which, in the judgment of Lynn White, Jr., lie at the root of our ecological crisis.[25]

Another major difference between Psalm 104 and the Genesis creation story deserves attention: the psalmist freely uses the mythopoeic language of the *Chaoskampf*. In describing how Yahweh "set Earth on her foundations" so that "she would be immovable forever," the poet says that Yahweh overspread the earth with *tehom* (deep, abyss; vv. 5–6). The waters, however, were not passive before Yahweh as in the Song of the Sea. They offered resistance; therefore Yahweh "rebuked" them, and they "took to flight" at the thunderous command of the Creator who assigned limits not to be transgressed (vv. 7–9). Here the mythopoeic language functions, not to portray the creation of a people or a well-ordered society, but to depict the order of creation. Every creature is assigned its proper place and time, and all function harmoniously in the wondrous whole: the springs that gush forth in the valleys, the birds that sing in the branches of the trees, the cattle that pasture in the meadows and the wild goats that cling to the mountain crags, the moon and the sun that mark the times and the seasons, human beings who go forth to their labor. Moreover, to human perception this is a meaningful, intelligible order; hence in v. 24 the poet breaks out in praise to the divine wisdom that is manifest in the cosmos.

> How manifold are your works, Yahweh!
> In wisdom you have made all of them.
> The earth is full of your creatures.

In this psalm creation-faith stands by itself, without being related to redemption. Contrary to von Rad, however, this does not mean that the psalm cannot be regarded as "wholly original to Yahwistic belief";[26] rather, here we find an authentic expression of Israelite faith at a relatively early period in the monarchy. We may well suppose that it was the sages of Israel, perhaps under the sponsorship of the royal court, who mediated to the Israelite cult influences from the surrounding culture. That would account for the affinities with the Egyptian "Hymn to the Aten," and the overtones of the Canaanite myth of the battle of the Divine Warrior against Sea or the chaos monster Leviathan who, however, is demythologized into a zoological curiosity, indeed Yahweh's plaything (v. 26; cf. Job 40—41).

The hymnic praise of Psalm 104 includes theological dimensions characteristic of wisdom. Wisdom is concerned not just with the "ordered functions" of the world but, as Hans-Jürgen Hermisson has shown (ch. 7 of this volume), also with "the foundation of the orders of the world," and these concerns prompt reflection on Yahweh's creative activity in the past as well as the continuation of that activity in the present.[27] Whereas hymns in the Zion tradition (e.g., Psalm 93) tend to speak of Yahweh's creative action as being repeated in the present, as the divine King overcomes the powers of chaos, in Psalm 104 statements like "Yahweh has founded the earth" (v. 4) or "Yahweh has made the moon" (v. 19) refer to "basic data of the past: the environment of the earth, like the changing of festival times and the times of the day, has been created by Yahweh once, and once and for all."[28] The mythopoeic language, in other words, expresses a cosmological interest, not just in the order of creation but in origination. Moreover, the poetic language also indicates the contingency of the cosmos or, in theological language, the radical dependence of all creatures upon the Creator. The powers of chaos are, to speak mythopoetically, pushed back and assigned their boundaries. The implication is that if the Creator's power were suspended chaos would return. The cosmos is not an autonomous whole, governed by its own laws, but is completely dependent on the God who transcends it. Moment by moment it is held in being by the sovereign will of the Creator. Even the regularities of "nature" are not iron-bound laws but are expressions of the Creator's faithfulness and trustworthiness (cf. Gen. 8:22).

This view of creaturely dependence is expressed magnificently at the very climax of Psalm 104. The Hebrew verbs (so-called imperfects) in the climactic strophe refer to action that is incomplete, continuing, frequentive; and this meaning can be rendered into English only by using the present tense.

13

All of them [animals and humans] look to you,
  to give them their food in its season.
When you give to them, they gather up;
  when you open your hand, they are satisfied to the full.
When you hide your face, they are disturbed,
  when you take away their breath, they expire
    and return to their dust.
When you send forth your spirit, they are [re]created,
  and you renew the surface of the soil.

Ps. 104:27–30

Here the creation verb *bara'* refers to *creatio continua*. Creation is not just an event that occurred in the beginning, at the foundation of the earth, but is God's continuing activity of sustaining creatures and holding everything in being.

IV *Creation as Origination*

So far we have seen that creation theology has a special accent in particular streams of tradition that can be traced through the OT – and beyond. In the Mosaic tradition, mythopoeic creation language is used to speak of the creation of a people who are given identity and vocation. In the royal covenant tradition, the language functions to show that the mundane social order is stable and wholesome by virtue of its relationship to the created order of the cosmos. And in Israelite wisdom, initially sponsored by the royal court, the language expresses cosmological interest in God's past and present creative activity. Needless to say, these traditions, with their special theological accents, were not isolated from one another; rather, they interacted and were interrelated, as can be seen from the psalms used in worship.

We turn now to another major theological tradition: the priestly circle that gave us the Torah in final form. In priestly perspective creation initiates a dramatic sequence of divine covenants: the Noachic (Gen. 9:8–17), the Abrahamic (Gen. 17:1–21), and the Sinaitic (Exod. 31:12–17), all of which are put under the rubric of "covenant in perpetuity" (*běrith 'ôlām*), that is, a covenant that is binding and lasting precisely because it is based on God's unconditional commitment.

Interpretation of the Genesis creation story (1:1—2:3) must be governed by two considerations. First, it must be studied as a discrete literary composition with its own structure, style, and dynamic.

It is a pericope that can be excised from its present context without damage to its internal coherence and integrity. Second, this literary unit must be interpreted contextually, that is, in terms of its function in the primeval history – and indeed, the entire Torah – that has been given to us by the priestly writer. The story may have been used once in a cultic setting, possibly as a festival libretto (Humbert); but it now functions within a scriptural context, and particularly within the primeval history that moves from creation to flood (Genesis 1—9).[29]

The priestly creation story of Genesis displays some of the cosmological dimensions that we have seen in other contexts, especially in Psalm 104. God's creation, first of all, is a cosmic order, which is without blemish and is harmonious in all its parts. The verdict of the divine Artist, upon perceiving the completed whole, was "very good" (Gen. 1:31). This, however, is not an ethical judgment but an aesthetic one. "The creation in itself is then neither good nor evil," observes J. Alberto Soggin, "it is only functional, responding to what God wanted it to be."[30] In priestly perspective the ethical problem is not emphasized until the time of Noah, when God perceived that the earth was filled with "violence" (6:11–12, the priestly introduction to the Flood story). And, of course, this creation theology, with its bold monotheism, led inevitably to the question of theodicy, evident in the various expostulations with God found in the OT, beginning with Abraham (18:22–33) and including such figures as Moses, Jeremiah, Habakkuk, and Job.

Second, the Genesis story portrays the radical dependence of the cosmic order upon the transcendent Creator. As Gunkel observed in his monumental study, there are traces of the mythopoeic language of creation in this story, even though there is no *Chaoskampf.* God created out of chaos (not *ex nihilo*), as shown by the prefatory verse that portrays the earth as once being a chaotic waste: stygian darkness, turbulent waters, utter disorder. In the mythopoeic portrayal, chaos is not destroyed but is only placed within bounds, although if God so determines, these bounds may be removed, allowing the earth to return to chaos, as almost happened during the Great Flood, according to the priestly view, when "all the fountains of the great deep burst forth, and the windows of the heavens were opened" (7:11). No language could portray more powerfully the contingent character of the creation. The cosmos is not eternal and self-perpetuating, as Greek philosophers maintained; it is sustained in being by the Creator. Were God to relax this upholding power, everything would lapse into chaos.

In various ways the Genesis creation story touches contemporary concerns. The *imago Dei* introduces the issue of the relation between man and woman in God's creation, both of whom are accorded equality of status.[31] Moreover, the elevation of *'adam*, consisting of "male and female," to a position of dominion over the Creator's earthly estate raises ecological issues such as the relation between animals and humans and the use, or exploitation, of earth's resources.[32] Further, the biblical doctrine of creation has implications for liberation theologies of the Third World.[33]

Another fascinating issue is the relation of the creation story to the new vistas of science, especially in view of the apparent dominance of the so-called big-bang theory of the origin of the universe. In a flamboyant essay, produced as a Phi Beta Kappa lecture for the American Association for the Advancement of Science (1978), Robert Jastrow, himself an agnostic, dared to suggest that developments in modern astrophysics bring us close to the Genesis view of the origin of the universe in a cosmic flash. In a much-quoted passage, which has brought smiles to many, Jastrow says:[34]

> For the scientist who has lived by his faith in the power of reason, the story ends like a bad dream. He has scaled the mountains of ignorance; he is about to conquer the highest peak; as he pulls himself over the final rock, he is greeted by a band of theologians who have been sitting there for centuries.

It is undoubtedly true that the mythopoeic language of the Bible leads us finally to the mystery of the origination of the cosmos: the mystery that Job (38:4–7) was asked to contemplate: the voice out of the whirlwind asks the question, "Where were you when I laid the foundations of the earth? Tell me if you have understanding!" (38:4). In recent years this has been a difficult matter for theologians, owing in part to the lack of adequate metaphysical categories. In a presidential address to the American Theological Society in 1971, George Hendry spoke about "The Eclipse of Creation" and chided theologians, especially biblical theologians, for reducing creation to redemption or creaturely dependence and for failing to deal with the biblical witness to creation as origination.[35] At least since Gerhard von Rad's 1936 essay dealing with the problem of creation faith in the OT, theologians have retreated from cosmology. This is true of both Karl Barth and Rudolf Bultmann, two biblical theologians who stand at opposite ends of the theological spectrum.[36] Claus Westermann, OT theologian, states flatly that "the stories of the origins are concerned with the subsistence of the world and of mankind, not with the intellectual question of the origin."[37] Westermann proceeds from a phenomenological understanding of myth which is set forth in his essay included in this volume.

Admittedly, the mythopoeic language of the Bible often expresses the existential apprehension of a world threatened by chaos, of human life in its limitation, of radical dependence on divine Power(s) and the cosmic order of reality. The theological question, however, is whether the creation story of Genesis 1 is only a mythical portrayal of what always is and what is timelessly true or whether, in addition, it speaks in its own way of origination.

This problem will never be solved by concentrating on the syntax of the initial sentence of the Genesis creation story. Grammatically, some translators can argue that "in the beginning" (*běrē'shîth*) introduces a circumstantial clause that precedes v. 3, "Then God said, Let there be light!" (as in NEB and NAB), just as well as others can maintain that the first Hebrew word of the Bible introduces an absolute statement that is prefatory to the story as a whole (as in RSV, JB, NIV).[38] However, the creation verbs that are used, *bara'* ("created") and *'asa* ("made"), indicate something more than "the subsistence of the world and humankind": they connote origination. Further, if the *toledoth* ("generations") formula in 2:4a actually introduces what follows, as it does in the other occurrences in primeval history and ancestral history, then the creation story is placed redactionally before the genealogical sequence and hence is prehistorical and even pretemporal.[39] Add to this the testimony of the Septuagint, which translates the first verse as an independent statement (*en archē epoiesen ho theos ton ouranon kai tēn gēn*), and we reach the plausible conclusion with Walther Eichrodt (see ch. 3 of this volume), that the first Hebrew word of the Bible refers to an absolute beginning.[40] It was therefore appropriate for the priestly redactors to begin the Torah story with creation, the liturgical sequence found also in Psalm 136.

It is another question altogether, however, as to whether this language, which is set in a mythopoeic context and which serves a doxological purpose, is related to the scientific view of the origination of the world in a flash of light, like a cosmic hydrogen explosion, at a sharply defined instant some sixteen billion years ago. Mythopoeic language cannot be converted into scientific language any more than poetry can be reduced to prose. It is hard to see how creationists can divest the creation story of its God-centered language and can propose teaching it, theologically denuded, as an alternative to a scientific hypothesis. Mythopoeic language provides a different approach to reality via the faculty of poetic intuition or imagination. While this approach may coexist with, and even be compatible with, the scientific method with its methodological limitations, it is questionable whether the two languages say the same things. The scientist is concerned with description and control, and is neutral about meaning, while the theologian is concerned with ultimate meaning and purpose. The scientist speaks of contingency (chance), whereas the theologian perceives that the earth and everything in it belongs to God and depends upon God constantly. The scientist may speak of a first cause in a chain of events, but the theologian declares that God, who transcends the whole cause-effect scheme, created the cosmos in freedom.

In any case the creation story, which now functions within the scriptural context of the priestly Torah and especially the priestly version of the primeval history, introduces a dramatic movement toward the near return of the earth to pre-creation chaos (the *tohu wa bohu* of Gen. 1:2), owing to violence. Violence is illustrated by incorporating into the priestly history selected episodes of the Old Epic (J) version of the primeval history: rebellion in the garden, fratricide in the first family, Lamech's measureless revenge, and the strange story of the breaching of the separation of heaven and earth by the heavenly beings who seized and had intercourse with beautiful human maidens (Genesis 2—3; 4; 6:1–4). Whether the problem of violence, which raises the whole question of theodicy, is dealt with satisfactorily in this narrative, is doubtful. At the climax of primeval history, however, the story speaks of a new beginning in God's purpose – indeed, of a new creation, as evident from the recurrence of motifs of the Genesis creation story such as the wind that dries the waters so that the dry land appears and the greening of the earth with vegetation again. Thus creation has a future – one might even say, an eschatological – horizon. In the comprehensive sense, creation deals with origination, maintenance, and consummation.[41]

V *Creation and New Creation*

These are precisely the theological dimensions found in the poetry of Second Isaiah, whose proclamation draws upon all Israelite traditions and fuses them in matchless synthesis. According to this anonymous prophet, Yahweh is "the God who made all things" (Isa. 44:26), who established the earth so that chaos does not prevail (45:18), who formed Israel as a worshiping community (43:21), and who even now is beginning to create something new in human history never heard of before (48:6–7). The question, much debated in recent decades, is how these dimensions of creation theology are integrated in the prophet's message. Gerhard von Rad, followed by a number of scholars, maintains that these lyrical poems are the supreme witness to how Israel's creation faith "is brought into harmony with soteriology." Creation, in his view, has only an ancillary function in the prophetic proclamation, that is, to provide support for faith in Yahweh's saving activity.[42]

It can be readily agreed that the poet appeals to Yahweh's wisdom and power as creator in order to awaken a disheartened people to believe that they, and all peoples, have a future in the divine purpose. The question is, however, whether creation is a "subsidiary theme" or whether, as P. B. Harner proposes, it plays "a major role" in the prophet's thinking.[43] This issue deserves reexamination if creation in a cosmological sense actually was integral to Israel's faith in earlier Israelite traditions.

A starting point for study is the prophet's proclamation that Yahweh is incomparable – the unique God beside whom there is no other (45:5), the one who is the first and the last (48:12). The question, "Who is like you, O Yahweh, in the heavenly council?" which was raised in Israel's hymns (Exod. 15:11; Ps. 89:6–8), is treated in two ways by the prophet. First, the poet Second Isaiah appeals to Yahweh's saving purpose in history, though with the special nuance that no other god has been able to announce a plan in advance and execute it (e.g., Isa. 48:14–16). This argument draws deeply upon the story of Israel's life, the "former things," though the prophet insists that "the new Exodus of salvation" will completely outshine anything experienced in the past.[44] At one point the prophet portrays the redemption of Israel at the Reed Sea in the mythopoeic language of the old creation myth. In an apostrophe to the mighty arm of the Divine Warrior the poet exclaims:

> Awake, awake, put on strength,
> O arm of Yahweh;
> awake, as in days of old,
> the generations of long ago.
> Was it not thou didst cut Rahab in pieces,
> that didst pierce the dragon?
> Was it not thou that didst dry up the sea,
> the waters of the great deep;
> that didst make the depths of the sea a way
> for the redeemed to pass over?
> Isa. 51:9–10, RSV

The creation of Israel, according to the prophet, was a historical witness to what Yahweh is on the verge of doing in the present. In a context where the event of the Reed Sea is recalled, we find this oracle:

> Remember not the former things,
>> nor consider the things of old.
> Behold, I am doing [or "making"] a new thing;
>> now it springs forth, do you not perceive it?
>
> Isa. 43:18–19, RSV

The second argument for the incomparability of Yahweh is based on the announcement that Yahweh alone is the creator who brought the cosmos into being and who maintains cosmic order.

> To whom then will you compare me,
>> that I should be like him? says the Holy One.
> Lift up your eyes on high and see:
>> who created these?
> He who brings out their host by number,
>> calling them all by name;
> by the greatness of his might,
>> and because he is strong in power
>> not one is missing.
>
> Isa. 40:25–26, RSV

Admittedly, this appeal to Yahweh as cosmic creator is intended to provide support for faith that Yahweh has not ignored Israel's "justice" (40:27–31). It is striking, however, that in passages like this (see also 42:5–9, 12–13, 18; 48:12–13) Yahweh's uniqueness is based on cosmic creation, without mention of the exodus tradition.[45]

These two arguments, that Yahweh is the creator of the ends of the earth (40:28) and that Yahweh has prophetically announced his saving historical purpose, converge to support the proclamation that Yahweh is the only God, the creator and the savior, to whom all peoples should turn.

> Turn to me and be saved,
>> all the ends of the earth!
> For I am God, and there is no other.
>
> Isa. 45:22

Because human history, not only the history of Israel but of all peoples, is given meaning and direction by the transcendent God, the Holy One, there is hope for the future. Yahweh is the one

who created the heavens (he is God!),
who formed the earth and made it (he established it;
he did not create it a chaos [*tohu*],
he formed it to be inhabited!)

Isa. 45:18, RSV

This God does not say to people, "Seek me in chaos" (45:19).

Here we find a complete synthesis of the theological dimensions of Israel's creation faith. The God who Israel worships and to whom she bears witness is the creator who originated the cosmos, who maintains order in the face of threats of chaos, and who created – and now re-creates – a people out of the chaos of bondage. In a time of historical tragedy, this people was called to bear witness to the "new thing" that God creates in history and to anticipate prophetically a new creation. The theme of the new creation was further developed in Trito-Isaiah (e.g., Isa. 65:17–25) and in later apocalyptic literature. And this creation theology was transposed into a new key in the New Testament.

NOTES

1 See the various essays in *Is God a Creationist? Religious Arguments Against Creation-Science* (ed. Roland M. Frye; New York: Charles Scribner's Sons, 1983).

2 The story is told, for instance, in Reginald C. Thompson, *A Century of Exploration at Nineveh* (London: Lusac & Co., 1929) 46–51.

3 Hermann Gunkel, *Schöpfung und Chaos in Urzeit und Endzeit* (Göttingen: Vandenhoeck & Ruprecht, 1895). Some of the theological reverberations were picked up in my book, *Creation versus Chaos: The Reinterpretation of Mythical Symbolism in the Bible* (New York: Association Press, 1967).

4 Langdon Gilkey, "Creationism: The Roots of the Conflict," *C & C* 42 (1982) 108–15, quotation, 108 [= *Is God a Creationist?* 56–67].

5 See, for instance, Mircea Eliade, *Cosmos and History: The Myth of the Eternal Return* (New York: Harper & Row, 1959); also Raffaele Pettazoni, "Myths of Beginnings and Creation Myths," *Proceedings of the Seventh Congress for the History of Religions* (1951) 67–78.

6 H. and H. A. Frankfort, et al., *The Intellectual Adventure of Ancient Man* (Chicago: Univ. of Chicago Press, 1946) 8.

7 See J. P. Hyatt, "Was Yahweh Originally a Creator Deity?" *JBL* 86 (1967) 369–77.

8 Albright's position is discussed in connection with Frank M. Cross's new interpretation in *Canaanite Myth and Hebrew Epic* (Cambridge: Harvard Univ. Press, 1973) 60–75. On the question of the identification of Yahweh with the Semitic

deity '*El*, see *inter alia*, Frank M. Cross, "Yahweh and the God of the Patriarchs," *HTR* (1962) 250–59; article on *"El", TDOT* 1 (1974) 242–61; Norman Habel, "Yahweh, Maker of Heaven and Earth," *JBL* 91 (1972) 321–37; Patrick D. Miller, "El, the Creator of Earth," *BASOR* 239 (1980) 43–46.

9   In "Creation and Liberation" (*USQR* 33/2 [1978] 79–99 [= ch. 8 of this volume]), George M. Landes emphasizes this point, while defending Albright's etymology.

10   Dennis J. McCarthy, S. J., "Creation Motifs in Ancient Hebrew Poetry," *CBQ* 29 (1967) 393–406 [= ch. 4 of this volume].

11   See Frank M. Cross, "The Song of the Sea and Canaanite Myth," in *Canaanite Myth and Hebrew Epic*, 112–44.

12   Umberto Cassuto, *A Commentary on the Book of Exodus* (ET, Israel Abrahams; Jerusalem: Magnes Press, Hebrew University, 1967, the first Hebrew edition appeared in 1951).

13   The English translation appeared in *The Problem of the Hexateuch and Other Essays* (New York: McGraw-Hill, 1966) 131–43 [= ch. 2 of this volume]. Von Rad's view is expounded by Davie Napier, "On Creation-Faith in the Old Testament," *Int* 10 (1956) 21–42.

14   See von Rad's 1964 essay, "Some Aspects of the Old Testament World View," in *The Problem of the Hexateuch*, 144–65. He wrote that "we are nowadays in serious danger of looking at the theological problems of the Old Testament far too much from the one-sided standpoint of an historically conditioned theology" and ignoring "the greater part of what the Old Testament has to say about what we call Nature" (144).

15   H. H. Schmid, "Schöpfung, Gerechtigkeit und Heil," *ZTK* 70 (1973) 1–19 [= ch. 6 of this volume].

16   This suggestion was made some years ago in my *Creation versus Chaos*, ch. 2, "Creation and Covenant," esp. 60–68.

17   See Richard J. Clifford, "Psalm 89: A Lament over the Davidic Ruler's Continued Failure," *HTR* 73 (1980) 35–47; also his paper presented to the Catholic Biblical Association (1983), "Creation in the Old Testament," 10–11.

18   See H. H. Schmid, "Creation, Righteousness, and Salvation" [= ch. 6 of this volume], 105.

19   George M. Landes, "Creation and Liberation," 79; or p. 136 of this volume.

20   Theodore M. Ludwig, "The Tradition of Establishing the Earth in Deutero-Isaiah," *JBL* 92 (1973) 345–57.

21   Loren R. Fisher, "Creation in Ugarit and in the Old Testament," *VT* 15 (1965) 313–24; "From Chaos to Cosmos," *Encounter* 26 (1965) 313–24. Arvid Kapelrud questions whether Canaanite theology really deals with creation in the proper sense in "The Relationship between El and Baal in the Ras Shamra Texts," *The Bible World: Essays in Honor of Cyrus H. Gordon* (ed. G. Rendsburg et al.; New York; KTAV, 1981) 79–85.

22   Bennie C. Ollenburger, *Zion, The City of the Great King: A Theological Investigation of Zion Symbolism in the Tradition of the Jerusalem Cult*, Diss., Princeton Theological Seminary (Ann Arbor: University Microfilms International, 1983) 86–96, quotation, 96.

23   Paul Humbert, "La relation de Genèse 1 et du Psaume 104 avec la liturgie du

Nouvel-An israélite," in *Opuscules d'un hébraïsant* (Neuchâtel: Université de Neuchâtel, 1958) 60–83.

24 It is difficult to see how some scholars maintain that the psalmist's interest is primarily historical: "the coming to be of a people, not just humanity in general but Israel who invokes the name of Yahweh" (Richard J. Clifford, "Creation", 14–15); or that here "the realm of nature is subsumed to the economy of history" (Samuel Terrien, "Creation, Cultus, and Faith in the Psalter," *Theological Education* 2, 4 [1966] 117–23; quotation, 123).

25 Lynn White, Jr., "The Historical Roots of Our Ecologic Crisis," *Science* 155 (March 10, 1967) 1203–7, and ibid. 156 (May 12, 1967) 737–38. For a theological response, see my essay, "Human Dominion over Nature," *Biblical Studies in Contemporary Thought* (ed. Miriam Ward; Somerville, Mass.: Greeno, Hadden Co., 1975) 27–45.

26 Von Rad, "The Theological Problem," 140 (pp. 60–61 in this volume).

27 H.-J. Hermisson, "Observations on the Creation Theology in Wisdom," in *Israelite Wisdom* (ed. J. Gammie, et al.; Missoula, Mont.: Scholars Press, 1978) 43–57 [= ch. 7 of this volume]. See also H. H. Schmid, "Creation, Righteousness and Salvation."

28 Hermisson, "Observations," 49; or see p. 125 of this volume.

29 For further discussion of the literary structure and dynamic of this pericope, see my essay "A Stylistic Study of the Priestly Creation Story" in *Canon and Authority* (ed. G. W. Coats and B. O. Long; Philadelphia: Fortress Press, 1977) 148–62. The function of this literary unit in the final context of the primeval history is discussed in my essay, "Creation and Ecology," *AJTP* 1 (1983) 14–30 [= ch. 9 of this volume].

30 J. Alberto Soggin, "God the Creator in the First Chapter of Genesis," *Old Testament and Oriental Studies*, BibOr 29 (Rome: Biblical Institute Press, 1975) 120–29; quotation, 126.

31 On Gen. 1:26–28, see my essay, "Human Dominion over Nature"; Phyllis Trible, *God and the Rhetoric of Sexuality* (OBT 2; Philadelphia: Fortress Press, 1978) 12–23. For a challenge to the view that the Priestly story sets forth the equality of the sexes, see Phyllis Bird, "Male and Female He Created Them: Gen. 1:27b in the Context of the P account of creation," *HTR* 74 (1981) 129–59.

32 See Karlfried Froehlich, "The Ecology of Creation," *TT* 27/3 (1971) 263–76; also my essay, "Creation and Ecology" [= ch. 9 of this volume].

33 See George M. Landes, "Creation and Liberation" [= ch. 10 of this volume]."

34 Robert Jastrow, *God and the Astronomers* (New York: Warner Books, 1980) 105–6.

35 George S. Hendry, "The Eclipse of Creation," *TT* 28 (1972) 406–25.

36 The views of Barth and Bultmann, and other theologians, are discussed and evaluated in Norman Young, *Creator, Creation and Faith* (Philadelphia: Westminster Press, 1976), chs. 5 and 7.

37 Claus Westermann, *Creation* (Philadelphia: Fortress Press, 1974) 120. See Westermann's essay in his introduction to *Creation* [= ch. 6 of this volume].

38 See, e.g., W. R. Lane, "The Initiation of Creation," *VT* 13 (1963) 63–73; Bruce

Waltke, "The Creation Account in Genesis 1:1–3, "a five-part essay in *Bibliotheca Sacra* 132/525, 526, 527, 528 (1975) 25–36, 136–44, 216–28, 327–42, and ibid. 133/529 (1976) 28–41.

39   A conclusion of my essay, "A Stylistic Study," 161.

40   Walther Eichrodt, "In The Beginning: A Contribution to the Interpretation of the First Word of the Bible," in *Israel's Prophetic Heritage* (ed. B. W. Anderson and Walter Harrelson; New York: Harper & Row, 1962) 1–10 [= ch. 3 of this volume].

41   See further my essay, "Creation and the Noachic Covenant," in *The Cry of the Environment and the Rebuilding of Christian Creation Tradition*, ed. P. Joranson and K. Butigan.

42   Gerhard von Rad, "The Theological Problem," 134–37 [= ch. 2 of this volume]. For scholars influenced by von Rad, see the bibliography under Werner Foerster, Rolf Rendtorff, John Reumann, and Carroll Stuhlmueller.

43   P. B. Harner, "Creation Faith in Deutero-Isaiah," *VT* 17 (1967) 298–306.

44   For further discussion of the argument from prophecy see Bernhard W. Anderson, "Exodus Typology in Second Isaiah," in *Israel's Prophetic Heritage*, 177–95.

45   Harner, who makes this point, observes ("Creation Faith," 302) that in these passages "creation faith is so closely interrelated with the idea of the uniqueness of Yahweh that it is indeed uncertain which is represented as the basis of the other."

1

The Influence of Babylonian Mythology Upon the Biblical Creation Story*

HERMANN GUNKEL

A Genesis is Not a Free Composition by the Author

My task here is to deal systematically with the question, until now [1895] so sadly neglected, of the relationship between the biblical and the Babylonian creation accounts. To this end it appears advisable, at the outset, to ascertain what can be said regarding Genesis 1 apart from Assyriological comparisons. [A discussion between Gunkel and Julius Wellhausen is omitted. (German, p. 5.)]

When it comes to the investigation of ancient legends, one must always make a sharp distinction between the present format of the narrative and its prehistory. With regard to each of the narratives in Genesis, once the literary state of affairs has been determined, it is the task of biblical research to go on and ask the frequently much more important question of whether or not something can be said about the earlier history of the narrative in question. As it turns out, one can often establish that material of more recent date and in later recension has been transmitted to us from long before the time when the material so preserved for us was actually written down in ancient Israel. What is more, there are strong grounds for supporting the assumption of just such a prehistory for Genesis 1.

Cosmogonies such as that offered by Genesis 1 are never the

* First published in *Schöpfung und Chaos in Urzeit und Endzeit* (1895) 3–120. Translated by Charles A. Muenchow. In the interest of brevity the block quotations of biblical texts have been omitted and replaced with simple references. Gunkel's text has been abridged at points, as indicated by editorial brackets.

products of an isolated individual. They always have a base in tradition. Likewise, the first reasoned attempts at explaining the world – attempts with which Wellhausen compares Genesis 1[1] – have grown out of mythological tradition.

In the same vein, in Genesis P has not generally put down its own, arbitrary points of view. Instead, it has reworked traditional material in line with the understanding of its own era. Fortunately, in many cases we still have parallels in J and E which allow us to make this determination. However, even the statements which are unique to P offer no exception to this rule. On the contrary, in many cases P goes back to a tradition parallel to the one reflected in our Pentateuchal sources J and E.[2]

Now it so happens that the investigator of legendary material can recognize certain features which allow him to establish whether a given narrative was blended together from older strands. It is the common fate of older narratives preserved in younger form that certain features, which once had a clear meaning in their earlier context, have been so transmitted in their newer setting as to have lost their meaningful context. Such ancient features, fragments of an earlier whole, are thus left without context in their newer setting and so appear hardly intelligible in the thought-world of the narrator. Such features betray to the investigator the existence of an earlier narrative, and they even suggest something of its particular traits.

To begin with, one such ancient feature is that of *chaos*. All of the other features, which together yield the view that the present order arose through a process of "separation," are of a piece with that one ancient feature. Even Wellhausen recognizes the feature of chaos as having been handed on to the narrator. And in fact, a notion such as this one – darkness and water at the beginning of the world – belongs to mythology and cannot be viewed as the invention of an author, least of all of a person such as the author of P. Added to that are the manifold parallels from pagan creation myths, which uniformly agree with the notion that the world was once only water and darkness.[3] One can further note the names *bōhû*, preserved via the Phoenician as *Báau*,[4] and *tĕhôm*, demonstrated to be very ancient through its lack of the definite article. Even apart from these considerations, however, we can see from the writings of early Judaism – above all from Deutero-Isaiah – how the notion of *chaos* simply does not fit with the Jewish concept of a freely acting Creator.[5] If it is the case, however, that a fragment of a cosmogonic myth is preserved in Genesis 1, then it is also no longer allowable in principle to reject the possibility that the whole chapter might be a myth that has been transformed into narrative.

The "brooding of the spirit upon the waters" also becomes a consideration. This feature, too, Wellhausen correctly reckons as among the preexistent starting points of P. The *rûaḥ 'ĕlōhîm* as used in the sense here is a *hapax legomenon* in the OT.[6] The Hebrews know only of spirits that "fall" upon a man and so work all sorts of wonders in and through him. They also know of the divine spirit that brings about the secret of life in the human body. But the *rûaḥ* of Genesis 1, the divine principle imparting form to the world – which finds parallels in the Phoenician *pneuma*[7] and the Greek *erōs*[8] – is a mythological conception. [A discussion of the cosmic egg is omitted. (German, p. 8.)]

It is also relevant to note what is said of the darkness in Genesis 1. It was not explicitly created by God, but rather it was simply there from the beginning. Light is created by God in response to the darkness which, in the beginning, "was upon the face of the deep." The author also avoids calling the darkness good.[9] All of this is also to be taken as an echo of ancient mythology, and at that of a mythology which speaks of deities of light. Certainly such a thought does not stem out of Judaism, where the concept of God much more closely corresponds to the words of Deutero-Isaiah: "I form light and create darkness" (45:7).

One can also find an ancient feature in Gen. 1:12: God himself did not "create" the plants and trees of the earth, but rather the earth caused them to spring forth at the command of God. This turn of phrase is all the more noteworthy in that it has no obvious parallel in the other acts of creation.[10] One is certainly justified in seeing here a reflection of a mythological way of viewing the earth. It is easy to explain why precisely this feature has been retained: it is anchored in the view that, just as the earth once brought forth its vegetation, so it does anew each spring.

Another ancient feature resounds when the "lights" of heaven are created for the purpose of "ruling" the day and the night. We know enough about the conceptual world of ancient Israel and of early Judaism to be able to place this expression in a broad context. The stars are mighty rulers (Isa. 40:26) – the stateliest metaphor for a king is to compare him with a star (Num. 24:17; Isa. 14:12) – who exercise lordship over the earth (Job 38:33), and to whom the peoples of the earth have been apportioned (Deut. 4:19). For the Hebrews, the stars have something of a divine quality: they are called the "stars of God" (Isa. 14:13), they are even "gods" (Isa. 24:21 in conjunction with Psalm 82), or at least "sons of God" (Job 38:7).[11] These notions are attested as very old in Israel on the basis of Judg. 5:20.[12] Now of course, in Gen. 1:16–17 any such mythological view of the stars, to say nothing of actual veneration of the stars, is far removed. In v. 14 the ancient notion that the stars bring about the seasons of the year is replaced by the notion that they are merely "signs" of the same. One can thus see that the notion of the "lordship" of the stars did not spring up on the basis of Genesis 1, but rather that it here faintly reflects a final reminiscence of an astral religion otherwise long since forgotten.

A whole series of ancient features has been preserved in the story of the creation of humankind. God said, "Let us make humanity in our image, after our likeness" (v. 26). Much discussed is the question of what the plural is here supposed to mean.[13] As it seems to me, the only possible explanation is the one already advocated by the Targum of Jonathan and by Philo,[14] namely, that God here included himself among the rest of the divine beings (*'ĕlōhîm*). In other words, originally presupposed here was a divine governing assembly, a "council of holy ones" (*sôd-qĕdōšîm*; Ps. 89:8[7]), a "divine council" (*'ădat-'ēl*; Ps. 82:1), such as is also described in 1 Kgs. 22: 19–22; Isaiah 6; Job 1; Dan. 7:10; Enoch 14:22–23, Revelation 4.[15] It is against such a background that the plural at Gen. 3:22; 11:7 and Isa. 6:8 – as well as here – is to be understood.

To be sure, in an ancient and still intact story it would be simply indispensable for some word concerning the other beings with whom God includes himself to precede such a "we." However, such a word is lacking in Gen. 1:26, as well as in 3:22 and 11:7. Such a state of affairs can only be explained like this: originally the full situation was either clearly stated or otherwise obvious in all three instances, but the previously indispensable material has fallen out in the course of transmission. The reason for such a falling out is not difficult to uncover. Narratives in which other *'ĕlōhîm* appear alongside Yahweh, even if only as his servants, had a polytheistic ring to them in the ears of a later time. After the rise of Judaism, any thought of a participation on the part of the spirits in the work of creation – which is however what the original setting of Genesis 1 related – was totally unacceptable (cf. Isa. 44:24). Now if the parallel passages at Gen. 3:22 and 11:7, which lie before us in a very old setting, have already experienced the same fate, then the conclusion follows that we must assume that the original recension of Genesis 1 dates from a very ancient time indeed. Even Job 38:7, which seems very archaic when compared with the present narrative of Genesis 1, no longer recognizes the "sons of God" as participating in the work of creation but sees them only as admiring spectators. This line of reasoning is strengthened all the more through the observation that any mention of angels is lacking elsewhere in P.[16] From this it follows that P on its own would never have been led to introduce other *'ēlōhîm* alongside Yahweh.

One comes to the same conclusion when starting from a consideration of the "image" (*ṣelem*) of God according to which humanity was created. Here also the story has been obscured; we do not directly discern what this image might be. It is not the rule of human beings over the animals, which is discussed in Gen. 1:26b and which is also brought into conjunction with the human likeness to God in Ps. 8:6–9 [5–8] and Sir. 17:3ff, because this is granted to human beings after their creation through a special blessing of God.[17] On the contrary, when it is stated in 5:1–3 that God created Adam after his own image, and that Adam begat Seth after his image, and when further it is stated (9:5–6) that both humans and beast are to have regard for the likeness of God that is in humankind and are to shun from violating it, then nothing other can be meant by the word *ṣelem* than the natural and obvious: the form of the deity, which resembles the human body – by which of course the similarity on the plane of the spiritual being is not to be excluded. Such a view was hardly any longer completely obvious to the author of P; the original narrative must have expressed it much more clearly.

That such a view hardly fits in with P and its time can also be deduced from the reinterpretation of Ps. 8:6–9 [5–8] in Sir. 17:3ff. That such a view would have been impossible in Hebraic antiquity, however, cannot be maintained. Hebraic antiquity always imagined Yahweh as humanlike. The notion of the deity as a fully spiritual being, without body, would have been totally incomprehensible to the ancient Hebrew; the aversion to depicting Yahweh was based on quite different grounds. Moreover, it is in the very nature of religion, once it has attained to a certain level of development, to imagine the deity as similar to a human being. Likewise the opposite notion, namely, that the human being bears the form of the deity, is also not infrequently attested in antiquity.[18] [A discussion of Wellhausen is omitted. (German, p. 12.)]

Furthermore, the very style in which Genesis 1 speaks of humanity – the words resound almost like a hymn in praise of human being, the image of the deity and the ruler over the animals – is to be understood throughout as reflecting ancient ways of thinking. Similarly ancient is the notion that the reproductive capabilities of human beings and their mastery over the animals were granted by a special blessing of God; antiquity sees in these phenomena great mysteries which can only be explained insofar as one makes reference to a primordial divine utterance that continues to be effective down to the present time. [...]

Likewise directing us to an ancient time is the notion that God deems each act of creation to be good. Here also there lies in the background an originally strong anthropomorphism: the possibility of failure. God considers each act of creation, testing how it has turned out; he finds each to be "good," which is to say successful. These are considerations which P certainly did not come up with on its own, and which it perhaps hardly even understood. And yet, such considerations lie behind its words.

The divine command in Gen. 1:29–30 that both human beings and animals are to be vegetarian, a command that was lifted after the Flood (Gen. 9:3–4), might initially strike one as an arbitrarily contrived theory about the history of human nourishment. This impression completely vanishes, however, as soon as one compares it with Isa. 11:6–8 (echoed in Isa. 65:25). Isaiah here describes the coming time of righteousness and peace as a time when the wolf dwells with the lamb, the leopard lies down with the kid, and "the lion eats straw like the ox." Such an image corresponds exactly to that which the creation narrative presupposes. One cannot regard this description as the prophet's own production. Were it that, it would be remarkably fanciful and hardly understandable as coming from such a man as Isaiah. The image only becomes conceivable when one recognizes that the prophet here takes up and uses for his own purposes an element that was presented to him by tradition.[19] He here cites the well-known myth of the golden age. (This myth finds a much fuller reflection in Isaiah than it does in Genesis 1. In Isaiah it is a poetic description of profound content; in Genesis 1 it has been collapsed into a simple command of God.) Any lingering doubt about the validity of this line of reasoning is silenced once one recognizes that similar descriptions also appear in Greek and Persian myths.[20]

The arranging of the acts of creation over six days, and the narrative of the institution of the Sabbath on the seventh which is bound up with this schema, is generally regarded as relatively late. Some have even gone so far as to believe that this seven-day pattern was secondarily introduced into P. Certainly it is true that particular emphasis on the sanctity of the Sabbath comes especially to the fore in our sources – to be sure, very incompletely preserved with regard to this issue – subsequent to the Exile. Furthermore, the arrangement according to the acts of creation which immediately inheres in the material does not seem to fit particularly well with a schema of six days.[21] The description of the first day, when light is created, yields a particular difficulty, for how is one thereby to think of the recurrent alternation between night and day?[22] Against this background one can perhaps also explain the circumstance that, in the present narrative, the stars are created only after the earth's vegetation. This peculiar sequence, which otherwise so clearly contradicts the nature of things and which we could hardly conceive of in a unified story, can perhaps be explained as follows: the introduction of the seven-day pattern into the material left no special day for the plants, which were then assigned to the earth and so appeared before the stars. On the other hand, the Sabbath was certainly a very ancient institution in Israel, and the question about the origin of this day's sanctity can be a very old question indeed. Furthermore, the view that God perhaps not only instituted the Sabbath by a command, but that it was God who celebrated this day at the beginning of the world, certainly leads us back to high antiquity. The anthropomorphic notion that God rested after the completion of work, a notion which fits in so poorly with the views of Judaism, could hardly have been invented by P. This notion must already have existed in tradition. In the light of all this, one has no grounds for regarding as postexilic the passage in Exod. 20:11, where the institution of the Sabbath at the time of the creation is presupposed.[23]

In sum, we can catch the echoes of a whole series of mythological features in Genesis 1. From this it follows that Genesis 1 is *not* the free composition of an author but is rather the deposit of a tradition. Furthermore, this tradition must stretch back to high antiquity.

We are now in a position to recognize a part of the history of this tradition, working backward from Genesis 1. Two distinct cosmogonies have here been combined. One of them thinks of the brooding spirit as the principle behind the origin of the world, the other the commanding Word of God. At some later time, the arrangement according to seven days, including the Sabbath, was added on.

On the basis of such considerations regarding Genesis 1, then, it is quite unlikely that the tradition therein contained could have arisen in Israel. To begin with, the parallels to Genesis 1 direct attention to the cosmogonies of other peoples. Further clues in this direction can be detected in the view that the world was once composed of water. Such a view obviously arose under the influence of a particular climate. Mythology imagines that the world first arose in much the same way that it is regenerated in each new year. At the outset all is water and darkness, but then the light appears and the water gets separated, some rising to the clouds and the rest sinking to the sea. Such a view only makes sense in a land whose main characteristics are determined by large outpourings of water, where the rain streams down from the sky in winter and mixes with the terrestrial waters to form a veritable "chaos," but where also the springtime issues in a dividing of the waters above and below. This interpretation becomes a certainty when one draws on that other creation narrative for comparison, namely, the one presently bound up with the Garden of Eden story. In that latter story, the earth is originally without vegetation because no rain has yet fallen (Gen. 2:5). A variant drawn from a separate tradition, now combined with the first, reports that Yahweh caused an 'ēd (water swell [RSV: mist]) to spring up out of the earth (Gen. 2:6). Both reflect Canaanite views: the water is not the enemy that must be dispelled for the world to arise, but rather it is the friend without whom the soil would bring forth no yield. Water is the blessing of the deity.[24] It is such a view of nature that Genesis 2 characteristically reflects. In Genesis 1 the deity conquers the waters; in Genesis 2 the deity creates them. The mythology behind Genesis 2 is thus Canaanite, but that behind Genesis 1 would be totally understandable in Babylonia.[25]

In this context it is instructive to note how the ancient Hebrews and the Babylonians calculated the beginning of the year. According to ancient Hebrew tradition, the year begins in the fall; according to the Babylonians it begins in the spring.[26] In Israel, one reckoned the rainy season as ushering in the new year, whereas in Babylonia the rainy season ended the old year. Now it is in keeping with the nature of the matter that the world was created in the spring. Accordingly, in Israel one would consider water as the initial creative act of the deity, whereas in Babylonia the initial creative act of the deity would be to bring the rainy season to an end. Applying these two views to the evaluation of Genesis 1 and 2 leads to clear results: the creation narrative in Genesis 2 corresponds to the Hebrew New Year and thus shows itself to be of ancient Canaanite origin, whereas Genesis 1 corresponds to the Babylonian system of reckoning.

The other features that we have pointed out in the foregoing as remnants of primordial tradition in Genesis 1 also point to Babylonia. The positive evaluation of the light and of the "lordship" of the stars suggests an astral religion – which is what the religion of the

Babylonians is known to have been. The case is similar with the myth of the golden age, of which a final trace is presently interwoven in the creation narrative: it can hardly have been originally Hebraic. For the ancient Hebrew, sacrifice and slaughtering of animals is so intrinsically bound up with the good life, and the ancient Hebrew legends so unabashedly date the slaughtering of animals to the earliest times (Gen. 3:21; 4:4; 7:2; 8:20–21), that we can hardly regard as anciently Hebraic the delicate sensitivities that seem to find a voice in this myth.

Without making use of the Babylonian cosmogonies, therefore, we have come upon our conclusion: the creation narrative of Genesis 1, even though relatively recent in its present format, is not a free composition of its author. Rather, it goes back to very ancient traditions, whose original setting we are quite likely to find in Babylonia.

B *The Babylonian Cosmogony*

The Babylonian cosmogony is known from Greek tradition through the reports of Damascius and of Berossus.[27] [The quoted reports are here omitted.]

The reports of Damascius and Berossus (*not* of Eusebius[28]) concerning the Babylonian cosmogony are everywhere confirmed by the cuneiform writings, at least insofar as they have been recovered. Parallels have even been preserved reflecting the notice of Berossus to the effect that images of the "creatures" were to be seen in the temple of Marduk.

We are indebted to George Smith for discovering the cuneiform creation story. The account, of ancient Babylonian origin and copied by Assyrian scribes for the library of Ashurbanipal, was found in 1873 in Kuyundjik, at the site of ancient Nineveh, among the ruins of the palace of Ashurbanipal. Supplements to the original find have since been forthcoming, and more can be expected. [A paraphrase of the Babylonian creation account is here omitted.]

The explanation of this myth was initially attempted by Jensen.[29] I hereby express my indebtedness to this researcher, all the while that I attempt to modify his results from the standpoint of a religio-historical method.

The narrative is obviously an etiological myth, a myth that attempts to describe the cause of a presently existing phenomenon, that aims to give the answer to a question. The creation myth owes its existence to the question of whence come heaven and earth and the deep, gods and plants and animals and human beings. This myth is therefore related to the many etiological sagas and myths of Genesis which explain the origin of extraordinary names, of mountains and springs and landscapes, or of anthropologic and ethnologic relationships.[30] The characteristic feature of etiological myths or sagas is that they answer such questions through the telling of a story.

In relating the story of the world's origin, the Babylonian creation myth thinks of that primordial origin as having taken place along the same lines as when the world arises anew in the spring of each year. The time before the world's creation is depicted as the most terrible winter that ever was. The powers of the deep were then in control, with water and darkness everywhere, until Marduk, the god of the sun that returns in force each springtime,[31] conquered Tiamat and split her carcass into the waters above and the waters below. The notion that there were waters up above, comprising half of the slain Tiamat, arises in part from deliberations on where the rain comes from.[32] However, such a view certainly also arises from the observation that, at the end of the rainy season when water seems to be everywhere, the sun breaks through and compels the waters to separate.[33]

It is fully understandable how the myth would express the terrifying impression that winter and chaos makes by thinking of the primordial sea as swarming with dreadful monsters. This sort of view is characteristic of myth. These monsters are now the zodiacal constellations. At first glance, that might appear most remarkable. However, the fact that these monsters are thought of as constellations might well be explained on the grounds that the stars are children of the night. That they have become specifically the constellations of the zodiac might stem from the fact that these groups of stars spend half the time beneath the horizon – in the realm of the dark and watery deep. At the same time, one can think of the difference between the freely wandering planets and the zodiacal constellations which permanently remain in their places. The planets are the greater and more powerful gods; the constellations are "fettered" in their service. Along this line of reasoning, the myth relates how Marduk bound the constellations of the zodiac.[34]

It appears to be the case that characteristics of the storm god as reflected in the myth of the victory of light have influenced the scene of the battle against Tiamat, when Marduk appears with the lightning bolt. Therefore the assumption lies readily at hand that Marduk, whose typical symbol was the lightning bolt,[35] was no less a storm god than was Zeus among the Greeks, even apart from his battle against Tiamat.

At the same time, the myth answers the question of how Marduk came by his present sovereignty. Since Marduk is the god of the city of Babylon, the myth also inquires after the origin of Babylon's hegemony.[36] Along this line one comes by the hypothesis that Marduk is a relatively new god who only at a later time became the peer of his "fathers" – indeed, became lord of the cosmos. In the myth, therefore, one finds reflected the historical fact that the city of Babylon became the dominant power in Babylonia at a relatively late date.[37] In other words, in this myth we possess the specifically Babylonian account of the origin of the world. In it the Babylonians proudly relate that their own god, Marduk, is lord of all because it was he who conquered the chaos and created the world. It was at that time that the gods, meeting in formal assembly (*puḫru*), granted lordship to Marduk, and it was at that time that he stripped Kingu of the Tablets of Fate. The claim and the proper right of Babylon to rule the world thus date from the very beginning of the world!

c *Other OT References to the Chaoskampf*

1 THE DRAGON TRADITIONS

Introduction

The difference between the Babylonian myth and Genesis 1 is so pronounced, in terms of both religious attitude and aesthetic quality, that at first glance the two seem to have nothing in common. One readily understands the disinclination of those who balk at even referring to the two accounts in one and the same breath. Consequently, before raising the question of a comparison of the Babylonian myth with Genesis 1, it is appropriate to inquire whether there are other points of contact between the Babylonian myth and the OT, apart from Genesis 1. At least initially, Genesis 1 should be left completely out of conssideration.

[In a lengthy discussion (German, pp. 30–82) Gunkel describes various reflections of Marduk's battle against Tiamat in the following passages and with regard to these particular dragonlike creatures of mythic origin:

(*a*) Rahab: Isa. 51:9–10; Ps. 89:10–15 [9–14]; Job 26:12–13; Job 9:13; Ps. 87:4; Isa. 30:7; Ps. 40:5 [4, where RSV reads "the proud"];

(b) Leviathan: Ps. 74:12–19; Isa. 27:1; Job 40:25—41:26 [41:1–34] Ps. 104:25–26; Job 3:8;

(c) Behemoth: Job 40:15–24; Enoch 60:7–9; 4 Ezra 6:49–52; Isa. 3:6 [where RSV reads "beasts"];

(d) The Dragon in the Sea: Job 7:12; Ps. 44:20 [19, where RSV reads "jackels"]; Ezek. 29:3–6a; 32:2–8; Pss. Sol. 2:28b–34;

(e) The Serpent: Amos 9:2–3.

Gunkel then offers the summary which follows.]

Summary

The mythological creatures (*ḥayyôt*, Ps. 68:31[30]; *animae*, 4 Ezra 6:49) bear these names:

(a) Rahab (*rahab*): Isa. 51:9; Ps. 89:11[10]; Job 26:12; Job 9:13; Ps. 87:4;; Isa. 30:7; Ps. 40:5 [4, *rĕhābîm*];

(b) Leviathan (*liwyātān*): Ps. 74:14; Isa. 27:1; Job 40:25—41:26 [41:1–34]; Job 3:8; Ps. 104:26;

(c) Behemoth (*bĕhēmôt*): Job 40:15–24; Isa. 30:6.

Appearing much like names of mythological creatures are these:

(a) Tannin (*tannîn* [without the article]): Isa. 51:9; Job 7:12; Ps. 44:20 [19, where RSV reads "jackels"]; Jer. 51:34; Pss. Sol. 2:29 (*ho drakōn*); (*hattannîn* [with the article]): Isa. 27:1 (*hattannîn ʾăšer bayyām*, "the dragon that is in the sea'"); Ezek. 32:2 (*hattannîn bayyammîm*, "the dragon in the seas"); Ezek. 29:3 (*hattannîn haggādôl hārōbēṣ bĕtôk yĕʾōrāyw*, "the great dragon that lies in the midst of his streams");

(b) Hayyot Haqqaneh ("the beasts of the reeds"): Ps. 68:31[30];

(c) Nahash: Amos 9:3 (cf. the context, *bĕqarqaʿ hayyām* ["at the bottom of the sea"]); Job 26:13 (*nāḥāš bārîăḥ* ["the fleeing serpent], cf. Isa. 27:1).

Appearing in significant juxtaposition are these:

(a) Rahab and Tannin: Isa. 51:9;

(b) Rahab and Nahash: Job 26:12–13;

(c) Leviathan and Tannin: Isa. 27:1;

(d) Leviathan and Behemoth: Job 40:15—41:26[34]; Enoch 60:7–9; 4 Ezra 6:49–52. In these passages Leviathan is king of the watery deep while Behemoth is ruler of the dry land. According to Enoch 60:7–9, Leviathan is of female gender and Behemoth is male.

The following are creatures subordinate to the dragons themselves:

(a) helpers of Rahab (*'ōzrê rahab*): Job 9:13;
(b) "enemies" (*'ôyĕbîm*) of Yahweh allied with Rahab: Ps. 89:11[10];
(c) serpents (*tannînîm*) allied with Leviathan: Ps. 74:13–14;
(d) terrors (*'êmôt*, cj.) allied with Leviathan: Ps. 104:26 [RSV: "ships"];
(e) every haughty one (*kol-gābōăh*) // all the sons of pride (*kol-bĕnê-šāḥaṣ*) – i.e., monsters over whom Leviathan is king: Job 41:26[34];
(f) "fish" of the streams: Ezek. 29:4, appearing as supporters (*sōmĕkîm*) and helpers (*'ōzrĕ'îm*) of Tannin: Ezek. 30:6, 8.

Leviathan is described as having many heads (Ps. 74:14), as being a sort of serpent (*nāḥāš*, Isa. 27:1), a twisted (*bārîăḥ*) and crooked (*'ăqallātôn*) serpent (Isa. 27:1), and as a fire-spewing crocodile (Job 41:9–12 [18–21]). Likewise the dragon (*tannîn*) is described as a scaly (Ezek. 29:4) crocodile (Ezek. 29:3–6a; 32:2–8). Behemoth of Job 40 also exhibits traits of the crocodile.

The connection between the dragon(s) and the sea is especially apparent in these cases:

(a) Isa. 51:9–10 (dragon, Rahab; waters of the great deep, sea);
(b) Ps. 89:10–11 [9–10] (sea and its waves; Rahab and the enemies of Yahweh);
(c) Ps. 74:13–14 (sea; dragons, Leviathan);
(d) Job 26:12 (Rahab; sea);
(e) Job 3:8 (Leviathan; sea);
(f) Ps. 68:31[30] (beasts of the reeds; sea);
(g) Job 7:12 (sea; dragon);
(h) Ps. 148:7 (dragons; deeps);
(i) Neh. 2:13 (well of the dragon [RSV: Jackel's Well]).

Consistently these creatures appear as aquatic monsters. They are in the sea (Isa. 27:1; 4 Ezra 6:52; Ezek. 29:3; 32:2), on the waters (Ps. 74:13), at the bottom of the sea (Amos 9:3), in the abyss of the sea (Enoch 60:7–9), or in the deep (Job 3:8; cf. v. 4). Leviathan appears as lord of the deep (Job 41:23–24 [31–32]) and of the underworld (Job 41:25 [33]), as a creature of the darkness, covered with gloom (Ps. 44:20 [19]), whose power is at work in the night (Job 3:8). Only Behemoth exercises lordship over the dry land (Job 40:19; Enoch 60:7–9; 4 Ezra 6:49–52). Because of this, it is supposed that there was some sort of juxtaposition of sea and desert during the time before the creation of the world (cf. Ps. 74:14–15; Ezek. 29:5; Pss. Sol. 2:30–31).

Appearing in conjunction with reference to the Nile are both the dragon (Ezek. 29:3–6a; 32:2–8) and Leviathan and Behemoth (Job 40–41).

A connection with the creation of the world shines through in some of this material, such as in Pss. 89:12–13 [11–12] and 74:15–17. The conquest of the dragon is seen as having taken place "in days of old," in "the generations of long ago" (Isa. 51:9; cf. 74:12 [*miqqedem*: "from of old"]). The dragon boasts concerning itself, "I created the streams" (Ezek. 29:3; cf. 32:2). Israel's religion ardently proclaimed the dragon to be a creation of Yahweh (Ps. 104:26); Behemoth is the firstborn of the creatures of God (Job 40:19).

The attribute characteristic of the dragon is arrogance (Ps. 89:10–11 [9–10]; Ezek. 29:3; Pss. Sol. 2:29; cf. Job 41:26 [34]). The dragon scoffs at God (*ḥērēp*; Ps. 74:18) and reviles God's name (*niʾēṣ*; Ps. 74:18; cf. Pss. Sol. 2:32–33). The uproar of the dragon ascends to the very heavens (Ps. 74:23; cf. the "raising up" in Job 41:17 [25]). It demands for itself the lordship over the streams, which it is said to have created (Ezek. 29:3), over the deep (Job 41:24[32]), and over both sea and land (Pss. Sol. 2:33). In its own domain the dragon wreaks terrible havoc (Ezek. 32:32). It causes "perpetual ruins" (Ps. 74:3); it muddies the water with its feet and stirs up the streams (Ezek. 32:2); it makes the deep boil like a retort for making ointment (Job 41:23[31]). Perhaps also reflecting the myth is Jer. 51:34, 44, which speaks of a kind of fodder with which the dragon gorges its belly but then must vomit out again. The dragon is quite simply the "enemy" (*ʾôyēb, ṣar*; Ps. 74:3, 10, 18). It is singularly the enemy of Yahweh (Ps. 74:4, 23), and its allies are the foes of Yahweh (Ps. 89:11[10]). The dragon is called the "evil-doer" (Pss. Sol. 2:1), the "impudent one" (Pss. Sol. 2:35). Paralleling these traits of the dragon is the raging (*šāʾôn*) of the sea, crashing against the land in its haughtiness (*gēʾût*; Ps. 89:10[9]), stirring up filth (Ps. 68:31[30]).

Against this background it is important to note the theme of Yahweh's vanquishing the monsters. At least one allusion permits the supposition that other gods (*ʾĕlōhîm*) had attempted to do battle with the monsters before Yahweh, but in vain (Job 41:17[25]; cf. v. 3[8]). Finally Yahweh could no longer idly stand by and calmly absorb the insult (Ps. 74:22) and the misery. Then he acted in "anger" (Job 9:13), but at the same time he "worked salvation in the midst of the earth" (Ps. 74:12). Yahweh is the good and gracious god who has overcome the evil, hostile being (Ps. 89:2–3, 15[1–2, 14]). In so doing he has revealed his "power" (Ps. 74:14; Isa. 51:9; Job 26:12; Ps. 89:10[9]; Job 9:13) and at the same time his "wisdom" (Job 26:12). His "arm" (Ps. 89:14[13]) was decked out "with strength" (Isa. 51:9). He proved himself as "ruler" (Ps. 89:10[9]) and "king" (Ps. 74:12; Pss. Sol. 2:34). The world thus gives reverence to Yahweh, the world which he created (Job 26:13; Ps. 74:15–17) and to which he gave substance and regularity (Ps. 74:17), the world which properly belongs to him (Pss. 74:16; 89:12[11]) who has no equal in the divine assembly (Ps. 89:7[6]).

The battle with the dragon is described in many places in the OT. One passage alludes to Yahweh's armour (Isa. 51:9); another refers to how the heavens were covered up during the battle (Ezek. 32:7). An angry, rebuking speech that likely preceded the battle is perhaps in mind in Psalm 68:31[30]. Yahweh's weapon was a sword (Isa. 27:1), or again a cord and hook (Job 40:25[41:1]), or elsewhere a fishing gaff (Ezek. 29:4), or even a net and a snare (Ezek. 32:8). Behemoth was captured with a nose hook (Job 40:24). With such weapons Yahweh "smote" (*māḥaṣ*) Rahab (Isa. 51:9; Job 26:12), he "crushed to bits" (*riṣṣēs*) the "heads" of Leviathan (Ps. 74:14). He fetched the dragon out of the floodwaters and slung it out onto the dry land (Ps. 74:14; Ezek. 29:5; 32:4) – where, being an aquatic monster, it was of course helpless. The various allies of the dragon were "scattered" (*pizzēr*, Ps. 89:11[10]; cf. also Ps. 68:31[30]); they fell at the feet of Yahweh (*šāḥāḥû*; Job 9:13). Elsewhere it is said that their heads were "broken" (Ps. 74:13); dangling from its scales, they were snatched up along with the dragon and cast upon the dry land (Ezek. 29:4–5). Described here and there with particular emphasis is the fate which the carcass of the dragon suffered. As the worst possible judgment upon the dragon's arrogance (Pss. Sol. 2:30–33), its body was reviled even after death ("pierced" [*ḥillēl*]: Isa. 51:9; Job 26:13; Pss. Sol. 2:30; "crushed like a carcass" [*dikkāʾ kěḥālāl*]: Ps. 89:11[10]); "crushed" [*dikkāʾ*]: Ps. 44:20[19; RSV: "jackels"]). The dragon's body was not buried (Ezek. 29:5; Pss. Sol. 2:31), but instead it was thrown into the wilderness where it was devoured by the wild beasts (Ps. 74:14; Ezek. 29:5; 32:4). The dragon's flesh covered the mountains and its blood filled the streams (Ezek. 32:5–6).

Such descriptions of the destruction of the dragon parallel the things that Yahweh is said to have done to the sea. For example, Yahweh dried up the sea, the waters of the great Tehom (Isa. 51:10). Yahweh calmed the sea (*rāgaʿ*; Job 26:12); he split it in two (*pōrar*; Ps. 74:13); he broke open streams and made brooks dry (Ps. 74:15). He dried up the rivers (Ezek. 30:12; cf. Jer. 51:36), making them flow smoothly like oil (Ezek. 32:13–14). Yahweh made the sea brighter than silver (Ps. 68:31[30]. [The Hebrew here reads literally "trampling down on pieces of silver;" the meaning is obscure]).

According to an alternate recension, the dragon was not slain but merely subdued. It was "brought to rest" (*rahab hammošbāt*; Isa. 30:7[emend.]). When Yahweh seized it, it acted very docile and became Yahweh's servant; Yahweh now holds it firmly by a nose ring (Job 40:26[41:2]). Occasionally Yahweh even plays with it (Job 40:29[41:5]; Ps. 104:26). The dragon lies at the bottom of the sea, but even there it must be obedient to Yahweh (Amos 9:3). It could become dangerous again at any time, and so Yahweh posts a guard over it (Job 7:12). According to another version, a magic spell stripped the dragon of its power. However, the beings who cast the spell on the dragon – following the mandate of Yahweh – are also able to rouse it (Job 3:8; 41:2[10]).

The nature of Yahweh's lordship over the sea monster parallels Yahweh's power over the waves of the tempestuous sea. Yahweh stills the waves (*šibbēăḥ*; Ps. 89:10[9]). The sea is kept calm by enchantment (*'ōrărê-yām*[emend.]; Job 3:8). The spirit of the sea keeps a tight rein on the sea (Enoch 60:16). The bars of heaven fear him (Job 26:13[emend.]). [Gunkel's treatment of five distinct variants of this myth in biblical texts and usages of it in O.T. literature are here omitted (German, pp. 86–90).]

2 TRADITIONS REGARDING THE PRIMEVAL SEA

By now we have more than once confirmed that the descriptions of the vanquishing of the dragon are paralleled by what Yahweh did to the sea in primordial times, as well as by what Yahweh still does to the sea in the present. Beyond that, we possess a number of poetic statements which, while speaking of the sea in the same way, do not explicitly draw on mythological notions regarding the monsters of the deep: Ps. 104:5–9; Job 38:8–11; Prov. 8:22–31; Jer. 5:22b; 31:35; 33:6–8; Ps. 65:7–8[6–7]; Sir. 43:23; Prayer of Manasseh 2—4.

[Gunkel describes the reflections of the traditions in the OT in two parts: I. Traditions of the overcoming of the sea in primordial time, especially in reference to Job 38, Prov. 8, Ps. 104 (German, pp. 91–99); II. Traditions of the primeval sea related to the endtime, or other reverberations: Ps. 46, Isa. 17:12–14, Hab. 3, Nah. 1, Ps. 18,

Ps. 77, Ps. 106:9, Exod. 15:7b, Isa. 51:9–10, and 59:15b–20 (German, pp. 99–110).]

We have attempted to pursue the traces of an eschatological use of the account of Yahweh's conquest of the sea. Now admittedly the clues we have followed are much less obvious than was the case with the eschatological interpretations of the chaos monsters. That lies in the nature of the material. Above all, we have had to proceed without benefit of the names of the chaos monsters. It is the names that so clearly point out the connection with the myth. Moreover, the images of the sea, which appear to have been derived from the myth, are not so unique that they would simply be inexplicable apart from the myth. It is with some caution, therefore, that I thus summarize the above observations:

(a) The chaos myth was present in Israel in a form which still mentioned the sea but in which the mythological figures of the dragons had fallen out;

(b) In its preserved form, the myth had the character of a hymn. Along with a series of explicit descriptions, we possess a number of hymnic allusions containing subdued echoes of the myth;

(c) As in the case of the chaos monsters, we can note an eschatological shift: there is talk of how, at the end of time, the sea will arrogantly storm against Yahweh's creation, but how then Yahweh's word of rebuke will put the sea to flight. This prophecy is then explained as being an image of the final onslaught of the heathen and of the great judgment of the peoples in the future. It seems that one particular prophet of great stature took the lead in so using the myth; the others followed suit. In the early apocalyptic writings, the image of the raging sea is a firmly fixed trait. Along with this core image, various particulars were carried over as poetic decorations or, as appropriate, allegorized. Even in the New Testament, among the other signs of the end, it is mentioned how the peoples will perish from the earth because of their trepidation at the raging of the sea (Luke 21:25 – incidently, the only passage in which the tumultuous sea of the future is not allegorized).

That is a historical development which is in itself probable and is, moreover, parallel to the tradition-history reconstructed for Rahab and his allies in every respect.

Luckily, with particular regard to the myth [as found, for instance, in Hab. 3, Nah. 1, Ps. 18 (cf. Ps. 77)], we have discovered these additional features:

—the "rebuke" (*gāʻar*) of Yahweh;
—Yahweh's acting before the break of day;
—Yahweh's coming with horses and chariot;
—Yahweh's coming in the thunderstorm;
—In all of this, Yahweh's weaponry will have been described in detail;
—It is easy to imagine the nature of Yahweh's weaponry in terms of the mythical parallels: Yahweh arms himself by putting on the weaponry associated with thunderstorms. This is how the Marduk myth describes the armor of God.

3   COMPARISON OF THE OT TRADITIONS ABOUT THE DRAGON AND THE PRIMEVAL SEA WITH THE BABYLONIAN TIAMAT MYTH

We have by now uncovered a long and rich history in Israel for the myth about chaos and the creation of the world. During the course of our investigation, we have established the existence of individual parallels to the Babylonian myth of Marduk and Tiamat. I will now summarize the chief points at which the two myths agree.

In both myths it is stated that, at one time in primordial antiquity, the universe consisted of water. This primeval sea is personified as a frightful being. The Babylonian name for this chaos monster, Tiamat, finds a close correspondence in the technical name for the primeval sea in Hebrew, *tĕhôm* – a name whose constant appearance without the definite article in Hebrew proves that it was once a proper name and was therefore used to designate a mythical figure. The familiar name of the chaos monster in Hebrew, *rahab*, is most likely also to be found in Babylonian, although it is not yet attested with full certainty. Both myths conceive of this monster as a dragon with many heads.

Alongside this monster are other creatures, similar to it, called the "helpers" of the dragon. One of these helpers plays a particularly important role. In the Babylonian myth it is Kingu who stands alongside Tiamat. In the Hebrew version, the following pairs appear: Rahab and Tannin, Leviathan and Tannin, Leviathan and Behemoth, Rahab and Nahash-Bariah. Kingu and Tiamat are mates, as are Behemoth and Leviathan according to Enoch 60.

Set over against these powers of the deep, in the Babylonian myth, are the deities of the upper realm, among whom is Marduk. In Israel, too, there occasionally appear other divine beings alongside Yahweh (Job 41:17[25]; 38:7; Ps. 89:7[6]), though naturally they are always inferior to Yahweh.

At some point these monsters of chaos rebelled against the power of the deities of the upper realm; they laid claim to world dominion for themselves. In the Yahweh myth, too, this arrogant and outrageous rebellion is a constant theme.

Before Marduk's intervention, several gods sought to do battle with Tiamat. There is perhaps an allusion to a similar course of events in the Hebrew myth in Job 41:3[11] and 17[25].

Finally, Marduk-Yahweh comes forward. His weaponry is described as he appears: he comes riding upon a horse-drawn chariot, with sword and net or with the terrifying weapons of the storm god. The agreement of both myths with regard to this latter trait is all the more significant in that it is not derived from an observation of nature – winter is not overcome by a thunderstorm. Rather, this trait has penetrated the myth from some external source.

Preceding the battle is an angry "rebuke." In the battle itself the god (Marduk; Yahweh) exhibits not only power but at the same time cleverness. In this the net plays a role. The "helpers" of the monster are also overthrown by the god; they "groveled before him." In the Babylonian myth Marduk let them off lightly; a Hebrew version of the myth makes a similar reference (Ps. 89:13[12]; Job 9:13).

The corpse of the slain monster is not buried – this is repeatedly emphasized in the Hebrew version. Rather, the world is formed out of its carcass by the chief god. Hebrew versions of the myth appear to derive the fertility of the land, which previously was sterile wilderness, from the blood and the decaying flesh of the dragon. The Babylonian myth relates how Tiamat was split into two parts, into the waters above and the waters below. A Hebrew version clearly stating the same is not to be found among the biblical passages cited above. However, Ps. 74:13 speaks of "splitting" the sea, and Job 26:13 knows of the "bars of heaven" [reading *bĕrîḥê šāmayim* for MT's *bĕrûḥô šāmayim*]. In any case, the creation of the world directly follows the conquering of the monster in the Hebrew version as well as in the Babylonian.

Both myths conclude on the same major note. The culmination of the whole Marduk-Yahweh myth is the idea that the deity who broke the destructive power of the pernicious monster and created this lovely world is, from now on, Lord and God. Let all joyously render him praise, the greatest among the gods!

43

From the Babylonian side we know of a variant in which Tiamat continues to conduct a reign of terror among human beings, which is to say within the course of history. We have found Hebrew parallels for this variant as well.

A further series of proofs is furnished by the later ancient Near Eastern materials which, on the one hand, are independent of the Babylonian traditions and, on the other hand, agree with the Hebraic materials in many ways. Extensive demonstration of this point would be extraneous to our main purpose here.

In conclusion, both myths (the Babylonian and the Hebrew) share all their main points in common. As a consequence, in the final analysis here we consider not two myths that happen to be similar but rather one and the same myth which is preserved in two different but related versions. When one stops to think about the immense difference between the Babylonian and Hebrew religions, one can hardly be sufficiently amazed at the strong similarity between these two versions of the myth.

The experts in these matters hardly need any proof as to which side is to be considered the borrower and which the originator. The Babylonian myth corresponds to the nature of the Mesopotamian climate and thereby establishes itself as genuinely Babylonian, while the Hebrew version must be judged to be decidedly non-Palestinian. Furthermore the Marduk myth, reflecting as it does a Babylonian sense of pride based on world domination, significantly predates the Hebrews as a people.

This, then, is the result of our deliberations: the Babylonian Tiamat-Marduk myth was taken over by Israel and there was transformed into a myth about Yahweh.

D The Babylonian Origin of the Genesis Creation Story

1 THE BABYLONIAN SOURCE

Having completed our digression, we now return to Genesis 1 and attempt to establish the relationship between this creation story and the Babylonian-Israelite creation myth as outlined above.

As was already obvious from a look at Genesis 1 alone (see above, pp. 25–32), this narrative is merely the Judaic reworking of much older traditional material that originally must have been considerably more mythological in nature. Various individual traits of Genesis 1 reflect a polytheistic origin; one feature in particular points to an astral religion; several motifs harmonize with Phoenician, Greek, and

Indic parallels. Likewise, both the Palestinian climate and the ancient Hebrew calendar argue against an indigenously Israelite origin of the Genesis 1 narrative. In fact, climate, calendar, and the echo of astral religion all point to Babylonia. It is now time definitively to confirm this supposition on the basis of a direct comparison of Genesis 1 with the Babylonian myth.

This myth bears precisely those traits that we have postulated for the *Vorlage* of Genesis 1; the characteristic features of the Babylonian myth clearly harmonize with Genesis 1. To be sure, the myth does not contain reference to the instituting of the Sabbath, but this segment also does not belong to the original core of Genesis 1. Furthermore, the parallels between the two touch only upon their introductions. This fact, however, results from our possessing only scant fragments of the actual creation account in the Babylonian myth.[38] In any case, the contacts between the two are particularly strong at the beginning.

In both accounts the world consists at the outset of water and darkness. Particularly striking here is the parallel with regard to the name for this primordial state of affairs; *tĕhôm* = Tiamat. The name *bōhû* is perhaps also Babylonian.[39]

The world comes into being in this manner: God separates the primordial waters into two parts by means of the heavenly firmament. Here the Israelite reader would naturally recall the role played by this feature in the Babylonian myth. We have already seen how, for Genesis 1, the feature of separation is specifically Babylonian and decidedly non-Palestinian. The agreement regarding this point is all the more striking in that the same feature appears nowhere else in the OT with the same clarity.[40]

According to Genesis 1 the creation arose through God's almighty Word. In the Marduk myth the effectiveness of the deity's word is likewise strongly emphasized (Tablet IV, 13–28; ANET, 66). Another parallel has to do with the creation of the animals: both accounts classify them in the same way (domestic animals, wild animals, and creeping things).[41]

A number of features in Genesis 1 are to be properly understood only on the basis of other Babylonian parallels. For example, in conjunction with the creation of the celestial bodies it is strongly emphasized that their function is to regulate the seasons. This emphasis is particularly striking in the context of Judaic tradition.[42] It is to be explained with reference to the Babylonian astral religion. Likewise, it is quite remarkable how in Genesis 1 light is created before the stars are called into being. In the Babylonian myth, too, light is to be regarded as already present before the appearance of Marduk, although Marduk subsequently creates the stars. This feature can be fully explained on the basis of the polytheistic Babylonian point of view according to which light partakes of the essence of the deities of the upper realm. As one of the youngest of the deities, however, Marduk himself will have come into being only after light was already there. Furthermore, the pronouncement by God at the completion of each of the acts of creation, namely, that they have been found to be good, finds its proper meaning through comparison with the Babylonian myth. In just the same way the Babylonian myth praises the bounty of the deity who smote the evil monster and created the good world.[43] In line with this, the predication "good" originally stood in contrast to the abomination of the primordial Tehom. That the darkness is not called "good" in Genesis 1 is therefore to be taken as a later echo of this view.

On the basis of these correspondences alone the conclusion would be quite probable that ultimately Genesis 1 goes back to the Babylonian creation myth. Moreover, this conclusion becomes considerably more certain when we recall all the many reflections of the Babylonian creation myth elsewhere in the OT, as established above. Against this background the interpretive situation is decisively altered. Now Genesis 1 is no longer an isolated passage, one for which any connection with the Marduk account would appear very strange indeed. On the contrary, Genesis 1 is but one link in a long chain; it is but one recension alongside so many others for which we have already established a common Babylonian original.

Consciously or unconsciously, the theologian will perhaps advance dogmatic objections against this historical thesis. He will direct attention to the unmistakably huge difference between the Babylonian and the biblical creation accounts. Insofar as he is inclined to acknowledge the partial correspondence between the two accounts at all, he will be partial to the thesis that we have here an ancient tradition that was common to both peoples but that was distorted by the Babylonians into mythological gibberish while it was preserved in its purity by the Hebrews. Such a thesis, however, is clearly refuted by the character of both traditions. As we have previously shown (cf. pp. 25–32), Genesis 1 is essentially a faded myth. Furthermore, as we have already seen (cf. pp. 31–33), convincing internal reasons compel us to seek the origin of the Israelite tradition in Babylon. For anyone willing to accord any significance at all to religio-historical observations, finally, it is the related OT material outside of Genesis 1 that becomes particularly instructive. It is these other passages which, in part, provide us with the intervening steps between Genesis 1 and the Babylonian myth; they show the path along which the Marduk myth was transformed into Genesis 1. Accordingly, it can be taken as assured that, ultimately, Genesis 1 is also of Babylonian origin.

2   THE CHARACTER OF THE REINTERPRETATION IN GENESIS 1

In order to comprehend something of the long history in terms of which Genesis 1 is to be understood, it is first of all necessary to establish the ways in which the rescension is indeed unique.

The difference between the Babylonian creation account and that of Genesis 1 is great; it could hardly be more pronounced. In the Babylonian account everything is wild and grotesque; it is barbaric, riotous poetry. In Genesis 1 everything is quietly solemn and elevated; it is expansive and occasionally somewhat pedantic prose.[44] There the gods emerged in the course of things; here God is one and the same from the very beginning. In the Babylonian account there is the deity who slays the monster in heated combat and forms the world out of its corpse; in Genesis 1 there is God "who speaks and it is so." (To be sure, the poetry of the original myth has almost completely vanished in Genesis 1. We do not regret that fact, however, for the account has thereby gained in being filled with the insights of a higher religion.)

The theologian will do well to treat the Marduk myth with respect. One does no honor to his parents by thinking poorly of his ancestors. In spite of that, however, we have a right to judge Genesis 1 quite differently from its ancient mythic forebear. Granted our scientific point of view has considerably distanced itself from the ancient point of view presupposed in Genesis 1. And likewise the supernaturalistic concept of God presupposed in Genesis 1[45] does not strike our own sense of piety as being the most lofty. In spite of everything, it remains true that in Genesis 1 we are able to encounter the God in whom we believe. All other cosmogonies are for us only interesting antiquities.

A historical-critical approach makes it impossible for us to view Genesis 1 as our parents did, namely, as the memorial of a special revelation which had been granted to the first human being. Unshakeable, however, remains our conviction that in the evolution of Israel's religion the providential will of the living God is revealed. It is the unassailable right and duty of the historian of religion powerfully to articulate this conviction with regard to each high point in history where the vista opens up in all directions. Genesis 1 is such a high point, a landmark in the history of the world, a monument of the revelation of God in Israel.

How does Genesis 1 relate to the "poetic recensions"? Genesis 1 is the only complete recension of the myth stemming from ancient Israel that we possess. All the others are no more than allusions to the myth, reminiscences of it, or applications in other contexts. The reason why no other full creation myth has been preserved is obvious. Permeated as it is by the Judaic spirit and being the fitting expression of the Judaic mentality that it is, Genesis 1 has simply supplanted all of the other recensions.

It is this completeness of Genesis 1 that explains how much has here been preserved which is lacking in the other recensions: the primordial darkness; the names *tōhû* and *bōhû*; the separation of the primeval sea; the pronouncing of names for the things created; the establishing of lordship for the stars; the import behind the divine "we" employed at the creation of humanity; the blessing pronounced upon animals and human beings; the motif of God's seeing "that it was good"; the institution of the Sabbath. In addition to these, there is a feature that seems to have penetrated the originally Babylonian material through Phoenician influence: the "brooding" of the spirit, along with its allied remnant of an account of a creation proceeding by spontaneous development. Finally there is a trait that probably stems from another Babylonian myth: that vegetarianism was the norm in primordial times.

If now Genesis 1 still contains so much ancient material, despite the inroads made by a Judaic reworking which, to judge from analogous material elsewhere in P, was relatively severe, then we can conclude that the *Vorlage* of Genesis 1 contained ancient features that were all the more pronounced. The old account of the creation of the world must have exuded a thoroughly ancient air, if even so energetic a reworker as P could not totally expunge the mythic traces. Many of the individual traces of antiquity must have been inextricably tied to the very heart of the material.

On the other hand, over against the other recensions Genesis 1 gives the impression of being in many ways quite modern. Genesis 1 is prose – only in vv. 2, 26, and 27 might there be echoes of poetry – while all the other recensions are thoroughly poetic. In this regard Genesis 1 shows itself to be the more recent, for the creation myth was by nature a hymn. This is not to say that the direct *Vorlage* of Genesis 1 was still written in verse, however. If I judge aright, even some of the sagas of J and E might be regarded as prose reminiscences of ancient songs.

If one further compares how the relationship of God to the chaos is described in the parallel recensions, one clearly recognizes a line of development. Along this line one notes how the Babylonian idea that chaos is even more ancient than the godhead itself is nowhere identifiable on Hebrew soil. Conversely, the ancient Babylonian notion of chaos monsters and of the deity's battle against them is preserved in some of the OT poetic recensions. To be sure, other OT poetic recensions have given up the personifying of chaos, but at least the theme of Yahweh's battle against the sea that once ruled also the land has been preserved. In Genesis 1, however, even this last remnant has disappeared. Here it is simply stated that God separated the waters under the firmament from the waters above the firmament. The primordial chaos monsters have been transformed into a remarkable sort of fish, which is to be included among the other created beings (v. 21). In ways like this we can observe the gradual receding of the mythological.

One arrives at the same result when comparing the remaining features of Genesis 1 with such ancient creation accounts as, for example, Prov. 8:22–31 or Job 26 and 38. In Genesis 1 we no longer hear of such things as "the pillars of heaven," "the wellsprings of the sea," or "the foundations of the mountains."

On the basis of such observations one comes to see that Genesis 1 is related to the poetic recensions somewhat like P in general relates to the parallel traditions in J or E: on the whole a strongly Judaicized reworking, sober prose in place of ancient poetry, at the same time a higher view of God replacing an earlier naiveté, and yet also individual features that are very ancient.

We have thus established the following religio-historical sequence:

1   the original Marduk myth,
2   a poetic recension of the Yahweh myth,
3   Genesis 1.

With specific regard to Genesis 1 the following steps have been uncovered:

1   The Babylonian myth was brought over into Israel.
2   There it lost much of its mythological character and almost all of its polytheistic nature.
3   In Genesis 1 the myth became as fully Judaicized as possible.

[Gunkel's discussion of the presumed date when the Babylonian material was taken over follows. (German, pp. 121–70)]

NOTES

1 Julius Wellhausen, *Prolegomena to the History of Ancient Israel* (ET by J. S. Black and A. Menzies, with a preface by W. Robertson Smith; New York: World Pub. Co., Meridian Books, 1957) 299.

2 With regard to the point of view here being maintained, it is a matter of indifference whether or not P might have drawn upon a source otherwise preserved for us only in fragments (e.g., Budde's J²); it is enough that P contains traditions that we know only from that source.

3 I cite creation myths of other ancient peoples following the synoptic arrangement of such material in August Dillmann, *Die Genesis* (KEH 11; Leipzig: S. Hirzel, 1892⁶) 4–10. In addition to the Hebrews and the Babylonians, the theme of chaos is found in ancient India, Greece, Egypt, and Phoenicia.

4 In Philo of Byblos; cf. Dillmann, *Genesis*, 7.

5 Cf. Dillmann, *Genesis*, 20. Wellhausen's view that the chaos of Genesis 1 had been created by God cannot be maintained, because the "heaven and earth" of Gen. 1:1 refers already to the ordered world (cf. Dillmann, *Genesis*, 16).

6 Psalms 33:6 (the breath [*rûăḥ*] of the mouth of God // his word) and 104:29–30 (the spirit of God creating life in the living creatures) do not belong here, contra Dillmann, *Genesis*, 19.

7 Cf. Dillmann, *Genesis*, 20.

8 Ibid.

9 Cf. Dillmann, *Genesis*, 21.

10 To be sure, similar echoes are to be heard in vv. 20 ("let the waters swarm") and 24 ("let the earth bring forth"). However, the similarities are obscured by the addition of the "so God created" in vv. 21 and 25.

11 Cf. also Deut. 4:19 in conjunction with 32:8 (reading *bĕnê 'ēl* with LXX; precisely the opposite corruption of the text is corrected by LXX at Amos 5:6 [not followed by RSV] and Hos. 10:15).

12 Enoch 82 shows that the view of the stars as governors over the seasons of the year was quite common in early Judaism.

13 See Dillmann's (*Genesis*, 31) explanation of "we".

14 Cf. Franz Delitzsch, *Neuer Commentar über die Genesis* (Leipzig: Dörffling und Franke, 1887) 64.

15 The same idea is presupposed in Jer. 23:18; Job 15:8; Dan. 4:14.

16 Dillmann, *Genesis*, 31.

17 Ibid., 32.

18 E.g., among the Greeks and Romans; cf. Dillmann, *Genesis*, 33.

19 Thus also August Dillmann, *Der Prophet Jesaia* (KEH 5; Leipzig: S. Hirzel, 1890⁵) 120; and Franz Delitzsch, *Biblischer Commentar über den Propheten Jesaia* (Leipzig, 1889⁴) 194; ET, 1890.

20 Dillmann, *Genesis*, 36.

21 The opinion of Julius Wellhausen (*Die Composition des Hexateuchs und der historischen Bücher des Alten Testaments* [Berlin: Reimer, 1889²] 187); Dillmann, *Genesis*, 15.

22 The deliberations of Dillmann (*Genesis*, 22) strike me as being much too complicated.

23 Karl Budde shows that the language of Exod. 20:11 also does not bear the stamp of P. See his *Die biblische Urgeschichte – Gen 1—12,5* (Giessen: J. Ricker, 1883) 494–95.

24 Cf. Immanuel Benzinger, *Hebräische Archäologie* (Freiburg: J. C. B. Mohr, 1894) 32.

25 Egypt, notable for its almost total lack of rainfall, falls outside the realm of consideration.

26 Benzinger, *Archäologie*, 199–200.

27 Damascii Philosophi Platonici. *Quaestiones de primis principiis* (ed. J. Kopp; Frankfurt: H. L. Broenner, 1826) 384. For an ET see George Smith, *The Chaldean Account of Genesis* (New York: Scribner, Armstrong & Co., 1876) 49–50. See further, P. C. A. Jensen, *Die Kosmologie der Babylonier: Studien und Materialien* (Strasburg: Trübner, 1890; Berlin and New York: Walter de Gruyter, 1974, photocopy reprint) 270–75.

28 Eusebius, *Chronicorum libri duo*, ed. A. E. Schoene (Berlin, 1875) I: 14–18. For interpretation of the text, see the critical comments of Alfred von Gutschmid in the Schoene edition; see also Budde, *Urgeschichte*, 476–85. For an ET see George Smith, *Chaldean Genesis*, 40–42. The rendering by Eberhard Schrader (*Die Keilinschriften und das Alte Testament* [Giessen: J. Ricker, 1883²] 12–14) is very imprecise.

29 Jensen, *Kosmologie*, 307–20.

30 Ibid., 308.

31 Ibid., 309. George A. Barton understands Marduk as a storm god who subdues the tempestuous sea ("Tiamat," *JAOS* 15 [1893] 14–15).

32 Thus Jensen, *Kosmologie*, 308.

33 Gunkel contra Jensen, *Kosmologie*, 308.

34 It consequently seems to me most likely that the primitive imagination saw the zodiacal signs as monsters in the heavens. Jensen takes a somewhat different view of the matter (*Kosmologie*, 89, 315–20; see also Heinrich Zimmern, *Die Assyriologie als Hülfswissenschaft für das Studium des Alten Testaments* [Königsberg, 1889] 14ff).

35 Cf. e.g., the stele of Esarhaddon from Zinjirli (published in the "Mittheilungen aus den orientalischen Sammlungen der Königliche Museen zu Berlin," Volume 11, plate 1 [cf. *ANEP*, plate 447]).

36 This connection was discovered by Alfred Jeremias (*Izdubar-Nimrod: eine altbabylonische Heldensage* [Leipzig: B. G. Teubner, 1891] 11. A.).

37 Cf. Hugo Winckler, *Alttestamentliche Untersuchungen* (Leipzig: E. Pfeiffer, 1892) 29, 33–34.

38   Contra Jensen, *Kosmologie*, 306.

39   Cf. Hommel, "Inschriftliche Glossen und Exkurse," 408ff.

40   The concept of "waters above" occurs in Pss. 104:3; 148:4; and Gen. 7:11; cf. 2 Kgs 7:2, 19; Job 38:25. The throne of God is set upon these waters – from whence comes the notion of the glassy "sea" in Rev. 4:6 and 15:2.

41   Cf. Jensen, *Kosmologie*, 293–95.

42   This emphasis is noted by Dillmann, *Genesis*, 27.

43   See Psalms 74 and 89. Compare Gen. 1:31 with Ps. 104:31.

44   Wellhausen, *Prolegomena*, 298–99.

45   Ibid., 298.

2

The Theological Problem
of the Old Testament Doctrine
# of Creation*

GERHARD VON RAD

The Yahwistic faith of the OT is a faith based on the notion of election and therefore primarily concerned with redemption. This statement, which requires no justification here, poses simply and precisely the problem with which we are here concerned. How are we to define theologically the relationship between this predominating belief in election and redemption, and that belief in Yahweh as Creator which is also attested by the OT? How far is the idea of Yahweh as Creator a relevant and immediate conception, over against his redemptive function?

This question, of course, is one of theology rather than of the history of religion, so that our task is that of investigating the specifically theological role of the doctrine of creation within the context of OT belief as a whole. To state the matter more precisely, the question we have to answer is whether this doctrine is related to that belief in redemption which dominates the whole of the OT, or whether it is independent of it; and here we meet with problems which are the subject of much controversy today. I will do no more than mention them.

Is the creation of the natural order by God adduced as a motive for faith, either in the prophets or in the psalms? Does the doctrine of redemption presuppose a doctrine of creation as its indispensable theological basis? W. Lütgert's work on creation and revelation[1] puts the case for this belief, arguing throughout from OT data. In his opinion the pronouncements of the prophets would have carried no conviction but for the self-evident testimony of the created order.

* First published in English in *The Problem of the Hexateuch* by G. von Rad (1966) 131–43. Original publication in German (1936).

In the prophetic proclamation of redemption the hearer recognizes again the Creator who is already known to him. If this is not a tenable view, then how is the doctrine of redemption related to the doctrine of creation, theologically speaking?

Before we face up to the immediate problem, let us make one brief preliminary observation. The most serious attack which the faith of Israel had to meet with regard to the conception of Nature came from the Canaanite Baal religion. The gravity of this crisis is known to us from Hosea and Deuteronomy, but evidently it does not occur either to Hosea or to the deuteronomic theologians to oppose the Nature religions on the grounds of the doctrine of creation, by pointing to the fact that Nature and all its forces are the creation of Yahweh. On the contrary, surprisingly enough, the theological objections to Canaanitish aberrations are constantly stated in historical terms, i.e., in terms of Israel's redemptive history. Yahweh both promised and granted the land to Israel, and so became the Giver of the blessings of settled life.

Most surprising of all is the use made of this thought in the prayer for offering first-fruits contained in Deut. 26:5ff. The worshipper does not give thanks for the fruits which the Creator has provided for him, but simply acknowledges that he is a member of the nation which God brought into the promised land by a historical saving act, thus making him heir to the blessings of this land.

From the earliest times this was Israel's view of Yahweh's relationship to the land, and to its way of life. This was the blessed plot given to the nation by the saving activity of Yahweh, the mighty Lord of history, and it still remained Yahweh's land. The statement of Lev. 25:23 – "The land belongs to me; you are guests and sojourners with me" – is extremely ancient, and underlies the whole law of land tenure in the OT. Nevertheless, it does not depend upon the doctrine of creation, but rests directly on belief in a historical act of grace on God's part. Nor does it lead into a doctrine of creation, since so far as one can see it is quite unrelated to it.

This purely negative conclusion serves as a further pointer to the peculiarity of the theological problem to which we now turn. We shall certainly have to correct radically the suspiciously simple picture of this matter which is drawn for us in many theological studies of the OT, and which is particularly widespread in the unlearned world as a result of the circumstance that Genesis 1 stands at the beginning of the Bible.

To this end we shall not follow the usual procedure of making the creation narrative of Genesis 1 the centre of the discussion. We prefer for our present purpose to start from the evidence for the doctrine of creation contained in the hymns of the Psalter and of Deutero-Isaiah, on the grounds that these hymns give more immediate expression to the religious actualities. They are theologically much less hidebound than the scholarly priestly code, whose course is dictated by a theological system.

Psalm 136 is a litany in praise of the marvellous acts of Yahweh. Verses 5–9 deal with the creation of the world, and at verse 10 the psalm abruptly changes its course in order to recount the mighty deeds of Yahweh in history. In this psalm, therefore, the doctrine of creation and the doctrine of redemption stand side by side, yet wholly unrelated the one to the other. Because of the rigid form of the litany, nothing of particular interest emerges from this psalm with regard to the relationship between the two doctrines which it embraces. We nevertheless observe that the doctrine of creation does not stand in isolation here; the hymn presses on beyond it to the saving acts of God, and we shall surely not be mistaken if we regard this second part as the climax of the psalm.

A very similar situation appears in Psalm 148. Here, too, the psalmist sings of the creation of the world and of the redemptive activity of Yahweh in two more or less unrelated sections. Psalm 33 must also be classed with these psalms. Once again the events of the creation are depicted, in language of great nobility: "By the word of Yahweh the heavens were made.... He commanded and it stood fast." Yet this hymn, like the others, does not linger over the thought, but goes on to sing of Yahweh's saving acts in history: "He has brought the counsel of the nations to nought ... blessed is the nation whose God is Yahweh." And here the singer comes to his main theme, moving on from God as Creator to God as Saviour, from protology to soteriology. (I trust that I may be allowed this rather crude theological terminology here. For the present purpose it serves to designate what are in fact the essential distinctions.)

If we now consider a typical hymn from Deutero-Isaiah, we are at once carried a step further:

Why do you say, O Jacob, and speak, O Israel: "My way is hid from Yahweh"?... Do you not know, have you not heard, that Yahweh is an everlasting God who has made the ends of the earth? He does not faint or grow weary.... He gives power to the faint, and to him who has no might he gives great strength. Even youths may faint and be weary ...   Isa. 40:27ff

We see at once that the doctrine of creation in verse 28 is not introduced for its own sake: it is not of this that the prophet wishes to speak to his people. The prophet speaks of God's redeeming grace, but he has to struggle against disbelief, and in order to arouse confidence in the unlimited might of his God he adverts to the fact of the creation of the world. He does precisely the same thing in the first Servant Song:

> Thus says Yahweh who created the heavens ... who spread forth the earth.... I, Yahweh, have called you. Isa. 42:5

The creation of the world is frequently mentioned in Deutero-Isaiah, with this purpose of providing a foundation for faith. How little the prophet is concerned with the doctrine of creation for its own sake is made very evident by the fact that in such texts he happily passes over the particular acts of God in creation and goes on at once to speak of manifestations of God's power in history (Isa. 40:21ff; 44:24ff; 45:12ff). Thus we can already at this stage make the important observation that at no point in the whole of Deutero-Isaiah does the doctrine of creation appear in its own right; it never forms the main theme of a pronouncement, nor provides the motive of a prophetic utterance. It is there, but as applied by the prophet in the course of his argument it performs only an ancillary function. It provides a foundation for the message of redemption, in that it stimulates faith. It is but a magnificent foil for the message of salvation, which thus appears the more powerful and the more worthy of confidence. Or is it something quite different?

Before we approach this very important topic, let us take a look at the doxologies in the Book of Amos.[2] Here too, undoubtedly, the psalmist hymns the power of the Creator with an identical theological purpose in view. The doxologies are theological accretions, arising from the reflections of a later writer. The affirmations made in the course of these doxologies have no specific message of their own which it is essential to include for its own sake, but, like the references in Deutero-Isaiah, perform only an ancillary function. Through them the prophetic pronouncement is universalized and so gains in profundity.

Let us, however, return to Deutero-Isaiah, for we have not yet come to the more fundamental theological aspect of the doctrines of creation and redemption. Let us for a moment consider the juxtaposition of creation and redemption which we find in the opening words of the prophet's oracles, a juxtaposition which has already become conventionalized and almost a formality:

But now thus has Yahweh spoken, he who created you, O Jacob, and he who formed you, O Israel, "Fear not, I will redeem you."

Isa. 43:1

or

Thus has Yahweh said, your Redeemer and the One who formed you from the womb ...

Isa. 44:24[3]

We are struck by the ease with which two doctrines, which to our way of thinking are of very different kinds, are here brought together. It is as if for Deutero-Isaiah the creation of the world and the redemption of Israel both exemplify the same divine dispensation, as if that which happened in the beginning of things, and those "new things" Isa. 42:9; 48:6 which are now about to happen to Israel, both result from one and the same divine purpose of redemption. And so in fact they do. If we read on from the texts quoted above, we shall be astonished to see with what forceful effect the doctrine of creation is here brought into harmony with soteriology:

I am Yahweh, who made all things, who stretched out the heavens alone, who spread out the earth. Who was with me? ... Who confirms the word of his servant ... who tells Jerusalem it shall be inhabited ... who says to the deep, "Be dry" ... who says to Cyrus, "My shepherd, he shall fulfil all my purpose."

Isa. 44:24–28

Yahweh the Creator, who raised up the world out of chaos, does not leave Jerusalem in chaos; he who dried up the elemental waters will also raise up Jerusalem anew. Here, obviously, the doctrine of creation has been fully incorporated into the dynamic of the prophet's doctrine of redemption. Let us then come at once to the passage in Deutero-Isaiah which is the most remarkable of all for our theological inquiry:

Awake, awake, put on strength, O arm of Yahweh, awake, as in the days of old. . . . Was it not thou that didst cut Rahab in pieces, that didst pierce the dragon? Was it not thou that didst dry up the sea, the waters of the great deep? that didst make the depths of the sea *a way for the redeemed to pass over*?

Isa. 51:9f.

What has happened here? Undoubtedly the prophet starts by

57

speaking of the creation of the world by Yahweh, but then by a grotesque foreshortening of time he brings this work of Yahweh into direct contact with that act of deliverance which took place at the Red Sea. He has accomplished what at first sight appears to be an incredible transposition from one category to another. But for Deutero-Isaiah the creation does not belong in a category distinct from that of the deliverance of the Red Sea! The prophet maintains with passionate conviction his belief that what appear theologically to be two distinct acts are in fact one and the same act of the universal redemptive purpose of God. At this point the doctrine of creation has been fully absorbed into the complex of soteriological belief, so fully absorbed indeed that the doctrine of creation and the doctrine of redemption are both included in the one picture of the battle with the primaeval dragon.

A further, rather different, aspect of the matter now becomes clear. It may have seemed surprising that Deutero-Isaiah should be so ready to show Yahweh as the Creator of Israel, the one who formed Israel from the first, rather than to refer to the notion of Israel's election. By contrast with the earlier prophets, indeed, there has been a complete change of front in Deutero-Isaiah. Instead of harking back in the familiar manner to the divine election of Israel, he prefers to speak of the creation of Israel. When Deutero-Isaiah says, "Thus has Yahweh said, your Redeemer and the one who formed you from the womb" (Isa. 44:24), he really *is* thinking of the miracle of creation, and not of the historical act of election; but to base his argument on the creation instead of on the fact of election does not entail any fundamental theological change of front, for as we have seen, Deutero-Isaiah is not in any way sidetracking the doctrine of redemption in so doing. His thought remains firmly within the sphere of soteriology. A particularly good example of this complete absorption of the doctrine of creation into the prophetic doctrine of salvation can be seen in Isa. 54:5:

> Your Husband is your Creator ... and your Redeemer is the Holy One of Israel.

Nevertheless, it cannot be claimed that this characteristic theological viewpoint is simply an instance of prophetic license which deviates from every allowable norm. If we turn once more to the psalter in the light of this deeper understanding of the matter, we find the same relationship between the doctrines of creation and redemption, at times in highly significant contexts. Psalm 89 in particular should be mentioned in this connection. Following on a formal introductory passage, the hymn begins with a recital of Yahweh's deeds in the creation of the world:

> Thou dost rule the raging of the sea.... Thou didst crush Rahab like a carcass ... the heavens are thine, the earth also is thine; the world and all that is in it, thou has founded them. The north and the south, thou hast created them.... Thou hast a mighty arm.

At this point, however, the psalm comes back with a jolt to its main theme, the covenant with David, the terms of which are now brought very insistently to Yahweh's remembrance. In this particular context the poet starts from the creation and reminds Yahweh of the mighty works which he accomplished at that time; but this is certainly not an irrelevant piece of verbiage, for all the facts adduced in the psalm, from the creation to the special promise of blessing on the throne of David, contribute to the one theme which the poet stated at the outset:

> I will sing of the manifestations of Yahweh's favour. Ps. 89:1

The creation itself, then, is to be accounted as one of the acts of Yahweh's favour, *ḥasĕdê* YHWH. This somewhat surprising suggestion appears in an unmistakable form in Ps. 74, where we read:

> Yet God my King is from of old, working *salvation* in the midst of the earth. Thou didst divide the sea by thy might; thou didst break the heads of the dragons on the waters ... thou didst cleave open springs and brooks ... thine is the day, thine also the night ... thou hast fixed all the bounds of the earth; thou hast made summer and winter.... Arise, O God, plead thy cause!

We need not bother about the details. Here we are interested only in seeing what is comprised in the notion of *yĕšu'ôt*, a word which one can translate only as "saving acts" – the creation of the world and the ordering of nature.

Let us pause here for a moment. We have found a great deal of evidence for the doctrine that Yahweh created the world, but we have not found the doctrine expressed as a religious actuality, standing on its own, forming the main theme of a passage in its own right. It has always been related to something else, and subordinated to the interests and content of the doctrine of redemption. We were indeed able to show, from passages which are certainly not to be dismissed as either far-fetched or insignificant, how the doctrine of the creation is at times altogether swallowed up in the doctrine of redemption. We do not hesitate to say, in fact, that we regard this soteriological interpretation of the work of creation as the most primitive expression of Yahwistic belief concerning Yahweh as Creator of the world. The belief finds expression almost exclusively in the mythological conception of the struggle against the dragon of chaos – a conception which Yahwism accepted at a very early stage, but whose originally independent status as a thing in itself Yahwism abolished.

I shall not deal extensively with the account of the creation in the Priestly writings. Genesis 1 is not an independent theological essay, but one component of a great dogmatic treatise which moves in ever-narrowing concentric circles. The writer naturally takes his own theological stand in the innermost circle, representing the redemptive relationship between Yahweh and Israel. In order to justify this relationship theologically, he starts from the creation of the world and shows how at each stage in the course of history new statutes and ordinances are revealed, which increasingly guarantee the redemption of the people of God.[4] Thus here, too, the creation of the world by Yahweh is not being considered for its own sake, nor as of value in itself. On the contrary, P's presentation of it, even in Genesis 1, is wholly motivated by considerations of the divine purpose of redemption.

So far as this particular issue is concerned, there is no deep theological cleavage between the priestly writer and Ps. 89 or Ps. 74. We must nevertheless admit that the drawing of these concentric circles represents a theological achievement of the first order, and the same may be said of the perspicacity of the theological distinctions by which the Noachic cycle is neatly separated from the creation story.

What remains to be said? We have still to discuss those psalms which are generally regarded as the main evidence for the OT doctrine of creation – Pss. 19, 54, and 8. In Ps. 19 we find a quite new phenomenon in the thought that the cosmos itself bears witness to God. It certainly cannot be said that this notion finds any very wide support in the OT. On the contrary, it occurs nowhere else with the same clarity. At the same time there is a striking degree of restraint here, in that the created order is not said to be a revelation of "Elohim," much less of Yahweh, but proclaims "the glory of El" (*kĕbôd 'El*), the word "El" being here the equivalent of "divinity." The most colourless possible word has been chosen.

In Psalm 104 this thought, so foreign to Genesis 1, occurs again. It is, however, much less directly expressed, in the form that by its wonderful nature the whole cosmos compels us to recognize the wisdom and the might of God.[5] It is particularly necessary, however, to compare Psalm 104 with Psalm 19, if only because in both cases there is real evidence for an unadulterated doctrine of creation which stands on its own ground. In these psalms the creation of the world by Yahweh actually supplies the main theme – a very striking phenomenon, in view of all the other evidence found in Yahwistic faith.

This encourages us to inquire into the origin of these psalms. It has long been accepted that neither Psalm 19 nor Psalm 104 can be regarded as wholly original to Yahwistic belief. It is hardly by accident that the first part of Psalm 19 has been truncated as it has, and it has long been held that here we have a fragment of an ancient Canaanitish hymn subsequently adapted to Yahwistic beliefs. It is equally widely recognized that the Hymn of Ikhnaton has at least influenced profoundly the writer of Psalm 104.

I would mention here that unrelated, isolated piece of evidence for the doctrine of creation in Gen. 14:19: "Blessed be Abram by El Elyon, Maker of heaven and earth." Here, too, we have nothing more nor less than a theological statement concerning the Creator of the world! Once again it can be shown that this notion stems from a non-Israelite source: in Philo Byblius we read that heaven and earth were created by *Elioun kaloumenos Hypsistos.*[6] There is food for thought here. I see no point in questioning the weight of this evidence. Yahwism actually did absorb these elements when it could easily have fended them off, as it fended off so much which was incompatible with itself.

I am concerned, however, to demonstrate that there is another quite different source for this kind of belief. Here we are dealing with conceptions and influences which do not spring in the first place from the heart of Yahwism, but rather come into it from outside. Yet Yahwism found in them an appropriate expression of its own religious belief that the world was created by Yahweh. Where did this belief originate? To answer this question we must call in evidence the wisdom literature of the OT for there, too, we find this independent doctrine of creation freely expressed.

As Fichtner has shown,[7] the belief in reward and punishment is based on belief in the Creator, not, as one would have expected, on belief in the righteousness of the God of the covenant. "He who mocks the poor insults his Maker" (Prov. 17:5). Let us look at the *Wisdom of Amenemope* (ch. 25): "Do not laugh at a blind man, nor jeer at a dwarf. Man is but clay and straw; God is the builder, who destroys and builds every day." There can be no doubt that this freely expressed reference to God as the Creator derives its stimulus from Egyptian thought. Again, in the teaching of Merikerê we read:

> Provision is made for man, the flock of God; he made heaven and earth for their pleasure ... he made the air, ... herbs and cattle, fowl and fishes, for them.[8]

Or in the great *Hymn of Amun*:

> Amun who made men and created the beasts ... who makes the fruit tree and the herb, and feeds the cattle ... etc.[9]

Here we have once again that readily intelligible, nonmythological mode of thought which has nothing whatever in common with stories of the struggle against the primaeval dragon. As we shall see, Ps. 104:10[10] and Psalm 8 also strongly reflect this outlook, which has as its interest the divine economy in this world. It expresses a rational, intelligible purpose, and is therefore concerned above all with those problems which force themselves upon our understanding and which compel our admiration, things very different from these portentous, bizarre elements which belong to the mythical cosmogony.[11] Are we not right to see here the influence of wisdom literature? In my opinion, what we have here is an Egyptian outlook passed on to Israel by travelling teachers of wisdom.[12]

Psalm 8 also belongs to the same complex of evidence for the doctrine of creation, which stems less from specifically Yahwistic beliefs concerning election and salvation than from a reasoned, reflective theology. The beautiful simplicity and originality of it must not blind us to the fact that the faith of the writer results from hard thinking: when I look at the sky, the moon, and the stars, when I reflect upon the wonder of the created order – how small man is! Yet this is the surprising and glorious thing, that God fences man round with his providential care and bestows on him his salvation. It is this sudden twist in the writer's thoughts about the cosmos which seems to me to be significant: the consideration of creation for its own sake is once again left behind. Here, too, it is no more than a starting point from which we go on to wonder at the miracle of God's providential care and of his purpose of salvation for mankind.

It is scarcely necessary to pursue the matter farther. Our main thesis was that in genuinely Yahwistic belief the doctrine of creation never attained to the stature of a relevant, independent doctrine. We found it invariably related, and indeed subordinated, to soteriological considerations. This is not to say, however, that it is necessarily of later origin. Evidently a doctrine of creation was known in Canaan in extremely early times, and played a large part in the cultus in the pre-Israelite period through mythical representations of the struggle against primaeval chaos. Yahwistic faith early absorbed these elements, but because of the exclusive commitment of Israel's faith to historical salvation, the doctrine of creation was never able to attain to independent existence in its own right. Either it remained a cosmic foil against which soteriological pronouncements stood out the more effectively, or it was wholly incorporated into the complex of soteriological thought.

A quite different strand of religious influence entered the Yahwistic faith in the form of wisdom-lore, a highly rationalized mode of speculation concerning the divine economy in this world which we may regard as being of Egyptian origin. At this point we are faced with unequivocal, self-justified statements of belief concerning the creation. That these documents should have been repeatedly cited as expressions of Yahwistic belief concerning the creation of the world by Yahweh does not betray a very profound knowledge of OT religion in those who have cited them. We would not, of course, in any way rob the evidence of its value, but we do maintain that in Israel quite obviously a very great many safeguards had to be established, some of them of primary theological importance, before this liberty of treatment could be achieved for an undiluted doctrine of creation; in other words, the doctrine of redemption had first to be fully safeguarded, in order that the doctrine that nature, too, is a means of divine self-revelation might not encroach upon or distort the doctrine of redemption, but rather broaden and enrich it.

I should like to close with the observation that it is impossible to arrive at an assessment of OT doctrine simply by using the methods of the history of religions. We made a great mistake in continuing for so long to judge the really quite slight significance of the doctrine of creation by the standard of importance of its later "development." Nor should our assessment depend on the fact that we now regard this doctrine as very ancient. Rather, what we have to do is to investigate the theological structure of the doctrinal statements of the OT.

NOTES

1   W. Lütgert, *Schöpfung und Offenbarung* (Gütersloh: Bertelsmann, 1934) 52, 56, 358.

2   Amos 4:13; 5:8f; 9:5f.

3   Cf. Isa. 44:21; 46:3; 54:5.

4 Cf. G. von Rad, *Die Priesterschrift im Hexateuch* (BWANT 65; Stuttgart: Kohlhammer, 1934) 188.

5 Cf. also Job 12:7–10, perhaps too Isa. 40:21.

6 C. Müller, *Fragmenta Historicorum Graecorum* (Paris: Ambrosio Firmin Didot, 1841) III: 111ff [Reprint: Frankfurt/M.: Minerva, 1975].

7 J. Fichtner, *Die altorientalische Weisheit in ihrer israelitisch-jüdischen Ausprägung* (BZAW 62; Giessen: Töpelmann, 1933).

8 H. Ranke, in H. Gressmann's *Altorientalische Texte zum Alten Testament* (2d ed., Berlin/Leipzig: Walter de Gruyter, 1926) 35.

9 A. Erman, *The Literature of the Ancient Egyptians* (ET, A. M. Blackman; London: Methuen & Co., 1927) 283.

10 Psalm 104 even contains an echo of the battle with the primaeval dragon, a feature not found of course in the Egyptian version. The fact is an indication of the manner in which in later times the small coin of the conception of creation could be admitted into almost any appropriate context.

11 There is a strong element of awe, therefore, at the very heart of what is actually a purely technical problem.

12 A similar process is at work in Prov. 8:22ff.

3

In the Beginning:
A Contribution to the
Interpretation of the First Word
*of the Bible**

WALTHER EICHRODT

Every reader of the Bible is familiar with the lapidary sentence with which its first chapter begins: "In the beginning God created the heavens and the earth." This opening of the creation story seems so appropriate that the consideration as to whether it misrepresents the original would appear offhand irrelevant. And yet this consideration goes back to the early Middle Ages, when the Jewish scholars Ibn Ezra (1167) and Rashi (1105) in their commentaries expressed the view that this sentence constitutes a relative indication of time, which either introduces the following verse ("In the beginning, when God created the heavens and the earth, then the earth was . . . ," as in Ibn Ezra) or reaches across the parenthetical vv. 2–3 ("In the beginning, when God created the heavens and the earth . . . then God spoke . . . ," as in Rashi). The principal reason for reducing v. 1 to a secondary stipulation of the following verse lay in the difficulty of harmonizing the assertion of v. 2 concerning the chaotic primitive condition of the earth with a comprehensive statement concerning the creation of the universe. Thus many Christian exegetes have followed one or the other proposed translation, usually that of Rashi.[1]

At the same time others, dealing with the exegetical difficulties in v. 2 in a variety of ways, held to the view that the first sentence of the Bible constitutes a fundamental statement of the activity of God the Creator who called all things into being[2] – an interpretation

* First published in English in *Israel's Prophetic Heritage* (1962) 1–11.

already attested in the Greek translation. It was acknowledged on all sides that the one translation was as defensible philologically and grammatically as the other. Reasons for the preference of one or the other interpretation of the text stemmed more from the history of religions or from theology, depending upon whether or not one wished to consider the priestly narrator capable of transcending, in principle, the level of OT statements concerning creation.

This line was first crossed by P. Humbert, who maintained that the understanding of Gen. 1:1 as a relative clause might well be established on linguistic historical grounds. He believed it possible to say: *"La seule traduction correcte est donc: 'Lorsque Dieu commença de créer l'Univers, le monde était alors en état chaotique, etc.'"*[3] This rendering of the result of his investigation is so keenly formulated that no exegete can ignore it. Were it sound, an age-old exegetical difference of opinion would have been solved. Thus it would be in the interests of all to examine it carefully. In so doing, we are certain to be acting in accordance with the wishes of this scholar, who is well known for his sagacious OT research.

Of the approximately fifty references to *rēʾšît* in the OT only twelve, according to Humbert, are to be understood in the sense of a temporal beginning, while three tend to express principle rather than time. At this point one might ask whether Gen. 10:10, Hos. 9:10, and Mic. 1:13 should not be reckoned with the twelve passages mentioned, Prov. 8:22 and Job 40:19 belonging to those passages where meaning is ambiguous. Nevertheless, since the question before us does not involve these passages, we do not wish to place particular emphasis upon them.

Of the passages which use *rēʾšît* in a temporal sense, only two display an absolute construction at first glance, namely Isa. 46:10 and Gen. 1:1. If it can be shown that in even the Isaiah passage no absolute statement of time is intended, then the evidence would seem complete that, on the basis of the use of *rēʾšît* in the entire OT, one can speak only of a relative beginning in Gen. 1:1 as well.

We must admit, of course, that we are not totally convinced of the cogency of this demonstration. In such an employment of OT passages, is not too little consideration given to the limited extent of the OT literature which has been preserved for us? And is it so irrefutably certain that a passage having as its author a thinker singular in many respects and unique in the OT may be understood only in terms of the twelve or fifteen passages – or, as the case may be, the only passage – from the prophet? In view of the available evidence, may one speak here of more than a high degree of probability? Yet even this would give the translator something to go on.

But it seems to us that in the evidence put before us certain important passages are lacking which ought not to be left out of consideration. Here must be mentioned above all the time indication *mērō'š* "from the beginning," which derives from the same root as *rē'šît*. It occurs four times in Deutero-Isaiah: 40:21; 41:4; 41:26; 48:16. Of these, the last two passages are to be understood in a relative sense according to the context. In 41:26 the term stands in parallelism with *mill^epānîm*, "long since," and refers to the beginning of Cyrus's intervention in the history of the Near Eastern states: that is, from the beginning he was accompanied by the prophetic witness to the role assigned him by Yahweh in the destiny of this people. Isaiah 48:16 must also be understood in this sense; the allusion to the prophetic witness that Yahweh alone directs the course of history is quite clear, despite the questionable text in v. 16c.

The situation is nevertheless different in the case of the first two passages mentioned. In 40:21 the parallel time designation *mîsudôt hā'āreṣ*, "from the foundation of the earth,"[4] is a clear reference to an absolute beginning. "From the beginning of the world" (Duhm) Yahweh, by virtue of his creative act, has proved himself the exalted one before whom all human greatness sinks into nothingness. And if, in 41:4, the amazing triumphal procession of Cyrus is referred to the God who called the generations "from the beginning," then an absolute beginning of history is meant, in which Yahweh allotted the peoples their task. The continuation in v. 4b, "I, Yahweh, the first, and with the last, I am the same," points toward the idea of the eternity of God and thereby derives from the act of creation in the beginning an inference of greatest significance for the understanding of the divine being.

That Deutero-Isaiah's allusion to an absolute beginning of the world is not an isolated one can be seen from Prov. 8:23, where *mērō'š* is unequivocally determined by the preceding *mē'ôlām*, "from eternity on," and by the following *miqqadmê 'éreṣ*, "from the primeval times of the earth." If this primordially created wisdom is given in the preceding verse the dignity of *rē'šît darkô* and *qédem mip'ālāw*, then the second designation may be translated with Köhler in a temporal sense as "the earliest of his works"; as for the first designation, one may waver between the translations "first-born" (cf. Sir. 1:4) and "unique evidence of His might,"[5] detecting also in this passage the transition mentioned by Humbert from the temporal to the material (*sachlich*) meaning of *rē'šît*. Accordingly, the temporal expressions in Sir. 24:9, *pro tou aiōnos ap'archēs ektisen me*, will be considered a translation of the Hebrew *mēʿôlām* and *mērōʾš*.[6]

It is worth noting that the words used here as adverbs of time may be used in an absolute as well as in a relative sense; for *mērōʾš* cf. p. 67 above; for *lᵉmîmê qédem* in the sense of *lᵉmērāḥôq* cf. 2 Kings 19:25; without *l*, Isa. 23:7; Mic. 7:20; and so on. In the strict sense of primeval time Isa. 51:9, *kîmê qédem*, is parallel to *dōrôt ʿôlāmîm*; Prov. 8:23, *miqqadmê ʾéreṣ*, cf. paragraph above; *mēʿôlām* absolute in Prov. 8:23, relative in Isa. 42:14; 47:7; and so on. It should be no cause for wonder, then, if something similar were the case with *rēʾšît*.

The use of *mērēʾšît* in Isa. 46:10 appears to be determined by its correlation with *ʾaḥᵃrît*. Does not here (as in Job 8:7; 42:12; Eccles. 7:8) a *terminus a quo* stand over against a *terminus ad quem* in order to denote a definite period of time? If so, the correlation would mean relation even in the case of a formally absolute construction of *rēʾšît*.[7] Nevertheless, the passage in Isaiah is completely dissimilar to the cited parallel passages, where a period within the earthly passage of time is clearly intended; one can claim the same for Isa. 46:10 only by disregarding the context. On the basis of v. 9 it is clear that the prophet thinks of something existent from primeval times, the *rîʾšōnôt mēʿôlām*. What is to be understood by this, as v. 9b states plainly enough, is the unique and eternal deity of Yahweh; and it is with this idea – already encountered in other passages[8] – that the prophet combines God's disposition over beginning and end. But one cannot refer this pair of words just to Cyrus's rise and ultimate success, of which v. 11 speaks. The power to summon Cyrus is deduced here, as in 44:24ff; 48:12–15, from the primordial majesty of Yahweh the Creator, who can make known from the beginning (*miqqédem*) that which has not yet been created (v. 10a) and who therefore causes the end to be proclaimed from the very beginning. Who or what proclaims, whether the works of creation themselves (Ps. 19:2f) or wisdom (Prov. 8:30f) or the morning stars (Job 38:4) – on this the prophet reflects little, just as in 40:21 he says little of who or what, from the foundation of the earth, is supposed to have brought men to the understanding of God's sublime majesty. It is enough that the transcendent God has determined the end together with the beginning, and therefore commands the entire development of the world. Here then is meant that broad perspective over earthly time which is possible for the Creator alone, and which allows him to declare his counsel irrefutable and his plans certain (v. 10b). The recognition of God's sovereignty through the force of his unique deity achieves particular significance for the historical moment in which the prophet and his followers live. Under the absolute power of disposal of the Almighty Creator the summons to the bird of prey has been issued, and the revolutionary event thus introduced will be carried through to the end (v. 11).

Here beginning and end do not comprise a specific period of time within history, but rather historical time as such. For it is the fundamental conviction of Deutero-Isaiah, determining all his prophetic utterances, that this historical time is *now*; arrived at the threshold of a new aeon, it realizes its *'aḥ^arît* in the fulfillment of the divine decision, through which the peoples – indeed, the whole cosmos – will be laid at the feet of God who alone rules the world (45:14–25; 51:6–8). Set in this larger context, the absolute use of *mērē'šît* might well be assured.

For that matter, neither is the absolute use of *b^erē'šît* in Gen. 1:1 so isolated and without analogy as one would like to pretend. Granted its complete independence, it nevertheless represents only one witness among several from the Exilic and post-Exilic period – a period during which a common spiritual concern, not previously evident, became active. One must simply accept, along with his pronounced peculiarity of thought and expression, the fact that the priestly narrator here makes use of the absolute form of *rē'šît* with the preposition *b* – a form which is no longer found elsewhere. In this case, linguistic history obviously cannot be the appropriate means of critical examination. In addition the question as to whether a reciprocal influence exists among the witnesses established in Deutero-Isaiah, in Proverbs, and in P, in which group Ps. 90:2 must also very probably be reckoned, scarcely permits an answer. Von Rad has rightly rejected the attempt to affix a precise date to the Priestly Document of the Hexateuch, a work strongly rooted in the priestly tradition which was preserved and handed down through the centuries.[9] It appears more important to seek out that place where, in such dissimilar documents, the idea of an absolute beginning of the earthly world finds expression with a kind of inner compulsion, thus adding to the linguistic-historical defense of the meaning of this controversial expression an intellectual-historical (*geitesgeschichtlich*) one.

This is probably easiest to do in the case of the prophet of the Exile, who at several points returns to this thought in his message. The indispensable help which he found here in his controversy with the pagan world view is evident. Rendtorff has demonstrated clearly how, in Deutero-Isaiah, the action of Yahweh the Creator is closely linked with his redemptive action toward Israel in the present and in the future; and how, through the focusing of the statements about creation upon Israel's existence, actual meaning for the present is won.[10] It is repeatedly emphasized that Yahweh alone, without help, stretched out the heavens and founded the earth (44:24; 45:12, 18); indeed, that the utmost opposites in nature and history – light and darkness, weal and woe – are comprehended in his creative will, revealing him as the only God and Lord (45:6–8). When in these contexts the prophet beholds the beginning of creation and the God who stands apart from it in sovereign freedom, he experiences in this vision the supreme moment of divine majesty in the universe: it is the eternal God who, unlike the pagan deities woven into their cosmogony, truly possesses transcendental majesty and therefore justly claims absolute power over the created world (40:21–24, 28;[11] 41:4; 45:6f, 21; 46:9f; 48:12f). No wonder that, in the face of the uncontradictable creative act of this eternal God, chaos vanishes. In 44:27 and 50:2f one may find perhaps traces of particular features of the chaos image. Yet even when this image emerges once again in the form of the mythical struggle against chaos (51:9f), it no longer possesses any intrinsic reality, but rather precludes the reference to the conquest of all historical forces which could challenge the salvation of Israel. From this God who stands above time, whose goodness and righteousness endure eternally (51:8; 54:8), come then in addition gifts of salvation which cannot be challenged by time: an eternal world (40:8), an eternal salvation (45:17; 51:6), an eternal covenant (54:10; 55:3). The prophet's assurance concerning the eternal God soars highest, however, where he describes the salvation also bestowed by God as superior to all the majesty of his creation (51:6–8). God's salvation will endure beyond the fall of this creation; it participates in the eternity of the Creator. Herewith the message of salvation for this God-despairing people first becomes secure against all apparent contradiction, because it is established in the being of God himself. The disciples of the prophet have drawn the conclusion to this message in their proclamation of a new heaven and a new earth (Isa. 65:17; 66:22). Thus it is an immediate concern of faith and no philosophical construction which points to an absolute beginning of this world and correspondingly to its end.

Apart from this aspect of his representation of the beginning of the created world – one governed by the idea of the divine act of salvation – the priestly writer seems inclined to a static interpretation of the creation as an event of the past, to be distinguished from the preservation of the world through divine providence. And yet on closer scrutiny it becomes clear that even Genesis 1 is not meant to make an independent statement concerning the origin of the world, but that it reflects a comprehensive view of God's action toward Israel. The dominant theme of the priestly narrative is preparation of the salvation realized in God's people as a divine gift of fundamental importance to the world, one which takes form little by little in ever-new divine ordinances and constitutes the deepest meaning of the course of history. The significance of Israel's salvation for the world finds reflection even in the choice of decisive manifestations in which P sees the divine revelation unveiled: creation, covenant with Noah, covenant with Abraham, revelation on Sinai. Whether the number four as the number for world and totality alludes already to the all-inclusive character of the history which here unfolds[12] must probably remain undecided. But in any case God's act of creation, by virtue of its position in this scheme, takes on the characteristic of an initial act in the working out of salvation, opening the way to man for fellowship with his God. The primordial action of God, through which he has determined the basic order of the earthly world, becomes in this way a permanent guarantee for the inevitability and eternal continuance of the salvation granted to Israel. The sanctification of the Sabbath as marking the completion of the miracles of creation clearly indicates the inner connection between the creation of the world and the open offer of divine grace to Israel. Though the source of grace here uncovered remains veiled to human perception, it nevertheless proclaims at the very beginning God's desire for fellowship with his creation, and especially with its appointed lord, mankind. From the beginning on, this creation appears to rest upon the rhythmic pattern of work and festive rest, with which it renounces all claim to self-value and lays down its strengths and achievements at the feet of the God who designed it for his praise and his adoration.

Here the priestly narrator manifests a view of world events which no longer acknowledges the cosmos to be significant in itself but subjects it at every moment to the omnipotent will of God the Sovereign, who wields it according to his purpose. In this context time, as the space within which all life is enacted, plays a significant role. At the time of the creation – indeed, based upon and insured by it – the seven-day week is established with the Sabbath as its conclusion. The stars, not created until the fourth day, have, in contrast to their worship in heathen practice, no other task than to confirm time as created and disposed by God along with the week of creation – to regulate the days, count the ages, determine years

71

and holidays – and in addition to this task of clear delineation to assist in the functioning of civic and cultic life. Thus the evaluation of time as the principle of order designed for God's creation establishes the total dependence of the created world upon the Lord, who stands apart from it in absolute freedom.

The idea of the absolute beginning of the created world thus proves to be a logical expression of the total outlook of the priestly narrator, an indispensable link in the working out of salvation on behalf of Israel in God's world order. What Deutero-Isaiah, in regarding the imminent consummation of history, grasps as a firm basis of faith makes it possible for the priestly writer to emphasize in concise form the divine transcendence over against the world of appearance. This transcendence makes all of the earthly world a mere reflection of its otherworldly glory, only in order to make known in the revelation to Israel the fullness of her redemption.

The wisdom teachers are already in an entirely different situation when they consider the absolute beginning of the world of creation. The broadening of the concept of *ḥokmâ* to a cosmic principle, to which the functional order of the earth is traced, and its elevation to a hypostasis which, at the creation of the universe, is used by God the Creator as the mediator of his will, necessarily led to the reflection on the first beginnings of divine creativity – where, of course, the idea of the world's proceeding from God appears as the effective force in question.[13] Not only is justice done to the transcendence of the divine being without denying his direct intervention in the internal events of the world, but also the authority of wisdom for human life is strengthened by its role as mediator in the formation of the universe, and so is made to coincide with the Word and the Spirit of God. Thus it is hardly surprising that expressions for the absolute beginning appear more and more frequently.

It should now be clear that each reflection on the beginning of creation exercises in its place an important function in the total view of the respective writer. If we understand *bᵉrēʾšît* in Gen. 1:1 as absolute, this is not an arbitrary judgment but is closely connected with the most important concern of the priestly conception of history. A relative interpretation of the expression would place an emphasis on the autonomy of the chaotic matter at the beginning of creation contrary to the whole concern of this creation story. The narrator is moved to reflection not by that which preceded the divine creation but by the fact that nothing but the autonomous decree of the transcendent God determined the form of creation. That the *creatio ex nihilo* thereby enters the picture is incontestable; indeed, other concepts in the priestly creation story, which we cannot examine in this connection,[14] point in this same direction. It is enough that the translation of the first sentence of the Bible, "In the beginning God created the heavens and the earth," proves to be the truly pertinent one, not only from the aesthetic-stylistic point of view but also from that of linguistic and intellectual history.

NOTES

1 Cf., among others, the commentaries of K. Budde, A. Dillmann, H. Holzinger, and S. R. Skinner.

2 Cf. H. Strack, H. Gunkel, O. Procksch, W. Zimmerli, G. von Rad, among others.

3 P. Humbert, "Trois notes sur Genèse 1," in *Interpretationes ad Vetus Testamentum pertinentes Sigmundo Mowinckel missae* (Oslo: Fabritius & Sønner, 1955) 85–96.

4 So most commentators read today. The article before *'ereṣ* may perhaps be omitted with the Qumran manuscript of Isaiah 1.

5 Cf. J. Savignac, "Note sur le sense du verset Prov. 8:22," *VT* 4 (1954) 429. J. B. Bauer, "Encore une fois Prov. 8:22," *VT* 8 (1958) 91f.

6 So V. Ryssel in E. Kautzsch's *Die Apokryphen und Pseudepigraphen des AT* (Tübingen: Mohr, 1900) I:353. See also Sir. 16:26; 34:27; 39:25, and the comments on these passages in R. Smend's *Die Weisheit des Jesus Sirach. Hebräisch und Deutsch* (Berlin: G. Reimer, 1906).

7 Cf. Humbert, "Trois notes," 87.

8 Cf. ibid., 4.

9 G. von Rad, *Die Priesterschrift im Hexateuch* (BWANT 65; Stuttgart: Kohlhammer, 1934) 189.

10 R. Rendtorff, "Die theologische Stellung des Schöpfungsglaubens bei Deuterojesaja," *ZTK* 51 (1954) 3ff.

11 On *'ēlōhê 'ôlām* cf. E. Jenni, *Das Wort 'ôlām im Alten Testament* (Berlin: Töpelmann, 1953) 68.

12 Cf. W. Zimmerli, *I Mose I–II. Die Urgeschichte I* (ZBK; Zurich: Zwingli Verlag, 1943).

13 Prov. 8:22f; Job 28:25–27; Sir. 1:4; 24:3, 9; Wis. 7:12, 15–22, 25f; 9:9.

14 On this point see W. Eichrodt's *Theologie des Alten Testaments*, Band 2–3 (Stuttgart: Klotz, 1961) 63–66 [ET: Theology of the Old Testament (Philadelphia: Westminster Press, 1964) 2:101–106].

4

"Creation" Motifs
in Ancient Hebrew Poetry*

DENNIS J. McCARTHY, S.J.

The OT scholar should be surprised when he finds that Ugaritologists
ordinarily deny that anything like a creation story has been found
at Ras Shamra.[1] It may well be true that nothing like the various
Egyptian cosmogonies, the Babylonian *enuma eliš*, or Hesiod's
Theogony have turned up in Ugaritic literature, and it is a limitation
of the definition of a creation story to this kind of thing which brings
about the reservations of the Ugaritologists. However, there is a great
deal about the struggle of the beneficent weather god, Hadd (mostly
designated by his title, Baal), to (re-)establish a proper order of things
which means assuring sovereignty for Baal and fertility for the earth.
This is exactly the sort of thing which we have taken for granted
to be creation myth since at least Hermann Gunkel's *Schöpfung und
Chaos*.

We deal with a picture of a divine struggle against chaotic forces
represented usually by the sea or the "waters," and we assume that
this is a creation story of a kind. This sort of story, which we may
call a *Chaoskampf*, is generally held to have three basic themes: (1)
the fight against chaos often represented by or personified as a
monster of the waters; (2) the conquest of this monstrous force by
a god who is consequently acclaimed king; (3) the giving of a palace
(temple) to the divine king. In fact, despite the doubts of so many
students of the Ugaritic texts about the occurrence of creation ideas
in them, these discoveries have actually confirmed most of us who
are primarily concerned with the OT in the conviction that some
such picture of creation was part of Canaan's legacy to Israel.[2]
Perhaps the problem the Ugaritologists find in identifying this sort

* First published in *CBQ* 29/3 (1967) 87–100. Before his untimely death in August
1983 McCarthy had revised and updated this essay in the light of more recent
Ugaritological studies.

of thing as creation is a good omen. It should give us pause. Are we so sure that the *Chaoskampf* with all its attendant themes is really a story of creation in any meaningful sense?

Perhaps we are asking the wrong questions of our texts. In fact, when it comes to creation we seem fated to do this in one way or another. The Christian is familiar with the firm teaching of the Church that God made everything without using any pre-existent materials. We tend to forget that the explicit and official formulation of this teaching has been governed by the actual situations which the Church has had to face. It has addressed itself to specific problems, particularly the recurrent challenge of gnostic dualism and the need to distinguish the trinitarian processions from the process of creation.[3] Hence the rightful insistence on *creatio ex nihilo* which denies both the existence of some sort of matter independent of God and the formation of the world as something which emanated (in the Plotinian sense) from God. However, apart from John,[4] dualism is not a biblical problem, and nowhere in the Bible are the special questions of developed trinitarian theology a concern. Addressing the scriptures directly (their implications are something else, but they are not the immediate concern of the exegete in this matter) for answers to questions not their own turns out to be fruitless, and yet we have asked our texts about *creatio ex nihilo* as though this was the concern of them and their authors.

Still, without going so far as the technical meaning expressed in terms drawn from philosophy, for us the word creation in its normal context must mean some sort of absolute beginning of our world, or we equivocate. Can we really say that this is what the *Chaoskampf* and all it implies is usually concerned with? In other words, when we speak of these things as creation motifs, are we in danger of introducing foreign elements, our own common sense notions even if not technical ones, into the understanding of the texts just as we do when we seek philosophy in them? It seems to me that in fact we are. In the OT the so-called creation motifs are introduced in function of something else, and we must wonder whether we are safe in speaking of creation here at all.[5]

The questions which bring out the motifs in the OT are various. There is the question of where salvation lies. There is the question of an orderly world of humans (secondarily of nature).[6] There is the question of identifying the true god (Deutero-Isaiah; 2 Macc. 7:28). There is the question of the proper cult (P). But where is the question of absolute origins as such?

Obviously, all of this is matter for many papers; we can deal only with restricted aspects here. We shall take only the first point: salvation and so-called creation imagery. This probably seems to be a commonplace. It is such, and one can find reference to it anywhere.[7] However, it is often rewarding to review the commonplace from the proper viewpoint. We may begin by noting the most influential study of the relation between the origin of things and salvation: Gerhard von Rad's brilliant analysis of the form of the Hexateuch and his conclusion that the primeval history is the genial addition of J as a kind of cosmic prologue for salvation history.[8] It is not without interest, then, that von Rad, following Hartmut Gese, now admits that the primeval history must have been part of Israel's basic account of itself even before J. This conclusion is based on the fact that the literary form of this account called for such a prologue.[9] Of course, if the primeval history was a given part of the genre rather than an addition to the basic historical credo by J as von Rad argued, it is harder to show that it is a brilliant stroke relating creation and grace as never before. Still, it can be shown that the genre has been adapted to a new purpose. Borrowed from tradition, it has been changed radically to provide a deepened understanding of God's dealings with his people.[10]

However, when we look at Genesis 2—11 from the special point of view we are adopting here, it is extremely difficult to speak of creation as being there in a meaningful sense. In the Yahwist parts of the primeval history, the only ones which interest us, there is no real concern for the origin of the world. All the interest is directed toward its good ordering. This is not *creatio ex nihilo* of course, but equally it has nothing to do with the *Chaoskampf* theme either. The order depends upon watering (rain) and man (cultivation): "When Yahweh God made heaven and earth no plant had yet sprung up in the fields because neither Yahweh God had brought rain to the earth nor had man worked the ground" (Gen. 2:4b–5). The familiar motif of the waters is there, but in unfamiliar guise. They are no force to be fought or contained. They are simply God's instrument, his contribution to an orderly world. Even in the flood story the waters are no raging monster; they are released to do their task quietly enough.[11] In all the talk of the struggle against a watery chaos which is supposed to have been of the essence of the *Chaoskampf* type of creation story, as far as is known to me there is no attention paid to the fact that in the only instances when the waters do get out of hand (and remember that they are supposed to threaten this yearly!)[12] they do so not as a force opposed to the divine but rather as the passive instrument of divine punishment.

In the OT version, in fact, they are used to overcome disorder, moral disorder it is true, but for the OT moral and natural order or disorder are a continuity,[13] and in any case we shall see that *Chaoskampf* motifs are commonly linked to moral or social order in the OT. The flood at least is there to purify, not pollute. The conclusion must be that the center of attention is the order of things, not their origins, in this use of the theme of the raging waters. In J, then, rather than speak of creation or cosmogony as the background for the OT drama of sin and grace one should speak of the order of things, cosmology in the root sense, if one will.

Thus the familiar struggle element is entirely absent from J. At most it gives us very early evidence (older than the document itself!) for an interest in the beginnings of the order of things, particularly the moral order. There is no mark of the mythic *Chaoskampf*, but then this section of Genesis has never been part of the argument for the occurrence and importance of the *Chaoskampf* theme in the OT. It is rather the poetry of the Hebrew Bible which has shown the creation struggle imagery.

In view of this, it is remarkable that the poetry which is identifiably oldest does not seem to have been studied systematically from this point of view. Yet much is gained if we can characterize the attitude to these most ancient texts. It may be that the forms found in later poetry, the kingship of Yahweh psalms for instance, are older as forms, for they surely antedate Israel itself. However, as we have them they are hymns modified by later use. They do not bear the linguistic marks of antiquity which other poems do, for example. If these latter tell us something about the use of the *Chaoskampf* theme in early days in Israel, about the meaning of the imagery borrowed from it and the purposes to which it was put, this direct evidence will show more clearly the meaning of the theme in Israel in the vital formative stages of Israelite religion than any extrapolation from later texts, even though this latter is integrated into a view of the theme as it was supposed to have existed outside Israel in earliest times.

The ancient poetry in question can be found in Genesis 49; Exod. 15:2–18; Deut. 32:1–43; Deuteronomy 33; Judges 5; 2 Sam. 22:2–51; and Psalms 29 and 68, materials which bring us back close to Israel's beginnings. Rather than take the older and relevant parts of these texts one by one in exegesis we shall address three basic questions to them. (1) What does God do in them which can be related to creation? This will come down to a discussion of certain basic vocabulary, the verbs used. Are they in fact ones also used of creation? (2) How does God act? Is the imagery used that associated with creation? (3) Why does he do it? This is crucial, for the purpose of an action will often reveal whether it is creation or not, and in what sense.

When we turn to the first question: what does God do, we find at once that certain of the actions predicated of him in these texts are associated with creation or at least production both in the Bible and at Ras Shamra. Among these are *qnh* (Ugaritic *qny*) and *kwn*.[14] In the ancient victory hymn in Exod. 15:2–18, v. 16b reads *'am-zû qanîtā*, "the people which thou hast gotten." In another old text, Deut. 32:6b, we have: *hălô'-hû' 'ābîkā qûnekā*, "Is he not thy father (who) got thee?"[15] It is well to retain here the double meaning in the rather old fashioned use of "get," for, though the root seems to mean "form" in a general sense, "acquire," or "be master of," the myths of Ugarit certainly demonstrate that it has the sense of "produce" and "procreate." This Ugaritic evidence points up the sexual overtones of the root *qny/qnh* as opposed to some more general note such as "make" or the like – the god is a father, not a manufacturer.

The other root, *kwn*, on the other hand, does not have this sort of overtone: the basic meaning is to "make firm," and so, among other things, "form," and "found."[16] This is clearly the case in Deut. 32:6, where it is part of a passage describing Yahweh's founding of Israel as a special instance of his universal activity of "setting the boundaries of the peoples, assigning them to the various sons of God."[17] Yahweh has formed a social order with each people given a proper place and guide.

These verbs do not exhaust the vocabulary pertinent to our investigation. On the contrary, though the ancient Israelite poems avoid a favorite word of the Ugaritic texts relating to origins, *bny* (Hebrew *bnh*), which is so common as an epithet of the high god El, *bny bnwt*, "creator of creatures," and do not apply its Hebrew cognate to Yahweh, they use what would seem a far less likely verb, *yld*, "bear a child." At Ras Shamra this was a cosmogonic or better theogonic word. For instance, goddesses bear a divinized Dawn and Dusk to El.[18] In Deut. 32:18 Yahweh himself is "the Rock (who) bore thee..., the God who was in travail with thee." The imagery is strong: "bore thee" (*yelādkā*) is parallel to *meḥollekā*, "writhe in the pangs of childbirth" literally, surely at first sight as extreme an anthropomorphism as one could imagine. But, of course, it is precisely a freedom from the basic anthropomorphic view of the divine current in the ancient Near East which permits this. A pantheon preserves the distinct sexual functions with its gods and goddesses. The one God of Israel is beyond anything like this, so far beyond that the poet can freely use the image of childbirth to emphasize the affective aspect, the love of Yahweh for his people, a love which like a mother's is unearned and even more intense for the weakling among her children, since the poet uses this image to introduce the section on the faithlessness of Israel which deserves and gets parental punishment.[19] This makes the usage here all the more poignant, for v. 18 resumes v. 6 with a new note. In the earlier verse we have to do with a section concerning the special marking out of Israel for Yahweh's favor among the nations, but the verbs used, *qnh* and *kwn*, though significant, are not especially colorful. The repetition of the title Rock (32:4) as well as the parallel in ideas between 32:6 and 32:18 form a kind of inclusion which brings us back to the earlier, happier situation, but by the change in tone also points forward to the judgment scene which continues the poem in v. 19ff. Hence the highly emotional figures; the measure of Yahweh's love and favor is the measure of Israel's guilt and punishment. This is the mood of Hosea 11, but in archaic form.

The conclusion at this point is clear. Yahweh is indeed spoken of in terms which, in one way or another, refer to the coming to be of things, and this vocabulary is the same as that of the Ugaritic texts when they speak of origins. However, the OT gives the words a particular focus. It uses the vocabulary to speak of Yahweh's favors to his people, his marking them out and making them a people (Deut. 32:6: *qnh, kwn*; Exod. 15:16: *qnh*) with emphasis on the love shown in all of this (Deut. 32:18: *yld*). Even at Ugarit these expressions were mostly used for the origins of man and the gods (though the latter may well be personified natural phenomena), of a kind of social order or at least of social beings rather than of a cosmos. Still there is nothing there about the formation of a god's people, nor of his loving and judging them. Israel seems to have done something quite new in applying these "creation" words to the description of its position as a saved and chosen people among peoples, all under God's guidance.[20] What is "created" is a social or political order. In Exodus 15 Israel is constituted a nation at Egypt's expense. In Deuteronomy 32 all nations have their place and their guides assigned them; a whole social order is brought into being.[21] We can and do call this sort of thing creative, but it is scarcely creation in any technical sense since it does not touch at all upon absolute beginnings of a whole world.

We find thus far that what Yahweh is described as doing when "creation" verbs are predicated of him is something quite different from what the divinity does in the supposed *Chaoskampf* creation myth. It is somewhat different when we turn to the *how* of things. The poetry makes ready use of the motifs associated with the *Chaoskampf*. This is obvious in Exodus 15. We have a battle in which the raging waters do indeed figure, the victorious god gains a temple, and he is acclaimed king. This is the very stuff of the creation myth in its classic formulation in *enuma eliš*. But here it is demythologized.[22] The waters are not the enemy but the weapon of God, and his temple is his own work. He is not subject to approval from on high, nor does he need a motion from the floor in a divine assembly[23]

This use of terms related to the *Chaoskampf* is not confined to this passage. The psalm in 2 Samuel 22 turns the imagery to a different purpose: "breakers of death" and "torrents" surround the afflicted king (22:6), but Yahweh the Warrior appears to confound and turn back the enemy (22:16). The imagery of the mighty sea is the same, but its function is different. Now it is not Yahweh's weapon as in Exodus but the symbol of the adversary he so easily puts down. Early in its history Israel is so free from seeing any reality in the *Chaoskampf* theme that it has become a mere source for figures of speech. Its language can be used now one way, now another as seems useful in a given literary situation, something hardly possible if it were felt to be a description of reality, for then the use of the language would have to be controlled by the reality behind it. The only consistency is the end to which the imagery is directed. Always it tells how Yahweh saved by producing or restoring order, whether it is by means of the waters or by saving from the waters which symbolize evil. The "creation" motifs have become images of salvation, and, of course, this became a tradition in Israel. In the psalms of lamentation, for example, the waters are a cliché for evil, and we shall find them appearing again as a weapon in God's hands. The point is that this turn was given to the imagery very early. Indeed, from its very first recorded use in Israel this is so.

One further instance of the imagery of the waters is worth noting. This motif from the *Chaoskampf* theme appears in Gen. 49:25 (= Deut. 33:13): *birkôt tᵉhôm rōbeṣet tāḥat*, "blessings from Deep lying in wait below."[24] The note of threat, even of recalcitrance, echoes faintly in that "lying in wait," a hint of an evil will in the waters, a hint all the more striking because it seems unconscious. It is just there. It serves no figurative purpose, it has no reason to be there except it be some traditional phrase or the like. The most one might say is that it emphasizes Yahweh's control even over difficult things, but this will hardly do in a context where there is no hint of any difficulties or opposition. This is as close as one comes to "rebellious waters" in the earliest poems, and it seems to be a case where the phrase is so trite it has lost any figurative meaning and its participle has become so colorless as to be equivalent of "being" or the like, even with the mild poetic figure of a personified Deep. Once more no battle, once more the waters are Yahweh's instrument, not enemy, and they are as mild as the brooklets they refer to, the blessings of springs in a dry country. So here too, in the realm of nature, the emphasis is on order for the benefit of God's people.

This same emphasis on order in society comes out in the motif of Yahweh the Warrior (Exod. 15:3) inseparable from much in the ancient poems. Now, obviously the idea of the *Chaoskampf* implies (a) warrior god(s), but nonetheless the divine warrior idea had its own independent and important place in Israel's traditions. In many ways it was the holy war led by Yahweh, God of armies, which made the people of Israel.[25] It would seem that this was combined with the other theme. The warrior god (*'îš milḥāmâ*) is described in images borrowed from the *Chaoskampf* theme, as is clear in Exodus 15, but especially in 2 Samuel 22 where the God who pushes back the waters and bares the foundations of the earth (10–16) is the one who trains the king to fight (33–37).

The same relationship appears in Judg. 5:20–21, where the very elements, the stars and the rain, are the weapons of Yahweh in the holy war against Sisera. This is not precisely the imagery of the *Chaoskampf*, as in the case of Exodus 15, but rather of the Lord of nature and man making use of the resources of his domain on behalf of his people.

This again brings us to a new theme. This is the god of the storm. Very early the description of the storm god's power was applied to Yahweh. Already in Ps. 68:5 Yahweh is the cloud-rider, an epithet of Baal at Ugarit, and in 2 Sam 22:11b–15 he moves on the wind with thunder and lightning.[26] However, the *locus classicus* here is Psalm 29. Yahweh shows his dominance through the storm. The emphasis is on the awesome power displayed in the thunder, the lightning, the blasts of the wind capable of smashing the mightiest giants of the forest. Awesomeness calls forth awe, and this terrible God receives it from the "sons of God" (29:1) as well as from men, and he receives it in his palace. Thus the result of the storm god's appearance at once ties into the complex of motifs associated with the *Chaoskampf*. The conqueror god receives homage and temple, but once again as in Exodus 15 the means are different. There the means were not any conquest of chaos but the formation of a people through the defeat of Egypt, but at least the imagery describing this defeat was borrowed in part from the traditions of the *Chaoskampf*. Here in Psalm 29 even the imagery is different. In a sense it is true that the picture is closer to the *Chaoskampf* in that the storm is real and belongs to the realm of nature, not merely figurative and pertaining to society as in Exodus 15. But this general connection proves nothing. The explicit topic of the psalm is the terrible power which the divinity shows in the storm. To be sure, the rainstorm could be beneficent. It was essential to the economy of Syro-Phoenicia, but this is not what the poet chooses to emphasize.

In the accepted analysis of the supposedly ubiquitous *Chaoskampf* theme this would be impossible. Such destruction wrought by water is not the manifestation and instrument of the divinity who will be king but of his monstrous opponent. Yet there it is; the storm god is acclaimed king, and this is in a hymn taken over almost without change from pre-Israelite sources.[27] This might be significant in several ways. It attests an attribution of kingship to the god of the storm by acclamation of the divine council, something which Ugaritic mythology usually allowed only to El.[28] It shows that the waters, even in their terrifying aspect, could be a divine instrument and bring a god to supremacy. If this is because of the concern with a rain economy as so often and persuasively argued by C. H. Gordon, it shows a concern with the order of things, an order maintained by violent divine power[29] but not in any way which resembles the workings of the so-called creation myth. In any case, what matters is the maintenance of the world of Syro-Phoenicia, not its origins. Granted that this psalm is a direct borrowing from Canaan, we have here an antecedent to some of the things which we have found in the ancient Hebrew texts we have examined. There is the use of the waters, natural phenomena, as divine weapons instead of making them symbols of inimical chaotic forces. There is the connection of this altered or new motif with the divine kingship.

Finally, to complete the survey of the means by which Yahweh is represented as achieving his purposes in our texts, the answer to our second question about how Yahweh acts, we must look at a further set of images commonly used. Regularly he is associated with mountains. He is the "One of Sinai," the one who "goes forth from Seir" (Judg. 5:4–5; Deut. 33:2). He comes with smoke and fire (2 Sam. 22:9; Deut. 32:22–25), and at his coming the earth is shaken to its foundations (Judg. 5:4–5; 2 Sam. 22:8). This calls to mind at once the account of the events on Sinai, especially Exodus 19, and the tradition associating Yahweh with mountains was constant (1 Kings 19; Psalms of Zion; Nah. 1:5–6). What is pertinent here is that the manifestations of the god from the mountain, fire, and the rest, are the instruments, the weapons with which he achieves his purposes. He destroys Israel's enemies (Judges 5; 2 Samuel 22) or he punishes his disloyal people (Deut. 32:22–25). This is the same figure as that of the waters in Exodus 15 or the storm in Psalm 29.

Probably Deuteronomy 32 and 2 Samuel 22 are most important here since the fire of the mountain god merges with the raging storm, and everything seems to have cosmic meaning. The foundations of the earth are consumed, the breakers of death turned back. So many motifs are crowded together here: mountain god, storm god, warrior god, *Chaoskampf*; but they are all symbolic, impressive figures of speech and thought for picturing the way Yahweh controls events among men. The point is always political or social order.[30]

We have not yet turned explicitly to our third question about the *why* of Yahweh's activities as depicted in our texts. Since the answer is so bound up with what he does and how he does it, in fact we have dealt with much of the answer. It is double: one object of it all is that Yahweh be acknowledged supreme, acclaimed king, the other that order be established for his people.

As for the first, we see Yahweh reigning in Exodus 15; Psalms 29 and 82; Deut. 32:2–3 and possibly Deut. 32:43.[31] The ancient Israelites saw no difficulty in picturing Yahweh as reigning in a divine council, since we must take a picture of him amid the sons of God in Deuteronomy 32 as somehow real if his special choice of Israel is to mean something. If it is an *empty* figure of speech, then the contrast between his taking Israel and the others' taking the other nations loses its force and election disappears. What appears to be unusual is the source of his reign. It is not the conquest of chaos in the manner of a Marduk in *enuma eliš*. It is simply his overwhelming power. This may be affirmed in violent imagery as in Exodus 15 or Psalm 29. However, in another image he is absolute ruler who orders society and its guardians as he will (Deut. 32:7–9) or nature and its powers as he wishes (Gen. 49:25). This is quiet superiority, but still total power. Once more the total expression cannot be simply subsumed under one head but the basic aim is clear amid the many images: Yahweh is absolute king of all.

If anything the other object of Yahweh's activities in our texts is even clearer. With imagery borrowed from almost any source at hand, including the *Chaoskampf* theme, they affirm that God controls events among men for the benefit of his chosen people.

In itself this is no very startling conclusion. The longing for order in human and natural affairs is characteristic of the laments of the ancient world, including Israel, and the praise of it rings in the Psalter (e.g., Psalms 8; 19). Here Psalm 104 is informative. In part very old, it has the special feature of uniting a *Chaoskampf* motif (putting down the rebellious waters: 5–9) with quiet praise of the order of nature (10ff). However, the union is not quite smooth and organic. One feels the abrupt change from the mythic imagery to the *Listenwissenschaft* of the ancient Near Eastern wisdom tradition.[32] Evidently it is not this wisdom tradition – though old in itself it is not part of the oldest Israelite traditions as handed down by the very ancient literature we have been studying – even united with hymns based on *Chaoskampf* motifs which is the original locus of Israel's articulated and (to it) self-evident concept of Yahweh as orderer.

Rather, the study of the ancient poems scattered in various books of the OT has shown them concerned with the events of Israel's historical relationship with Yahweh and points in another direction. Israel was thoroughly at home in the imagery of the *Chaoskampf* from the earliest evidence for it in Israel. This ease with mythic imagery seems to come precisely because it was seen as having nothing to do with a story of real, ultimate origins. The origins which counted for Israel were political and social, ultimately religious because these things were not separated, and these origins were seen to be the mighty work of Yahweh in choosing and saving Israel, protecting it, and punishing it if proper order called for it. Connected with this was the proper allotment of places to the other nations. All this could be and was described in the imagery of battles involving nature, especially the waters, which could symbolize Yahweh's enemy or instrument involved in the real task, bringing about the desired order among men. Other imagery could be and was used; the divine warrior, the storm of God, the God of the mountain, the divine king who could and did extend his order to the "sons of God," the guides of nations, and thus all mankind. What we have here is not evidence for any real belief in a *Chaoskampf* with its attendant pantheon, forces on the same plane as God. Quite the contrary, as was mentioned earlier, the freedom in using *Chaoskampf* imagery in different, even contradictory, ways shows that there was little feeling of a religious reality behind it. Rather it was simply a convenient source of tropes.

This is borne out by the complex mixing of motifs which we have found. Warrior, mountain, and storm god motifs are all used along with those from the *Chaoskampf*. This sort of mixing is usually seen as representing the breakdown of a form. Be that as it may, the fact confirms the point already made: there is little or no effort to use all these ideas and images as consistent, independent wholes. Rather they are merely sources for means to describe what is important, and this once again is the proper ordering of the world of men.

Thus the evidence hardly indicates a need for demythologizing in the sense of a working away from a belief in the *Chaoskampf* and all its characteristic apparatus. The evidence is that such "demythologization" was there from the first because Israel was interested in historical, not cosmic origins, and so it could use the mythic themes without hazard.

Once more, if we ask the proper questions, it would seem that we get answers. We should not ask about creation as such from these texts. It may be that there are relics in them left over from myths about absolute origins, though it seems to me that this idea forces the meaning even of the supposed myths. The problem arises because we extend the meaning of all the myths since there is always for us the question of absolute origins. In fact, the ancient Israelite poems we have looked at do indeed contain material usually associated with the *Chaoskampf*. However, because the poems speak not of absolute origins but rather of the origins of the social order as Israel found it and understood it, these relics do not speak of world origins, if they ever did anywhere. They speak of God's saving Israel, and it may be misleading to seek more from them.

NOTES

1 For discussion and references see Loren R. Fisher, "Creation at Ugarit and in the Old Testament," *VT* 15 (1965) 313–24, and "From Chaos to Cosmos," *Encounter* 26 (1965) 183–97. Fisher suggests that we distinguish between *theogony* and *cosmogony* and that we can find the latter in Ugaritic texts. He would call this creation because it is the typical thing we call *Chaoskampf* here, a struggle of a young god, Baal, against hostile waters (Yam, the sea god) leading to his acclamation as divine king. This calls for more discussion than can be given here. It must suffice to notice that the struggle is between adversaries for control of an apparently organized world, and that there is no hint that the winner constructs a new order as Marduk does in *enuma eliš*: this hardly conforms to what are usually considered creation or even cosmogonic ideas in the ancient Near East.

2 For an argument in this sense see Lucien Legrand, "La création, triomphe

cosmique de Yahvé," *NRT* 83 (1961) 449–70 (*TD* 11 [1963] 154–58), who feels that the creation theme was so inviting and dangerous because of its Canaanite origin that it was allowed into the canonical writings only in late times. We shall see that this reservation is hardly correct.

3   The classic official Catholic text is the decree of the 4th Lateran Council (A.D. 1215) condemning the dualism of the Cathari (*DS* 800); on the Fathers and the problem of procession and creation see H. A. Wolfson, "The Meaning of *ex nihilo* in the Church Fathers, Arabic and Hebrew Philosophy, and St. Thomas," in *Ford Festschrift: Medieval Studies* (ed. U. T. Holmes, Jr., and A. J. Denomy, C.S.B.; Cambridge: Harvard Univ. Press, 1948) 355–67.

4   The concern with the gnostic dualist crisis in John is widely affirmed: e.g., by Frederick C. Grant, *JBL* 86 (1967) 92–93 in reviewing the JB, ed. Alexander Jones.

5   As implied in the first note, I believe that the Ugaritic materials show that the so-called creation motifs borrowed from Canaan are also in this class. Not only do they not speak of creation by progressive emanation from some primordial thing (Fisher's theogony), but they do not really tell of a struggle against chaos and the formation of an ordered world consequent on victory over that enemy. At most they speak of a struggle for control of the world and its organization. This, however, is matter for another article hopefully to appear soon.

6   This is characteristic of much in the Psalter, where the laments imply that sin creates disorder and the royal psalms (note especially Ps. 72:1–7) see the king's justice (right order) as being in the same line as and even the cause of right order in nature.

7   For example and more or less at random: T. Boman, "The Biblical Doctrine of Creation," *CQR* 165 (1964) 140–51; A. Jepsen, "The Scientific Study of the Old Testament," *Essays in Old Testament Hermeneutics* (ed. C. Westermann and J. L. Mays; Richmond: John Knox Press, 1963) 280.

8   G. von Rad, "Das formgeschichtliche Problem des Hexateuch," in *Gesammelte Studien zum Alten Testament* (TB 8; Munich: Chr. Kaiser, 1958) 71–75.

9   *Int* 16 (1962) 21.

10   See H. Gese, "Geschichtliches Denken im alten Orient und im Alten Testament," *ZTK* 55 (1958) 127–47: the literary form called for a "Golden Age" at the beginning of things but J has made it a time of sin; this is developed in detail elsewhere by me, cf. "The Word of God and 'Literary Embellishment,'" *RRel* 24 (1965) 771–84.

11   It is not surprising that the waters are not represented as a personal monster in Genesis, but the same thing is true of the Babylonian deluge story where, if the *Chaoskampf* idea were as ubiquitous as is often claimed, we should expect something different. This is another of the bits of evidence calling for a review of our ideas of ancient cosmogonies and cosmologies in general.

12   This, of course, is the basic idea behind the *Chaoskampf* concept: the representation of the annual vegetation cycle in the guise of a divine battle against the ruin which threatens when the vegetation dies: see T. H. Gaster, *Thespis* (Garden City, N.Y.: Doubleday & Co., Anchor Books, 1961²), for a study of

the ancient near Eastern material from this point of view; more general: Mircea Eliade, *Cosmos and History: The Myth of the Eternal Return* (New York: Harper & Row, Torchbooks, 1959).

13 See above, n. 6.

14 On these roots in Ugaritic and "creation" see M. H. Pope, *El in the Ugaritic Texts* (VTSup 2; Leiden: E. J. Brill, 1955) 50–54, though one cannot follow his overemphasis on the sexual aspects of the roots. *Qny* certainly has this aspect, but not always; see for the neutral meaning "create," F. M. Cross and D. N. Freedman, "The Song of Miriam," *JNES* 14 (1955) 249, n. 57 with references, and F. M. Cross, "Yahweh and the God of the Patriarchs," *HTR* 55 (1962) 240, n. 70; also the bland use in I Aqhat 220: *d yqny ddm*, "who possesses/owns (i.e., is master of) fields." *Kwn* is certainly neutral, though it may have a sexual sense in context. Its basic meaning is established by the new text in *PRU* II:188 (RS 15.128), lines 6 and 9, where it is a question of *establishing* guarantees.

15 For the antiquity of the poem in Deuteronomy 32 see O. Eissfeldt, *Das Lied Moses, Deuteronomium 32, 1–43 und das Lehrgedicht Asaphs Psalm 78 samt einer Analyse der Umgebung des Mose-Liedes* (Verhandlungen der säch. Akad. zu Leipzig, Phil.-hist. Klasse, 104/5; Berlin, 1958); W. F. Albright, "Some Remarks on the Song of Moses in Deuteronomy XXXII," *VT* 9 (1959) 339–46; G. E. Wright, "The Lawsuit of God: A Form-Critical Study of Deuteronomy 32," in *Israel's Prophetic Heritage* (ed. B. W. Anderson and W. Harrelson; New York: Harper & Row, 1962) 26–67. The first two opt for a date as early as the eleventh century B.C.; Wright sees later redaction of earlier material, but the texts which concern us belong to this older material (see below, n. 21).

16 See above, n. 14.

17 Reading in 8b *bᵉnê 'ĕlōhîm* with LXX for MT *bᵉne yiśrā'ēl*, a reading confirmed from Qumrân; see G. E. Wright, "The Lawsuit of God," 28, n. 8.

18 C. H. Gordon, *Ugaritic Textbook* (Analecta orientalia 38; Rome, 1965) Text 52, called by Gaster, *Thespis*, 418–35, "Poem of the Gracious Gods." Gaster points out, probably rightly, that there is a burlesque element in the text we have. This, though, implies something serious to be burlesqued. [See now A. Caquot and M. Sznycer, *Textes Ougaritiques I. Mythes et Legendes* (Paris, 1974) 364–65: there is humor but no buffoonery; J. Gibson, *Ugaritic Myths and Legends* (Edinburgh: T. & T. Clark, 1978) 29–30, seems to agree. Thus later Ugaritological studies confirm what follows in my original notes 14–18]. Insofar as this deals with natural phenomena we might speak of a cosmogony; insofar as they are personified and deified, a theogony. This ambiguity seems inevitable in the ancient stories of origins.

19 Verse 18 is evidently old: witness the ancient title, Rock, and El (not Elohim), the lack of connectives and of the article. We may assume that the less colorful parallel, v. 6, which also lacks some connectives, is also ancient.

20 Perhaps we should add to the "creation" words the very name Yahweh if, as has been persuasively argued, it is a causative of the verb "to be" and so means "he makes to be." See F. M. Cross, *HTR* 55 (1962) 252–54. Note 123 is important for showing through parallel forms that the idea was not too "abstract" and "metaphysical" for the ancients.

21 This is not a common OT idea, but it does occur in another form in Amos 9:7. Does Amos's insight into Yahweh's universal love and providence depend somehow on the view couched in more mythic terms in Deuteronomy? The idea is very old, as it occurs in the fourteenth-century Egyptian hymn to Aton (see *ANET* 370b) where, as here, it is entirely disassociated from any *Chaoskampf* motifs.

22 See on this Cross and Freedman, *JNES* 14 (1955) 239–40.

23 As did Baal at Ugarit: Text 51, IV–V (*ANET* 133), and Marduk at Babylon: *enuma eliš*, VI, 49ff (*ANET* 68).

24 On the date of this text see H.-J. Zobel, *Stamesspruch und Geschichte* (BZAW 95; Berlin: Töpelmann, 1965) 59–61, and F. M. Cross, *Studies in Ancient Yahwistic Poetry* (Baltimore, 1950) 226–27. The translation in the text here of course takes $t^e h \hat{o} m$ to be personified as is indicated by the primitive ideas in the phrase. On this see F. M. Cross and D. N. Freedman, "The Blessing of Moses," *JBL* 67 (1948) 206, n. 44. This of course, refers to the entirely parallel text of Deut. 33:13.

25 The basic work on this idea has been that of R. Smend, *Jahwekrieg und Stämmebund* (FRLANT 84; Göttingen: Vandenhoeck & Ruprecht, 1963), and *Die Bundesformel* (Theologische Studien 68; Zurich, 1963).

26 For the dates of 2 Samuel 22 (Psalm 18) and Psalm 68 see H. J. Kraus, *Psalmen* (BKAT 15/1; Neukirchen-Vluyn: Neukirchener, 1961²) 136–51, 464–77, with extensive references to the literature. The basic study of 2 Samuel 22 remains F. M. Cross and D. N. Freedman, "A Royal Song of Thanksgiving: II Samuel 22, Psalm 18," *JBL* 72 (1953) 15–34; see also D. N. Freedman, "Archaic Forms in Early Hebrew Poetry," *ZAW* 72 (1960) 103.

27 On this see M. Dahood, S.J., *Psalms I: 1–50* (AB; Garden City, N.Y.: Doubleday & Co., 1966) 175–80, with extensive references.

28 See W. Schmidt, *Königtum Gottes in Ugarit und Israel* (BZAW 80; Berlin: Töpelmann, 1961) 20–21, and "Jerusalemer El-Traditionen bei Jesaja," *Zeitschrift für Religionsund Geistesgeschichte* 16 (1964) 308.

29 This interpretation is now confirmed from the Ugaritic "Palace of Baal" story: Gibson, *Ugaritic Myths*, 9, 13–14, and, with nuances, Caquot and Sznycer, *Textes Ougaritiques I*, 188–89.

30 We might note that this mixture of motifs is not peculiar to Israel. Apart from the kingship in the divine council and the mountain god aspects they are all applied to Baal in Ugaritic literature. He is even associated with a mountain (Schmidt, *Königtum Gottes*, 23–27), but this is the seat of kingship, and he manifests none of the fiery attributes of the God *as he* comes from the mountain in the OT. Even so, we should note this pre-Israelite mixture of motifs. Such mixing of literary phenomena is generally held to be part of the declining stage of a form, and this should call our attention to the fact that we should not assume pure forms at the start of OT literature. The Hebrews borrowed wholesale from an advanced culture, and this example shows what is evident anyway: much that they borrowed was far past the stage of pure forms. This is borne out by the mixed state we find in the forms of the oldest Israelite texts.

31 On the reconstruction of Deut. 32:43 in this sense see G. E. Wright, "The Lawsuit

of God: A Form-Critical Study of Deuteronomy 32," in *Israel's Prophetic Heritage*, ed. B. W. Anderson and W. Harrelson (New York: Harper & Row, 1963) 33. On Psalm 82 see, besides the commentaries, G. E. Wright, *The Old Testament against Its Environment* (SBT 2; London: SCM Press, 1950) 30–41.

32 See W. Schmidt, *Die Schöpfungsgeschichte der Priesterschrift* (WMANT 17; Neukirchener-Vluyn: Neukirchener, 1964) 42; H. J. Kraus, *Psalmen* II:709.

5

Biblical Reflection on Creator-Creation[*]

CLAUS WESTERMANN

It is both remarkable and undeniable that the passages dealing with Creation and primeval time which at the high point of the Enlightenment had been dismissed as utterly outmoded, have found a hearing once more in the second phase of the technological age. When the astronauts read out the story of Creation from the first chapter of the Bible before setting off for the moon, this was neither emotion nor enthusiasm. Rather, the words of the Creation narrative were suited to the event. In this spirit they were read, in this spirit they were heard by thousands. The achievements of science and technology in the first phase of the technological age gave rise to arguments for questioning the belief in Creation. An achievement in this same area in the second phase provides the occasion for the recitation of the Creation story.

It is a fact that the Creation belief long ago faded into the background of the Church's preaching and theology. The Creation narratives of the Bible were accepted for a long time without question as accounts of an actual event. These stories, together with the first sentence of the Creed, "Creator of heaven and earth", formed the reliable, unshakable foundations which supported all thought and talk about the beginning of the world and of man. The shaking of the foundations began with the rise of the natural sciences. They shook not only belief in the Creator, but also the picture of the world which had remained unaltered since ancient times. Inexorably the new picture of the world prevailed, and the Christian Church step by step gave up her initial opposition. But the new world-picture questioned the biblical account of the creation of the world and of man. The result was a growing wave of opposition on the part of

[*] First published as "Introduction" to *Creation* by Claus Westermann (1974) 1–15. Original publication in German (1971).

the Enlightenment to the biblical statements on Creation, an opposition which, with all the soul-searching of the Enlightenment, brought light where darkness had been. The light of science clarified the origin and development of the world and of man, and drove out the darkness of primitive myth and clerical obscurantism. In fact, the biblical Creation accounts offered the most welcome target to enlightened and atheistic polemic, the high points being Haeckel's *World Riddle* and, in more recent times, *Universe, Earth, Man*, a publication authorized by the German Democratic Republic. The attacks of the Enlightenment, with its glorification of the natural sciences and its ridicule of the nursery tales of the biblical–ecclesiastical tradition, have now run their course, and the emotion has evaporated. The time is past, too, when the attitude of the Church in the face of these attacks was largely that of defence. This attitude had become more and more entrenched as it maintained that the Creation accounts in the Bible had nothing at all to do with scientific knowledge: they dealt only with religion and belief; the discussion was concerned with salvation. This defensive, apologetic attitude was basically determined by the other side, by the attackers. It is time to see and to acknowledge this.

From the time of Kepler, Galileo, and Copernicus right up to the formation of the Marxist materialistic ideology, the Church had no serious encounter with the all-conquering scientific explanation of the origin of the world and of man. One stood by the validity of the biblical Creation accounts and the belief in the Creator. At the same time one acknowledged more or less openly the scientific explanation of the origin of the world and of man. There was, however, no serious concern to build a bridge between the scientific explanations of the world and the biblical account of Creation. While acknowledging this, one must point out the following: in the course of the nineteenth century, and beginning with Schleiermacher, the new theology in the Evangelical Church concentrated more and more on man. There is a direct line from Schleiermacher through Harnack to the existential interpretation, which has been looking for meaning in the biblical texts in so far as they shed light on man's understanding of himself in his present situation. To speak of God the Creator and to acknowledge him as "Creator of heaven and earth" lose all meaning in this context. And does not this line of thought follow the very same direction as the polemic of the Enlightenment which directed itself against the biblical reflection on Creation? Under the dominant influence of a theology which limits its thought and concern to the existential situation of the individual, has not this reflection on Creator-Creation become a sort of cult of the dead past?

We must go a step further: the new theology with its concentration on man bears the mark of a renewal of the Reformation theology. Nowhere, however, has it been clearly stated that everything that the Reformers said of man and of his state before God, of justification, faith, the kingdom of God, stands on the utterly unshakable foundation of its belief in Creation. It has not been noticed that when this foundation is no longer there, then the basis of all that the Reformers say of man and his relationship to God has been whisked away. In other words, once theology has imperceptibly become detached from Creator-Creation, the necessary consequence is that it must gradually become an anthropology and begin to disintegrate from within and collapse around us. Today's theology takes its point of departure from the very place where the reflection on Creator-Creation began to vanish and dissipate itself. One can be even more precise: it began where the theology and teaching of the Church took only a defensive stand against the scientific explanation of the world and of man and had no renewed, vital presentation of the biblical reflection on Creator-Creation to set against it. The process can be readily explained. When the theology and the preaching of the Church are concerned only with salvation, when God's dealing with man is limited to the forgiveness of sins or to justification, the necessary consequence is that it is only in this context that man has to deal with God and God with man. This means that God is not concerned with a worm being trodden to the earth or with the appearance of a new star in the Milky Way. And so the question must be put: what sort of God is he who does everything for the salvation of man but clearly has nothing at all to do with man in his life situation? What can be the meaning of a salvation history which has nothing at all to do with real history? Science has now stepped in as lord of the domain which man used to refer to Creation. What remains for God? This is the reason why some say "God is dead" and why many more say "The word 'God' has no longer any meaning for me". And so it is an illusion to try to modernize a soteriology which has been cut off from reality and to up-date it in modern jargon. This is of no help. The matter stands or falls with the question, is God concerned with the real world which surrounds us? Is he Creator or not?

We must begin where, at the break-through of the natural sciences, the Church failed, and ask what was the reason for the failure. It can only be that at the time of the condemnation of this breakthrough there prevailed an understanding of Creator-Creation that was both fossilized and untrue to the Bible. What was wrong? We can answer in two ways. A teaching on Creation had been constructed out of the narrative of Creation and the praise of the Creator. This meant a teaching which had laid down a seven-day Creation programme, or a definite way of conceiving things: for example, the heavens were a solid body. This was a serious misunderstanding of the biblical reflection on Creator-Creation. This reflection is presented in the form of stories told from different points of view which give rise to different presentations. The biblical statements on Creation had been limited to texts which seemed to be required for the teaching on salvation (i.e., limited to Genesis 1—3); what followed in chs. 4—11 seemed without meaning for Creation.

These are but indications. But they are enough to show the attitude with which the churches defended against the natural sciences a teaching on Creation which did not in its essential points correspond to the biblical reflection on Creator-Creation. A thorough revision has not yet won through: it is pending.

The Bible speaks of Creation in this way: the narrative says that God created the world (man) and that the response to this act was the praise of the Creator. It must be noted, however, that the Bible is not proposing an article of faith. An article such as we find at the beginning of our confession of faith would be impossible in the OT. The OT never speaks of belief in the Creator: there never occurs a sentence such as "I believe the world was created by God," and Creation or belief in Creation never occurs in the confessions of faith of the OT (von Rad's "historical Credo," e.g. Deut. 26:5–9).

One can easily see the reason: for the man of the OT it was not possible that the world could have originated in any other way. Creation was not an article of faith because there was simply no alternative. In other words, the OT had a different understanding of reality from ours, inasmuch as there was no other reality than that established by God. They had no need expressly to *believe* that the world was created by God because that was a presupposition of their thinking.

This has had two consequences for the reflection on Creator-Creation which must be clarified:

1   The question, *how* did God create the world, could never have been a question of faith for the man of the OT. There could be quite different opinions about this. And so the OT reflection on Creator-

Creation is many-sided. The process of Creation has not been and cannot be established definitively: each age can only express it in a way intelligible to itself. Consequently the OT presents not one but many Creation accounts. The old approach to Genesis understood the first two chapters as a coherent account which related the creation of the world and humanity (1:1—2:4a) and then a more detailed account of the creation of humankind (2:4b–24). Historical-critical examination of the OT discovered that the two accounts, 1:1—2:4a and 2:4b–24 (with ch. 3) belonged to two different sources, the latter to the older source, J (Yahwist, tenth–ninth centuries B.C.) and the former to the later source, P (Priestly Code, sixth–fifth centuries B.C.). This was the first step in scholarly inquiry into the reflection on Creator-Creation in the OT. This separation of the two Creation accounts into two literary sources is one of the most important and most assured results of the literary-critical examination of the OT. It was established that ancient Israel spoke of Creation in different ways at different times. The OT knew no definitive teaching on Creation. The reflection on the Creation could vary. The most striking difference between the two presentations is that the older account describes the way in which God created in a manner quite different from the later account. In the old account there is God's action, the forming of the man from clay and of the woman from the rib of the man; in the later account, Creation is by word: God spoke and so it happened. But the investigation of the Creation texts did not end there. Literary-critical research was taken a step further by the study of the history of tradition. It was recognized that the texts which have come down to us have had a long oral tradition, and that the written sources where we meet these traditions are the final stage of a long process of tradition which must itself be examined.

The approach of the reflection on Creator-Creation changes notably in the OT. It is now recognized that in Israel there were not just two accounts of Creation, an older 2:4b–24 and a later 1:1—2:4a, but a long series extending through the whole history of the tradition. There were successively and side by side several presentations of the story of Creation in ever new forms. The Creation account in Genesis 1:1—2:4a was not the work of one author in the sense that this author wrote the whole story as an original composition. The author was one in a long chain of successors; he was at the same time one who received tradition and one who shaped what he received into a new form. The construction of the narrative of ch. 1 clearly betrays a prehistory. In this presentation of Creation by the word an older presentation has been resumed in which the Creator did not speak, but acted. An older account of Creation by action is to be recognized behind the later account of Creation by word. And the earlier Creation account bears even less the marks of one single mould. It too grew out of a long prehistory, traces of which can be recognized.

We are not however restricted to the first three chapters of the Bible in our examination of this prehistory. There is a whole series of passages from other parts of the OT, especially from the Psalms, Job, 2 Isaiah, and the Wisdom literature, which enable us to reconstruct the history of the tradition of the reflection on Creator-Creation, uncovering a variety of possibilities and a wealth of presentations and arrangements.

2   The second consequence extends even further the circle of the reflection on Creator-Creation. Because it was not properly speaking a question of belief peculiar to Israel, there could be no definitive separation of the world in which she lived from the surrounding world, and from the world which preceded her. There are always, of course, differences in the way in which the Creator is spoken of. But Israel was always conscious that in its reflection on Creator-Creation it was united with its surrounding world. All peoples who bordered on Israel, and of whom Israel had knowledge, shared the common conviction that human beings must be understood as creatures of God and the world as a creature of the divine.

A clarification is required in the face of our present-day situation. In recent times it is precisely the belief in Creation that has become the object of the sharpest polarization. Atheistic and anti-Christian propaganda has always made the belief in Creation the object of its attack. The denial of God was and is the denial of the Creator which accompanies the explanation that the natural sciences give of human origin and of the world. It is the biblical formulation therefore that became the decisive point of dispute; and this should never have been, inasmuch as on this very point the people of God were essentially at one with other people. The tradition of the Christian Church can take little credit here. It is neither necessary nor correct from the biblical viewpoint to concentrate the conflict on this area. That such has happened is partly due to an erroneous development within the Church and Christian theology.

The biblical reflection on Creator-Creation is recognizably and in many ways related to the reflection on Creator-Creation in the world which surrounded and preceded Israel. When we examine these relationships we must again distinguish two stages which correspond to the two stages in the growth of the biblical reflection on Creator-Creation.

1   The acknowledged fact that not only the Bible but the whole world had something to say on Creator-Creation, on the making of the world and of man, scarcely concerned Christian theology and the exegesis of the biblical texts. There was, however, an explanation that seemed to account quite adequately for this lack of concern. From Rom. 1:18–20 one concluded to a primitive revelation which, broadly speaking, was distorted and veiled among the pagans, but of which traces remained. It was because of this primitive revelation that one explained a knowledge of Creation among the peoples of the earth, albeit distorted and corrupt, but the situation was changed when writings were discovered, in the lands surrounding ancient Israel, which bore a striking resemblance to the biblical Creation and Flood stories. The Babylonian cuneiform texts which were found towards the end of the last century raised the question of the relationship between the biblical and Babylonian writings, of their interdependence, of their relative age. And so arose the long-standing dispute which reached its climax in the Babel-Bible controversy. The result was to concede that a dependence of the Babylonian texts on the biblical texts was impossible, while a dependence of biblical on Babylonian texts was possible or probable. As a result of this concession many exegetes became entrenched in a certain defensive attitude, striving to demonstrate the spiritual and theological superiority of the biblical texts without being aware of the real problem which had been thrown up, namely, that to appraise the biblical texts by comparison with the non-biblical texts is really to renounce the unique importance of the biblical texts.

2   The extra-biblical Creation stories had now to be examined further. In the first stage, the extra-biblical parallels had only been cited when they imposed themselves and just could not be overlooked. On the whole, comparison had been restricted to individual texts, so that usually a biblical excerpt was set beside a non-biblical excerpt. But this method was soon seen to be insufficient. Serious misunderstandings and false conclusions can only be avoided by going on to study and understand the extra-biblical texts not in isolation, but in and out of their own immediate and broader contexts, just as is done with the biblical texts.

96

It was here that research in the history of religion, oriental studies, and mythology came to the aid of biblical scholarship in a quite surprising way. It was discovered that the texts which had been compared with the biblical Creation accounts were themselves part of a long and varied tradition in which Creation stories occurred in not one but many forms. One can trace a history of the Creation motif from early Sumerian through Babylonian and Assyrian right down to the later versions written in Greek. A most stimulating perspective presents itself. The study of this history of tradition, however, has only just begun. Nevertheless the state of biblical research has been changed at one stroke. The inquiry into the meaning and import of the biblical Creation story has broadened greatly. It is no longer a question of the rather limited and quite unproductive problem, what is the relationship of Genesis 1 to the Babylonian epic in *Enuma Elish*, which also deals with Creation? The question is now: what is the relationship of the biblical reflection on Creation in its broadest compass to a history of reflection on Creation stretching over thousands of years, as we meet it in the succession of Sumerian, Babylonian, and Assyrian texts?

The circle must be widened even further. A striking parallel has now appeared in Egyptian temple texts from Memphis; it touches the very important matter of Creation through the word. How does one explain the occurrence of the motif of Creation through the word in both places?

But the limits of the inquiry have not yet been reached. It appears that the Creation traditions of the high cultures of the Mediterranean world have their roots in traditions still more ancient, going right back to primitive cultures. Let one example suffice for the moment: the imagery of the Creation of man out of mud or clay or dust occurs together with the motif of the life-giving breath in Sumerian and Babylonian myths just as it does in many primitive Creation narratives. How is this striking agreement explained?

The agreement is not limited to striking individual similarities. A further observation must be made: a consideration of the Creation stories in the context of the account of the origins, that is of Genesis 1—11, shows that the motifs of this narrative are distributed across the whole world. This is most striking in the motifs of the Creation and the Flood which are found in the stories of early times of people on all continents. It is the same with other motifs of the account of the origins, as H. Baumann has shown quite impressively in his book *Creation and Primeval Time of Man in the Mythology of the African Peoples* (1936; 1964²). He has set out the African myths of primitive time according to the motifs of the biblical accounts of the origins. There, too, occur the motifs of the first offence, the origin of death, the origin of civilization, fratricide, the building of a tower. With such far-reaching agreements in the motifs, the earlier explanation of historical dependence is quite inadequate. The starting point must be that the many-sided and distinctive occurrences of the same motifs of the origins, spread over the whole earth, have arisen quite independently. The conclusion is unavoidable that mankind possessed something common in the stories about primeval time. The narratives express an understanding of the world and of man which in its broad lines and in an earlier epoch was common to races, peoples, and groups throughout the whole world. However much the civilization and thought of the different groups of men have diversified in their later developments, and however broad has become the gap between the different civilizations, there is in the narratives of the primeval periods a common basis of thought and understanding which can have an even further and deeper meaning for the future of mankind. And so the question becomes more pressing: how did these narratives of primeval time arise? Do the narratives themselves allow any conclusions at all as to their origin? Are there still traces of their original meaning?

The answer is, "yes". It has been discovered that the story of the Flood, which is worldwide, is still received today in certain places in the context of definite rites which serve either to ward off another flood or to give protection should such occur. We know from the Babylonian Creation myth that it was recited at the New Year feast, a feast which as a whole served to commemorate the renewal of the world. These two examples show clearly that the reflection on Creator-Creation took place in the context of the primeval myths; it was the reflection of threatened man in a threatened world. The Creation myths then had the function of preserving the world and of giving security to life.

The current interpretation of the reflection on Creator-Creation must therefore be thoroughly revised. We have regarded the Creation narratives as an answer to the question "whence?", i.e., what is the origin of the world, of man? It is an intellectual question asking after the first cause. But the history of tradition shows that the Creation narratives became intellectual problems only at a later stage. It was not the philosopher inquiring about his origins that spoke in the Creation narratives; it was man threatened by his surroundings. The background was an existential, not an intellectual problem.

Let us now make clear what this means for the modern discussion about the Creation faith. The controversy was: did the world originate just as the Bible and the Church say it did, or as the natural sciences say? Such a statement of the question misunderstands the biblical reflection on Creation. Both attacker and defender share the misunderstanding. There is no purpose in pursuing this controversy further. The question of the present-day meaning of Creation must be stated in an entirely new way.

The relationship of narrative and action, or, to use technical terms, of myth and ritual, uncovers the true and original meaning of the narrative of the origins. The rediscovery of the real significance of myth is a positive result of modern research into the history of religion. It can only be outlined here. The Christian West first encountered myth as stories about the gods characteristic of and developed in pagan polytheism: as such, myth was completely rejected. And since the Enlightenment myth so understood has been thought of more and more as opposed to history. Mythical presentation of an event, in contrast to a historical presentation, has been judged quite "unhistorical." The adjective "mythical" has come to be used for the unreal, the unhistorical, or the untrue.

It was this aspect of myth and the mythical that came into biblical scholarship and played a special role in Rudolph Bultmann's demythologizing of the NT. The notion was purely negative. Myth was utterly false; it was to be overcome and dismissed. There was no inquiry into the real meaning and original function of myth. In such a radical rejection of everything mythical the question could not even arise. It is significant that this demythologizing was concerned basically with the mythical world picture as presumed in the language of the NT. The demythologizing programme therefore came to grips with myth only in its secondary stage, where it explained the mythology of the world and of man. It knew nothing of the primary stage.

The newly acquired understanding of myth has altered the situation. It was realized that myth had been misunderstood by setting it in opposition to history, that myth belonged originally to the context of survival, an expression therefore of one's understanding of existence, of one's understanding of the existence of the threatened-self (and this is precisely the goal at which the existential interpretation aims with its demythologizing). Reflection on Creation meant to rehearse (i.e., to repeat by narrative), in the present world and in man's dangerous situation, the beginning, when what now is came to be. Relationship with the beginning meant relationship with the basis of the world, and the repeated making present of what had happened at the beginning meant a reiteration of the reality by virtue of which the world continues to exist.

Myth must be regarded as a reflection on reality, as a presentation of what has actually happened. Such a presentation of what actually happened accorded with man's understanding of existence and of the world in the early period. To oppose myth and history in such a way that history presents what actually happened, while myth presents fiction, is utterly unhistorical. It is much more perceptive to see that in the early period of mankind it was not possible to speak of what actually happened in any other way.

The way is then cleared for an understanding of the biblical account of the origins, of the biblical reflection on the Creator-Creation. And one can understand why the Bible knows no doctrine about Creator-Creation, but only tells stories about it. Only in the narrative, only in the rehearsing, can Creation be repeatedly made present. Only in the narrating can Creation become real again. When the Creation narratives of an earlier stage of man's history are preserved in our Bible, then there is preserved with them the continuity between later epochs and generations and that earlier stage. In other words, in the Creation narratives of the Bible the history of mankind is preserved as a whole, as a continuum, as a meaningful continuity in such a way as to preserve for the future early man's understanding of reality – that is, of existence and of the world.

So the biblical reflection on Creator-Creation takes on a new meaning. The mythical stage is succeeded by one that is characterized by the ever-inquiring intellect. Out of the questioning of threatened man in a threatened world arose the question about the beginning and the end, about coming into existence and ceasing to exist. Limited man asks about and beyond his limitations, about his own and the world's coming into being. But this intellectual inquiry preserves within it the original inquiry of threatened man in his threatened existence, as he asks after the beginning as ground and support of his continuing in the present. The original inquiry about the ground and support of his existence is common to all mankind; it occurs in all races, civilizations, and religions; it belongs to man's being.

It is only in the secondary stage, when the intellectual inquiry about the "whence" comes to the fore, that the way is gradually opened to distinguish knowledge and belief, religion and philosophy. The reflection on Creator-Creation precedes this separation, preserving within itself, still undivided, religion and science, religion and faith. The real meaning of the biblical Creation narrative and of the reflection on the primeval period (Genesis 1—11) lies in this, that in it the remembrance of mankind's history is preserved as a self-contained whole, and that present-day man experiences himself as part of mankind's history. These chapters record for the future that the decisive points of human existence are the same for all mankind; that all races, all peoples, all human groups understand themselves as men in the world in essentially the same way, and that religions, outlooks, philosophies, and ideologies all go back to one beginning where they are all rooted in the same question.

In the first eleven chapters of the Bible the inquiry about the whole is compressed out of millennia-long tradition into an inquiry about the beginning and the end, and is bound up with the question of the history of mankind which is centred in the history of God's people.

The uniqueness of the biblical reflection on Creation and the primeval period lies precisely in this bond. The first chapters of the Bible are conceived as a constituent part of the Pentateuch [Torah] in the middle of which is set the account of the liberation from Egypt and the encounter with God on Sinai, the foundation of Israel's history. The boldness of this conception is that the constricted history of a small people is presented as the leading, saving, preserving action of the same God who created the world and man. And so the reflection on Creation and the primeval period extends to the broadest limits of an activity of God which is experienced and witnessed by those who encounter this same God as their saviour. The path of this small people with its experience of the great deeds of God, with its drama of guilt and forgiveness, with its high points and low points, with the word of God and man's response, has its origin in God's activity towards mankind aand the universe, and will sometime find its way again into the concourse of his universal action.

6

Creation, Righteousness, and Salvation:*

"Creation Theology" as the Broad Horizon of Biblical Theology[1]

H. H. SCHMID

In recent decades the concept of creation has been largely ignored in theology. According to the broad *communis opinio* it has been agreed that a theology of creation does indeed belong to Christian theology but that it must be accorded a secondary position to christology or soteriology. One who tries to give more weight to creation theology is immediately suspected of promoting a "natural theology," which at least since the early days of dialectical theology has been considered theologically suspect. In a similar fashion the concept of orders, which formerly was closely connected with creation theology, has almost completely vanished from theological literature. The reasons for this are well known and do not need to be discussed here. Futhermore, in recent years other themes in vogue have been pushed to the forefront of theological discussion: peace, justice, and on another basis cybernetics, sociology, and the like. These themes seem to have little to do with creation, so that in these discussions too silence about the theme of creation has prevailed.

A series of exegetical observations in the fields of both the OT and the NT prompt the question as to whether the subject of creation theology ought not to be considered once again and thus bring to an end this unfortunate period of silence. The purpose of this essay, then, is to assign to creation theology a much more central theological significance, indeed, to see it as the broad horizon of biblical

*First published in *ZTK* 70 (1973) 1–19. Translated by Bernhard W. Anderson and Dan G. Johnson. In the interest of brevity several lengthy notes, as well as Part II of the text, have been omitted.

theology. In doing this we shall try to avoid those paths which in recent decades have rightly been regarded as erroneous.

I

Let me begin with a few considerations based on the exegesis of the OT. OT scholarship is nearly unanimous in regarding creation faith in ancient Israel as chronologically late and theologically secondary. This view is completely in line with the general judgment about creation theology. Again and again it is said that in the OT extended statements about Yahweh's creation of the world appear in the later texts: Second Isaiah, the Priestly writing, and in late Psalms. To be sure, Gerhard von Rad[2] held substantial reservations about this unqualified judgment, but *de facto* he has contributed to establishing the view. He maintained that in the center of OT texts dealing with creation, even in later texts, creation faith nowhere achieves an independent status. When the OT speaks of creation, according to his view, it does so solely in connection with faith in Yahweh's saving activity in history. Older expressions of creation faith, originally dependent on Canaan, he designated merely as "foils"; and the independent creation texts of wisdom literature he could only regard as having significance during a time when faith in Yahweh's saving activity had been absolutely ensured. So for von Rad at least, it was beyond question that the primary and central salvation faith had essential priority over the secondary creation faith.

Does an investigation of the texts of the OT support this view? A few observations from the field of the history of religions of the ancient Near East will serve to initiate our discussion.

There were no cultures of the ancient Near East that did not speak rather extensively of creation in various literary forms and contexts. One of the most pregnant forms for speaking about creation was myth. The myth of creation had its setting in the annual ritual of the New Year's festival. Only through the recitation of the myth, so it was assumed, was the assurance given that the new year would begin its course anew and that there would be a revival of nature and fertility.

Already a first point becomes clear. In the ancient Near East creation faith did not deal only, indeed not even primarily, with the origin of the world. Rather, it was concerned above all with the present world and the natural environment of humanity now.

A second point is related to this. The order established through creation and newly constituted every year is not only the renewal of nature; it is just as much the order of the state. This is seen, for instance, in the use of the motif of the battle against chaos (*Chaoskampf*) which belongs to creation typology. (Von Rad talks about "the struggle between Yahweh and Chaos." [*Theology* I:151]. Eichrodt refers to "the struggle with Chaos" [*Theology* I:229].) In Mesopotamia, Ugarit, and Israel the *Chaoskampf* appears not only in cosmological contexts but just as frequently – and this was fundamentally true right from the first – in political contexts. The repulsion and destruction of the enemy, and thereby the maintenance of political order, always constitute one of the major dimensions of the battle against chaos.[3] The enemies are none other than a manifestation of chaos which must be driven back.

There is a third point: legal order belongs to the order of creation. Take as an example the beginning of the prologue to the Code of Hammurabi:

> When lofty Anum, king of the Anunnaki,
> and Enlil, lord of heaven and earth,
> the determiner of the destinies of the land,
> determined for Marduk, the first born of Enki,
> the Enlil sanctions over all mankind,
> made him great among the Igigi,
> called Babylon by its exalted name,
> made it supreme in the world,
> established for him in its midst an enduring kingship,
> whose foundations are as firm as heaven and earth –
> at that time Anum and Enlil named me
> to promote the welfare of the people,
> me, Hammurabi, the devout, god-fearing prince,
> to cause justice to prevail in the land,
> to destroy the wicked and the evil,
> that the strong might not oppress the weak,
> to rise like the sun over the black-headed (people),
> and to light up the land.[4]

Anu, Enlil, and Ea make up the triad of cosmological deities; Marduk is the warrior against Chaos. Also Šamaš, who according to the relief on the stele transmits the law to the king,[5] is the sun god and, thus, a cosmic deity.

That the founding of the city of Babylon was understood to be closely connected with the creation of the world is seen not only from this text but also with great clarity from the *Enūma elish*.[6]

Hammurabi's giving of the law comes in this creation context, and so does every ancient Near Eastern legal code with the same structure. The law enacts the establishment of the order of creation seen in its juristic aspect. In short, ancient Near Eastern cosmic, political, and social order find their unity under the concept of "creation."

This may be confirmed from several different angles. Only from this background is it possible to understand, for instance, why in the whole ancient Near East, including Israel, an offense in the legal realm obviously has effects in the realm of nature (drought, famine) or in the political sphere (threat of the enemy). Law, nature, and politics are only aspects of one comprehensive order of creation.

An even clearer confirmation of the close connection between the cosmic and the ethical-social order comes from the realm of the ancient Near Eastern wisdom. That creation plays a central and primary role in this sphere is so well known that it is unnecessary to demonstrate the special character of so-called nature wisdom. Also well known is the fundamental significance of the ethical-social dimension in wisdom, the realization of which is nothing other than the realization of the original order of creation. This was given conceptual expression in ancient Egypt, where Maat, the concept for the order of creation, is at once the central concept in both legal literature[7] and wisdom literature.[8]

This comprehensive character and this fundamental appreciation of the order of creation found vivid expression in the kingship ideology of the ancient Near East. As incarnation or son – in any case the representative – of the (creator-) deity upon the earth, the king was understood to be the earthly guarantor of the order of creation. Upon him and his acts depend the fertility of the land as well as the just social and political order of the state.[9] Apart from this reference back to the order of creation it is impossible to understand the numerous forms and formulations based on kingship ideology.

To this way of thinking about creation also belongs that view which scholars designate as "the connection of act and consequence."[10] Whoever transgresses against this order inflicts on it objective damage that must be repaired again. The act must fall back upon the actor or otherwise be "expiated." It is not accidental that the Hebrew term for this is *šillēm*, "to make intact," "to restore *šālôm*." This connection, of course, is known from the sphere of blood revenge;[11] but it is also the basis for wisdom texts and legal literature as well insofar as every legal code of the ancient Near

East, including those in the OT, is concluded with a more or less extended formula of blessing and curse and many of them are introduced with an express reference to creation deities. Whoever does what is right conforms to the created order – understood to be fundamentally *heilsam* [wholesome, healthful] – and hence stands under the blessing. Whoever acts wrongly must in some special way bear the consequences of this deed and thus stands under the curse. In some ancient Near Eastern texts, as well as some in the OT, the relation between act and consequence is effected automatically, by inner necessity. In other texts the (creator-) deity is the executor. There is no substantial contradiction between the two, so long as the inner force of the order of creation and the action of the creator god are not differentiated. In this way people of the ancient Near East understood broad areas of life and many events within the horizon of creation faith.

So much for the ancient Near Eastern background. How is this subject treated in the OT? To begin with, we may presume that it would be unusual if Israel, who in many respects was an oriental people alongside her neighbors, did not basically share this thinking, even though expressing it in her own way.

With that in mind, let us consider as a case in point the *preexilic prophets*. What others have noticed previously is becoming clearer all the time: in their proclamation the preexilic prophets very seldom referred to faith in Yahweh's saving historical deeds in the sense of a "historical credo." They expose the false behavior of the people and their leaders, indicating that the judgment of Yahweh will and must come on account of this. Here we see the basic structure of the act-consequence syndrome. Some have raised the question about the source from which the prophets drew the criteria for their accusations. E. Würthwein[12] and R. Bach[13] propose that in the case of Amos it was the sphere of law; and H. W. Wolff[14] suggests wisdom as a source. Reasons can be adduced for both points of view. However, we must go beyond both of those positions. The prophets follow the general knowledge of the time and criticize the people in terms of what is "order" in the sphere of interpersonal relationships. And this is the same order that is found in the context of creation faith as well as in the sphere of law and of wisdom.[15] Moreover, it was assumed in creation-thought, as well as in wisdom and in law, that these orders could not be violated with impunity. To be sure, the circumstances in which the prophets appeared, the radical consistency of their indictment of the people, and the deadly earnestness with which they demand righteousness and justice

106

comprise a specifically Israelite phenomenon quite without any ancient Near Eastern parallels; nevertheless the substance of their proclamation, the horizon and even the logic thereof, is that of the general Near Eastern view of the order of creation.

Various passages in the preexilic prophetic books expect that in the time after the divine judgment there will be an inbreaking of a new era of salvation. [Questions about the literary authenticity of the relevant texts may be left open at this point.] The *exilic and postexilic prophets* argued in a similar fashion. Second Isaiah begins with the announcement that Israel's debt has been doubly paid and that salvation is close at hand (Isa. 40:1ff) This announcement accords with the thinking about creation sketched above: once the marred order is restored through punishment (here the exile), the world returns again to its order, it again becomes whole and healthy [There is no single English equivalent for the German adjective *heil*, which connotes wholesome, healthy, harmonious, whole, orderly.] Whenever portrayals of this blissful (*heil*) future rework motifs dealing with primeval time, the connection with creation faith is obvious. However, in an indirect way this connection can be seen in numerous other passages: in those cases, among others, where salvation (*Heil*) is described with the concept of *ṣĕdāqă* (righteousness).[16] In these instances "righteousness" is not understood narrowly as a legal matter, but as universal world order, as comprehensive salvation. Here too the basic structure of the prophetic message corresponds essentially with the ancient Near Eastern view of creation.

The *Deuteronomistic History*, as evidenced for instance in the books of Kings, agrees with the proclamation of the prophets. At many points in the history it is shown that Israel, almost without exception, refused to hearken to the prophets, that therefore the blame for the exile lay not with Yahweh but with Israel itself. It is well known that the theology of the Chronicler carried this theme to extremes. The Deuteronomistic way of thinking understands every particular trespass as a concrete example of disregard for the first commandment. In this regard, a specifically Israelite tenet of faith lies at the center of the argumentation; nevertheless, it is given concrete meaning and binding force consistently within the act-consequence connection inherent in creation.

That basic elements of wisdom and law in the OT belong to this world of thought has already been indicated and need not be repeated. Here too the concepts *ṣedeq*, *ṣĕdāqâ*, and *ṣaddîq* – among others – play a dominant role; the emphasis, however, is not upon specific acts of justice but, rather, on aspects of the one, harmonious (*heil*) order of the world.

Claus Westermann has designated the narratives dealing with *Primeval History* as, almost without exception, narratives of sin and punishment.[17] One can readily agree, but what does this mean? Nothing other than that these narratives also are based on the act-consequence connection (evident in wisdom, law, creation) and are constituted by it. Yahweh is the one who executes this connection.

From all of this we may conclude that, for extensive and major literary contexts of the OT creation-faith in the broad sense is not simply a "foil";[18] rather, this faith centrally determines their content. But what does this mean for the *theology of history in the OT?* Does not the latter reflect a mode of thinking and experience that has a quite different, specifically Israelite character? I maintain that in this area too there are tremendous and fundamental affinities with the general oriental (and perhaps even the general human) horizon of thought sketched above.

This is seen most clearly in those cases where historical experiences are expressed with the help of motifs drawn from creation typology. Take, for instance, those passages in the Psalter and in Second Isaiah where the exodus is portrayed in terms of the *Chaoskampf*[19] or where Second Isaiah's announcement of the imminent historical events exhibits creation motifs.[20] Here we do not find that creation motifs have been transferred secondarily to historical statements. The situation is quite the opposite and completely in accord with ancient Near Eastern parallels: views of creation provide the framework within which assertions about history are made.[21] One is reminded of Isaiah's concept of "the work of Yahweh" which, as H. Wildberger has shown,[22] designates simultaneously and indistinguishably the creative and the historical action of Yahweh. In this view, history is understood as the implementation of creation and the actualization of the order of creation.

This also becomes clear in many *older historical traditions* which are conceived from the viewpoint of the act-consequences connection that accords with creation. By way of illustration consider a few particular traditions from the Ancestral History (Genesis 12—50). In Genesis 12 the Pharaoh offends against a married woman. Immediately he is beset with plagues, and the matter must be set aright, the world must be brought back to order. In Genesis 13 Abraham and Lot divide the land. Abraham is magnanimous, greed is far from his mind – and that is rewarded. It only goes to show that wisdom is part of the basic order of this world (Prov.

21:26; 28:25). The people of Sodom and Gomorrah (Genesis 19) sin greatly, and consequently they are destroyed. Only Lot acts righteously, and therefore he is saved. The list of examples could easily be lengthened to include, for instance, the many narratives that tell about unexpected reward for proper behavior. H.-J. Hermisson[23] has provided some examples from the Davidic Court History under the title, "Wisdom and History." And Gerhard von Rad has already called our attention to other examples from the Joseph story.[24] The order of creation provides the basis and the content for innumerable individual traditions.

How shall we understand the basic theological motif of the Yahwistic Ancestral History, namely, *the Promise*? Is not the Yahwist's view alien to this sphere of thought from the very outset? The content of the promise is the assurance of possession of the land, the pledge that Abraham's descendants would become a great people, and the bestowal of the divine blessing, understood concretely as increase, fortune, and prosperity. These three elements of the promise describe what, according to the general view of the ancient Near East, constitutes a people. That the existence of a people would be guaranteed by the deity was an unquestionable assumption in the whole ancient Near East, so long as the religions were national religions and the gods were national deities. That assumption pertains to the foundation of the world order, insofar as one's particular world and the absolute world were seen to be basically identical. How the promise assuring such a fulfillment was articulated in Israel, and how in different epochs of Israelite history one lived in and from this promise, certainly found expression in ways that were distinctively Israelite. However, the fundamental idea was conceived from the view of the order of the world, given with creation, the establishment of which was guaranteed by the Promise, or the covenant with the ancestors.

Our last example is the confession that Israel was "brought forth out of Egypt," which Martin Noth regards as the primary article of Israel's faith (*Urbekenntnis*).[25] In the Yahwistic narrative the exodus is presented as the first part of the fulfillment of the promise to the ancestors; and that means, as already indicated, the establishment of what appears in the whole ancient Near East as harmonious (*heil*) world order: that God creates and maintains the existence of the people. In the Deuteronomistic literature the exodus theme receives a special emphasis. Here it is very closely linked with the keeping of the commandments, the law, and with the promise of blessing. The legal material in many parts of Deuteronomy, as is well known, can hardly be distinguished from comparable material of the ancient Near East. Even the structures of Deuteronomic legal thinking (blessing, curse) correspond to analogous views of the ancient Near East.[26] The blessing involved in obeying the commandment is nothing other than the harmonious (*heil*) world order given in creation. But what is the meaning of the close uniting of this view with the exodus kerygma? Previously I said that, in the ancient Near East, it was myth that constituted world order (corresponding to creation). The OT is far removed from the mythical view of reality in essential matters. The place of myth, at least here in Deuteronomy, is taken by history. No longer is it myth, but rather a shared history, which is the sign and pledge that God supports the world order and intends to bring it into realization. Here one may speak with good reason about a specifically Israelite theology of history. Yet history has theological relevance only and precisely because it gains meaning in the context of thought about the order of the world which phenomenologically is bound with creation.

To round off the discussion let us consider finally those parts of the OT in which we may discern the *emergence of an eschatological faith*. It has long been recognized that there is a close relation between views of creation and consummation. The salvation (*Heil*) expected at the end of history corresponds to what the entire ancient Near East considered an orderly (*heil*) world, including the view of the pilgrimage to Zion to do homage to the God enthroned there as King.[27] What the so-called messianic prophecies attributed to the King of the end time is expressed *materialiter* in what in the thought of the ancient Near East, based as it was on mythical-magical presuppositions, was expected of the reigning king. This is the new dimension in the eschatological horizon: in the course of time there was an increasingly sharpened awareness of the difference between the world of creation and that which can be realized in history. Consequently the period of salvation was postponed into an ever-receding future and eventually was expected to be the in-breaking of a completely new eon. To be sure, even this experience was not completely alien to ancient mythical thinking. For the continual attempt by means of magic to induce reality in the direction of an orderly (*heil*) world shows that one was already somewhat aware that the orderly (*heil*) world cannot be identified with the actual world.

Now to summarize: wherever we looked we saw, to be sure in manifold variations but still with great clarity, that the controlling background of OT thought and faith is the view of a comprehensive world order and, hence, a creation faith in the broad sense of the word – a creation faith that Israel in many respects shared with her environment. It must have become clear, however, that this does not amount to putting the faith of the OT on the same level as the religions of the ancient Near East. On the contrary: in this way the unique elements of Israelite religion stand out more clearly against the ancient Near Eastern background.[28] To be sure, it is not as Gerhard von Rad perceived: that Israel first of all began with a more or less purely historical faith, and later combined with this soteriological faith other ancient Near Eastern traditions, such as the creation faith. Just the opposite: Israel participated fully in the thought world and in the creation faith of the world of the ancient Near East and understood – and indeed could only understand – her particular experiences of history and experiences of God in this horizon.[29] As would be expected, Israel's historical experiences necessitated some modifications, but that was the case also with other cultures of the ancient Near East which likewise gave their own relatively independent expression to the common way of thinking. In short, it has been shown that, contrary to what von Rad's position would logically lead us to believe, Israel did not create from her own faith a peculiar realm of life and experience. Rather, from the outset Israel's experiences occurred in the context of and in vigorous engagement (*Auseinandersetzung*) with the already given sphere of the common ancient Near Eastern way of thinking, particularly creation thought. [Part II, in reference to the NT, has been omitted.]

III

All factors considered, the doctrine of creation, namely, the belief that God has created and is sustaining the order of the world in all its complexities, is not a peripheral theme of biblical theology but is plainly the fundamental theme. What Israel experienced in her history and what the early Christian community experienced in relation to Jesus is understood and interpreted in terms of this one basic theme.

Therefore it seems to me to be of the highest significance that the description of the order of creation in the Bible and the description of creation found in the surrounding countries are largely in agreement. What creation – that is, orderly and harmonious (*heil*) world – is, or should be, is a general human perception, to which *mutatis mutandis* the Enlightenment also came in a new way centuries later. Specifically the elements of this view are: (a) the judgment about how this orderly (*heil*) world can be attained; (b) why the breakthrough of this orderly world has not yet occurred; and (c) what people can cling to in the meantime so as not to resign or give up. The essential exegetical work must begin with the treatment of these three questions. The task cannot be pursued further now; it must suffice first of all to show what the problem is.[30] Nevertheless, a few more lines should be added to the discussion.

IV

In considering the possible consequences of these findings for systematic theology I would like to begin, not with a technical discussion in the field of systematic theology, but rather with an attempt to develop them along the lines of exegetical results.

To recapitulate: the basic theme of ancient Near Eastern views of creation was the question about the orderly (*heil*) world, the question of a comprehensive righteousness according to the presuppositions of the time. This is precisely the theme of the Bible too, both in the OT and the NT – not the least under the catchword "righteousness." This thematic congruence is not accidental but arises necessarily from the fact that the message of the Bible touches people in their world and in the fundamental questions of human existence.

Broad lines of continuity run from the extrabiblical question about righteousness to the biblical question about righteousness. In general, ancient views and those of the Bible agree to a considerable extent on how the true righteousness, the orderly (*heil*) world in itself, is to be described.

I jump now to the present. It is undeniable that the theme of a comprehensive righteousness, of the orderly (*heil*) world, is also one of the main themes – if not the major theme – of our own time. After the NT and above all in the wake of the Enlightenment the content of this theme, over against the ancient parallels, has shifted. For us the world has become universal, and so has the demand for righteousness. No longer can we be concerned only with the correct order of our own nation; rather, the correct order of the whole world must come into view. Also the description of social righteousness has been broadened on the basis of the view of general human rights. Nevertheless, the lines of continuity that run from antiquity to the present cannot be overlooked. Ancient insights concerning the interrelatedness of justice, politics, and nature have found new relevance today. The problem as such remains the same. If we want to continue what has been accomplished by the bearers of biblical tradition, then our concepts of righteousness, based on current presuppositions, must be the ground on which we theologize responsibly about God's righteousness and God's salvation. Just as the Bible could share contemporary notions of the proper world order to a great degree, so today's theology can take up contemporary descriptions and make them its own.

To be sure, neither the description of this world order nor the endeavor to achieve it constituted the specific elements of the biblical message. The world order only provided in the first instance the horizon and the material point of reference for the biblical message. For today's discussion this implies that modern theology must certainly come to terms with contempory conceptions of righteousness; but the specifically theological contribution in this process is not evident so long as, in the name of God or of theology, one only describes the present-day concept of peaceful order and calls for its realization. Those who go no further than this – and there are many who do not – remain at the stage where once the nonbiblical people of the ancient Near East remained and where today many of our contemporaries remain, especially those who are heavily influenced by the Enlightenment.

What might be the specific contribution of theology in our time? Let me make a couple of suggestions. In line with, for instance, the preexilic prophets or Paul's discussion in Romans 1, theology would have to point out and consider the obvious discrepancy between the evident demands of a universal righteousness and the actual possibilities and performances of human beings, including Christians. The description of this discrepancy would be the ground for theological and anthropological statements. In this connection it would also be appropriate to deal with sin, taking into account the circumstances of judgment. Also, this would be the place to consider concretely the assurance of forgiveness. In this way theology would speak about the theme of the righteousness of the world in terms of the righteousness of God.

On the basis of the background of the biblical experience of God in history, both the history of Israel and the history of Jesus Christ, theology could show the possibilities of living in and with the unrighteousness of the world and yet holding fast to the assurance and the claim of righteousness. Here it would be possible to speak, for instance, of the grace and faithfulness of God, as well as the specific elements of God's demand. In this way the basic principles of the way to righteousness, which are hidden to the unbeliever, might

113

be discovered. In this case, too, discussion would deal with the theme of the righteousness of the world in terms of the righteousness of God.

Theology needs to consider in special degree the significance of the fact that, in the course of the biblical history of faith, righteousness came to be conceived eschatologically in an ever-more-consistent manner. Gradually it was freed from connection with the creation of the world in the beginning of time and came to be more closely bound with the theme of the eschatological new creation. In this horizon theology should consider what the insight into the temporary and broken character of the world implies for the question of righteousness. It could thereby free us from dogged striving toward the realization of the ultimate righteousness at any cost and from the frustration that necessarily arises from it. It could give courage for the fragmentary – in full awareness of sin that abides. Finally, it could encourage deeds of righteousness even in those cases which do not lead visibly to success but whose effects are hidden or even end in failure. This would then not be far removed at all from the righteousness meant, for instance, in the Sermon on the Mount. In any case, however, the theme of the righteousness of the world would be considered once again centrally in terms of the righteousness of God.

Thus the theological theme of the righteousness of God does not stand in opposition to the theme of the righteousness of the world, as is often asserted. Just the opposite: only the theme of God's righteousness makes it possible to speak *coram deo* properly of the righteousness of the world, about which all of us must speak because it is the fundamental problem of our human existence.

It should be clear that even with all these considerations, we are still dealing with our initial theme of creation theology. Though in various ways, every expression of human thinking has to do with the question of the proper understanding of the world and its orders, and thus with the question of justice and righteousness in the comprehensive sense of the word. Wherever this was done in a religious dimension, one spoke in some way about "creation" and in that connection made some assertions about the origin of the world. The question as to whether priority lay with assertions about order or assertions about creation cannot be decided any more than that famous question of whether the chicken or the egg came first. Assertions about order and about creation are two aspects of one and the same complex of problems. In this worldwide discussion, the bearers of the biblical message have lifted their voices and have brought before us their own conceptions of how the world is to be understood as creation, that is, as related to God. We have seen that the central themes of the biblical message throughout move within the horizon of this one fundamental question. And a theology which understands itself in terms of this stream of tradition should not proceed in any other fashion. All theology is creation theology, even when it does not speak expressly of creation but speaks of faith, justification, the reign of God, or whatever, if it does so in relation to the world. And it must do that as long as it makes any claim of being responsible.

NOTES

1 An address given at a conference of Reformed Theological Professors held in Wuppertal, 29–30 September 1972. [Published first in *ZTK* 70 (1973) 1–19; also in H. H. Schmid's collection of essays, *Altorientalische Welt in der alttestamentlichen Theologie* (Zurich: Theologischer Verlag, 1974) 9–30. In these essays Schmid has further developed his thoughts, especially in "Jahweglaube und altorientalisches Weltordnungsdenken," 31–63, and in "Altorientalische Welt in der alttestamentlichen Theologie," 145–64.]

2 Gerhard von Rad, *Das theologische Problem des alttestamentlichen Schöpfungsglaubens* (BZAW 66; 1936) 138–47 [=*Gesammelte Studien zum AT* (TBü 8; Munich: Chr. Kaiser, 1965³) 136–47. The 1966 translation of the essay appears in this volume as ch. 2]. Cf. also his *Theologie des AT* (Munich: Chr. Kaiser, 1969⁶) I:149–67 [ET *Old Testament Theology* (New York: Harper & Row; Edinburgh: Oliver & Boyd, 1962) I:136–53].

3 Cf. F. Stolz, *Strukturen und Figuren im Kult von Jerusalem* (BZAW 118; Berlin: Walter de Gruyter, 1970) 12–101.

4 Translation according to *AOT*², 380f [=*ANET*, 164].

5 *AOB*² Nr. 318; *ANEP* Nr. 246, p. 77.

6 Table 6, lines 35ff in *AOT*², 122f; lines 47ff in *ANET*, 68f.

7 Cf. e.g., E. Otto, *Prolegomena zur Frage der Gesetzgebung und Rechtssprechung in Ägypten* (MDAI.K 14; 1956) 150–59: "The central concept, around which all the powers of government are oriented and which in the juridical sense may be regarded as the most general element of law, is Maat" (150).

8 Cf. e.g., H. Brunner, *Die Weisheitsliteratur* in Handbuch der Orientalistik (ed. B. Spuler; 1952) I/2:90–110, esp. 93: "The central concept of wisdom teaching is that of Maat, 'law', 'justice', 'the primal order' "; S. Morenz, *Ägyptische Religion* in Die Religionen der Menschheit (ed. C. M. Schröder; Stuttgart: Kohlhammer, 1960) 8:120: ". . . the Egyptian ethic and its innermost aspect is Maat."

9 For further evidence see H. H. Schmid, *Gerechtigkeit als Weltordnung* (BHT 40; Tübingen: Mohr/Siebeck, 1968) 24–46. From the OT, cf. Ps. 72, for example.

10 Cf., among others, K. Koch, "Gibt es ein Vergeltungsdogma im Alten Testament?" *ZTK* 52 (1955) 1–42 [=*Um das Prinzip der Vergeltung in Religion und*

Recht des AT (WdF 125; Darmstadt: Wissenschaftliche Buchgesellschaft, 1972) 130–80. ET: "Is There a Doctrine of a Retribution in the Old Testament" in *Theodicy in the Old Testament*, ed. J. L. Crenshaw (IRT 4; Philadelphia: Fortress Press; London: SPCK, 1983) 57–87]. See also the astounding statement by von Rad (see above, n. 2): "The belief in retribution is based ... on faith in the creator (thus not, as one might expect, on faith in the justice of the God of the covenant)."

11 Cf. H. Graf Reventlow, "Sein Blut komme über sein Haupt," *VT* 10 (1960) 311–27 [=WdF 125 (1972) 412–31]. See also, K. Koch, "Der Spruch, 'Sein Blut bleibe auf seinem Haupt' und die israelitische Auffassung vom vergossenen Blut," *VT* 12 (1962) 396–416 [=WdF 125 (1972) 432–56].

12 E. Würthwein, "Amos-Studien," *ZAW* 62 (1949/50) 10–52, esp. 40–52.

13 R. Bach, "Gottesrecht und weltliches Recht in der Verkündigung des Propheten Amos" in *Festschrift G. Dehn* (1957) 23–34.

14 H. W. Wolff, *Amos' geistige Heimat* (WMANT 18; Neukirchen-Vluyn: Neukirchener, 1964. ET: *Amos the Prophet: The Man and His Background.*

15 Cf. H. H. Schmid, "Amos: Zur Frage nach der geistigen Heimat des Propheten," *WuD*, NF 10 (1969) 85–103.

16 Isa. 45:8, 23f; 46:12f; 51:6, 8; 54:14, 17.

17 C. Westermann, "Arten der Erzählung in der Genesis" in *Forschung am AT* (TBü 24; Munich: Chr. Kaiser, 1964) 9–91, esp. 47–58; cf. *Genesis* (BKAT I/1; Neukirchen-Vluyn: Neukirchener, 1966) 66–77.

18 Cf. von Rad, [see above, n. 2], 146.

19 So possibly Ps 74:13ff; cf. H.-J. Kraus, *Psalmen* (BKAT 15; Neukirchen-Vluyn: Neukirchener, 1960) I:517; cf. Ps. 77:17ff; Isa. 51:9ff.

20 Cf. e.g., Isa. 44:24ff; 45:11ff.

21 Von Rad (see above, n. 2), to be sure, continually speaks of the close juxtaposition and interrelation of creation faith and salvation faith in Second Isaiah (R. Rendtorff does so even more clearly in "Die theologische Stellung des Schöpfungsglaubens bei Deuterojesaja," *ZTK* 51 [1954] 3–13), but he assumes that we are dealing with two originally separate strands (*"metabasis eis allo genos,"* 140).

22 H. Wildberger, *Jesajas Verständnis der Geschichte*, VTSup 9 (Leiden: E. J. Brill, 1963) 83–117; also his *Jesaja* (BKAT 10/3; Neukirchen-Vluyn: Neukirchener, 1968) 188f.

23 H. J. Hermisson, "Weisheit und Geschichte" in *Probleme biblischer Theologie. G. von Rad zum 70. Geburtstag* (ed. H. W. Wolff; Munich: Chr. Kaiser, 1971) 136–54; esp. 137–48.

24 G. von Rad, "Josephsgeschichte und ältere Chokma," VTSup 1 (1953) 120–27 [=*Gesammelte Studien zum AT* (TBü 8; Munich: Chr. Kaiser, 1965) 272–80. ET: "The Joseph Narrative and Ancient Wisdom" in *The Problem of the Hexateuch and Other Essays* (New York: McGraw Hill; Edinburgh: Oliver & Boyd, 1966) 292–300].

25 M. Noth, *Überlieferungsgeschichte des Pentateuch* (Darmstadt: Wissenschaftliche Buchgesellschaft, 1960) 52. [ET: *A History of Pentateuchal Traditions* (trans. B. W. Anderson; Chico, Calif.: Scholars Press, 1981) 49.]

26 Cf. M. Noth, "Die mit des Gesetzes Werken umgehen, die sind unter dem Fluch" in *Gesammelte Studien zum AT* (TBü 6; Munich: Chr. Kaiser, 1960) 155–71. [ET: "For All Who Rely on the Works of the Law Are Under a Curse" in *The Laws of the Pentateuch* (trans. D. R. Ap-Thomas; Philadelphia: Fortress Press; Edinburgh: Oliver & Boyd, 1966) 118–31].

27 Cf. F. Stolz, see above, n. 3, 76f, 94.

28 Where specific matters are relevant they have been indicated above at appropriate points. To consider them in greater detail lies beyond the scope of this essay.

29 Here again it must be emphasized that it is not responsible exegetically to subsume the creation thought of the OT and that of the ancient Near East under the catchword "Protology." Cf. above, n. 21.

30 [Notes on the limitations of this essay, the theme of creation vis-à-vis the theme of order, and on the necessity of treating creation theology as an essential aspect of fundamental theology are omitted.]

7

*Observations on the Creation Theology in Wisdom**

HANS-JÜRGEN HERMISSON

"The wisdom of the OT stays quite determinedly within the horizon of creation. Its theology is creation theology."[1] These two sentences by Walther Zimmerli formulate in an almost classical way a generally accepted conviction. However, anyone who sets out consequently to look for the theology of creation in the "proper" wisdom writings will arrive at a result which is disappointing at first. Among the numerous proverbs of the older proverbial wisdom he will find a small number in which Yahweh is named as creator of the poor and the rich, of eye and ear, and even of the culprit.[2] He will find a few remarks by Ecclesiastes about the work of God, which is opaque to man;[3] and even the great poem of wisdom in Proverbs 8, the central section of which (8:22–31) lists the events of creation somewhat broadly, does not want to speak in the first place about the creation of the world, but about the creation of wisdom *before* the world and about wisdom's resulting superiority (so, too, Sirach 24). Proverbs 3:19–20 also has been formulated in the interest of wisdom: it was through wisdom that Yahweh founded the earth, and thus the significance of wisdom is stressed again. Things look different in the Book of Job, particularly in the hymnic passages, which are probably secondary,[4] and above all in the concluding speeches of God (Job 38—41); but of this, more later. Lastly, the hymnic praise of the God of creation takes up ample space in Jesus ben Sira,[5] and beyond that the subject of creation is a basic theme of his theology.[6] However, Jesus ben Sira's book is a late fruit of OT wisdom, and one with which someone wanting to speak about Israel's wisdom will hardly begin.

Someone glancing thus at the evidence might further gain the

* First published in English in *Israelite Wisdom* (1978) 43–57. Several lengthy notes have been abridged.

118

impression that here one is dealing only with the much discussed phenomenon of a supposedly late theologizing of an originally quite secular wisdom. But as Gerhard von Rad has already shown,[7] this is not so; rather that which becomes the explicit theme only in late texts has long been implicitly presupposed in the older wisdom. Therefore the two sentences by Zimmerli quoted in the beginning are indeed right. But it is not unimportant to see that Zimmerli gives a negative rather than a positive reason for this statement: the God of *Israel* is nowhere mentioned in the older wisdom literature, and this gap is then filled "occasionally" by predication of the creator.[8] This presents an important problem of wisdom theology which will have to be discussed again briefly at the end. But before we can ask about wisdom in OT theology, we first have to ask about the place of creation theology in wisdom. If the topic of creation has been at least presupposed from the beginning, and later made explicit, then one must be able to say what significance it has for wisdom and whether in functioning thus it also has to take a special form. The main part of this study is devoted to the second question, the question about significance may be briefly presented first.

I

As is well known, wisdom searches for the knowledge of order, or, for those to whom this seems too rigid, for a certain regularity within the diversity of the phenomena of the world. This world, however, is *unitary*. Although for us it may customarily divide into nature, regulated by (seemingly firm) natural laws, and history, which is more or less contingent, ancient wisdom starts from the conviction that the regularities within the human and the historical-social realm are not in principle different from the ones within the realm of non-human phenomena.[9] Therefore "nature wisdom" and "culture wisdom" are not as far apart as it may seem at first. Knowledge of the world and the education of man belong together. The endeavor to recognize the regularities in this unitary world is the appropriate context for wisdom to ask about creation,[10] for it involves the actual correspondence between the created world and the knowledge of it, and, therefore, the necessary conditions for proper knowing *and* for proper conduct (inasmuch as *knowing* [e.g., the good] and the *doing* of it are not already identical!). What God created "in wisdom"[11] can also be comprehended and stated in the sentences of wisdom. There must be correspondence here or there will be no true knowledge. If, for instance, it were at all thinkable that God created the world as chaos – which however is a *contradicto in adjecto!* – any question about regularity would be senseless. "In wisdom" then means more than "not chaotic." It also says something about the intelligibility of the world,[12] and, indeed, for this, the perfect expression was found in Proverbs 8. Here wisdom was personified for the purpose of being able to address man; however, it is the same wisdom which is present in the created world as regularity, purposiveness, and therefore also as beauty. Thus Proverbs 8 talks about creation when it talks about wisdom: about creation with respect to its intelligible orders, to which man is to adapt himself.[13]

II

If the creation theology of wisdom has its place and its special function in the close relationship between an effective knowledge and human education, it has to be expected that it also takes a special form. Now, "theology" is hardly presentable in the form of individual (and originally quite independent) proverbs; therefore, if only on the ground of their conformity to the literary type, one must not expect too much of the older collections of proverbs, and must look for other texts. Still we may begin with a brief glance at the sporadic mention of the creator in Proverbs 10–29.

Four of the seven proverbs in question should be taken in one group. All of them speak about Yahweh's having created the poor as well as the rich, and even the oppressor:

> He who mocks the poor insults his Maker.... (17:5)

> He who oppresses a poor man insults his Maker,
>> but he who is kind to the needy honors him. (14:31)

> The rich and the poor meet together;
>> the Lord is the maker of them all (22:2)

> The poor man and the oppressor meet together;
>> the Lord gives light to the eyes of both. (29:13)[14]

As one can easily see, these proverbs form two pairs, the second member of which varies a previously formulated insight; thus, 17:5 is probably the original version over against 14:31 (correspondence of verbs!). But what do such proverbs say? Taken by themselves, they are ambiguous; but in the context of wisdom this wide scope of usage and meaning can be discerned more precisely. One should not understand them as the expression of a social order stabilized by a creation ideology, for it is a misinterpretation of wisdom if it is credited with the stabilizing of an unchangeably rigid order.[15] Wisdom is much more reserved: it does not even try to *understand* the phenomenon of poverty, but it says that the poor are to be respected. One could apply wisdom sentences and ask: Is it not his own fault – through lack of wisdom, through laziness, etc.? No, says wisdom, even with his poverty the poor man is God's creature; therefore, whoever mocks the poor man insults his creator. The variant text (14:31) goes a step further by implicitly warning not to oppress the poor man but to have mercy upon the needy. The sentence about the poor man and the oppressor seems to be the most scandalous: is this said out of cynicism or resignation in the face of reality? Perhaps it is indicative that creation is not explicitly mentioned here. "The Lord gives light to their eyes" does mean the granting of existence, to be sure, but it also signifies the dependence and limitation of the oppressor – certainly not his justification.

The "ethical world order" has been portrayed much more satisfactorily in the following proverb:

> The Lord has made everything for its purpose,
> even the wicked for the day of trouble. (16:4)

This may already be an apologetic in view of the question why in a meaningfully arranged world there is also evil, there is the wicked. However in the world of the old wisdom it certainly is a satisfying answer, not an expedient one. The boundaries are only starting to become visible: the Lord has made *everything* for its purpose. This is the principle, the rule, and the proverb goes only one step further: not even an element as disturbing as the oppressor is an exception. Creation is the basis not only of regularity, but of a meaningful and satisfactory order of events in the world, a purposefulness of created beings and things.

It would seem that the following proverb was also conceived from the idea of right fulfillment of purposes, of ordered functions:

> A just balance and scales are the Lord's
> all the weights in the bag are his work. (16:11)

The sentence also has an ethical implication (the implicit admonition to commercial honesty) and thus corresponds to Prov. 11:1 ("False balance – abomination to the Lord ..."). But here again the proof of a meaningfully functioning individual order in Yahweh's (creation-) work has priority. Therefore one could have formulated

121

it: Who falsifies the balance offends against an order of corporate human life which was established and guaranteed by the creator. This formulation has not been made, at least not in the tradition passed on to us, because it was naturally presupposed and, certainly specified in a proverb like this one – *sapienti sat.*

The final saying once again deals with the aboriginal business of wisdom, with knowledge:

> The hearing ear and the seeing eye,
> the Lord has made them both. (20:12)

Applied to the individual and his participation in knowing, this means something like predestination:[16] only those can hear and see to whom it is granted by Yahweh. Principally it means – and this will be placed in the foreground here – the ability to know is not an autonomous quality of man, but it is just as much Yahweh's creation as the world which he made in its regularities. For this very reason, however, knowing is possible at all; for the same creator created the "world" and the organs of cognition adequate to it.

The texts which we have viewed so far thus confirm at first only the image of Yahweh's creative activity as the foundation of the orders of the world: meaningful and rational orders, and also at the borderline of cognition, a knowing which itself was created by Yahweh and thus properly associates with the orders and "functions." One can add that such activity of the creator obviously persists. Creation did not only happen at the beginning of the world, but takes place continuously; therefore, the orders have not become rigid, but necessarily remain flexible. If "activity of the creator" is understood in this broad sense (or if Yahweh is principally understood as the creator), one can probably refer to further sayings; however, this does not alter the fact of the relative scarcity of such statements. Certainly the wise were far from explicitly seasoning their moral teachings each time by referring to the orders of creation.[17] Finally it can be observed that the sentences pointing to the creator in the older part of the Book of Proverbs generally deal with the creation of man, with human situations, or matters within man's sphere of activity. This, however, is not to be evaluated in the sense of a fundamental differentiation between man and nature (and correspondingly of natural wisdom and cultural wisdom), but it simply serves a purpose, since knowledge of the conditions of the world has to guide human behavior directly. For this there are, of course, more immediate and more remote objects of knowledge. But if we are searching for statements in which the broader connection between moral teaching and creation stands out more clearly, we will be forced to leave the area of short proverbs and look for wisdom texts which speak directly and pointedly about creation.

III

Apart from that late and mature product of Israelite creation theology, which appears in Genesis 1 as a didactic, historical tale, Israel spoke about Yahweh's creation activity above all in hymnic praise. There is at least one hymn which was definitely composed in the handwriting of wisdom: Psalm 104.[18] As is well known, the psalm begins with the heavenly activities of the creator God (v. 1–4), moves from there to the foundation of the earth through the expulsion of the original floods (v. 5–9), continues with the life-giving irrigation of the earth through brooks and rain (v. 10–12 + 13–18) and links with this the placement of plants and animals within their environment (esp. v. 11–12 + 16–18). Verses 19–23 then deal with the coordination of the creatures with their times – night and day. Verses 24–26 – after an exclamation of astonishment at the multitude of Yahweh's works – occupy themselves once again with the sea and its inhabitants, and v. 27–30 finally describe the permanent dependence of all life upon Yahweh's creative activity, until the hymnic coda (*Abgesang*) concludes the entire psalm (v. 31–35).[19]

What reminds one of wisdom in this psalm? Whoever is only looking for the vocabulary, may be comforted by *ḥokmâ* in the central and all-encompassing v. 24. But actually there is much more. If one first examines the middle section of the psalm in that regard, it seems to offer a perfect example of that "nature wisdom" which is described in 1 Kgs. 5:13 (English 4:33) as Solomon's special skill,[20] although here not in a style of sober statement, but of hymnic usage. If "Solomon" made proverbs "from the cedar that is in Lebanon to the hyssop that grows out of the wall" (1 Kgs. 5:13), one may find in the psalm the same assignment of beings to their local and temporal realms: the badger to the rocks, the stork to the cedar trees, the lion to the night, and man and his work to the day. Naturally, then, there is more here than the mere compilation of creatures and environments. The meaningfulness of such coordination becomes evident, too: in this world and its manifold spaces everything is well arranged ecologically. There is even more: everything fulfills its purpose in this world, as is shown especially by the statements about the beneficial effects of water from springs and from Yahweh's heavenly chambers. Psalm 104:13–15 may be read as a perfect example of a whole chain of consecutive purposes. This points to man again, just as v. 23 also is directed to the time of man. It corresponds indeed with the often noted "anthropocentric" character of wisdom, however in such a way that man is introduced without strain into a wonderfully ordered world – a world which moreover does not only exist for the sake of man, but in which everything has a meaning – even such a bizarre creature as Leviathan out there in the distant ocean whom God created as his toy.[21] A world thus meaningfully ordered in all its parts is beautiful in the eyes of the Hebrews – beautiful in its intelligible functioning. Thus the form of the creation statement corresponds thoroughly with the declaration by Ecclesiastes: "He has made everything beautiful in its time (*yāpeh bě'ittô*)" (Qoh. 3:11), although not with his following statement about the works of God being indiscernible; for to the poet of Psalm 104, as well as to the old wisdom, the world as creation is intelligible enough.

Only in passing let me point to the well-known relationship between Psalm 104 and the Egyptian solar hymnody (especially from the Amarna Age).[22] Here too "wisdom" recommends itself as the place of tradition and as the place for taking over features of foreign culture.[23] Now and again the relationship between the psalm and the "catalogue science" of the onomastica (passed on in Egypt and Mesopotamia and probably to be presupposed in Israel) has been pointed out.[24] In this also a relation to wisdom would come into play. However, some reserve is advisable here: in any case the psalm is not interested in a *successive* order of things, and, with the exception of the widespaced movement from heaven to earth, the phenomena seem to be listed more by random association than with a side-glance at a catalogue of things. (For instance, the poet goes from mentioning the rain, to the cedars of Lebanon, and from there, on the one hand, to the birds nesting in them, and, on the other hand, to the mountain animals, etc.)

The poet of Proverbs had formulated, "The Lord has made everything for its purpose. . . ." (16:4). Is not Psalm 104 the comprehensive presentation of such a wisdom concept of creation? The meaningful, purposeful ordering of things and spaces and creatures first reaches its goal indeed in the hymnic form of presentation, for in it the ordered world appears as the result of a continuous devotion of the creator to his creation. Here, too, then we find the continuation of Yahweh's creative activity which we encountered already in Proverbs.

But this does not apply to all parts of the psalm. In two places the style shows obvious deviations from this psalm's mode of expression, which uses mostly participial and imperfect constructions. We are referring to the two verbs in the perfect in v. 5 and v. 19, each of which introduces a new paragraph: "He has founded the earth . . ." and "He has made the moon. . . ." Although it is customary to adapt the two verbs to the style and context and read them as participles,[25] this is hardly right. For obviously the poet wants to speak here about the basic data of the past: the environment of earth, like the changing of festival times and the times of the day, has been created by Yahweh once, and once and for all, and this work continues in existence even where Yahweh "hides his face" (v. 29): He renews the face of the ground (v. 30), but he does not have to found it anew.

This becomes especially clear through the example of the earth. The poet uses here the old mythical motive of the chaos struggle – a noticeably adapted, tamed version, but that is not the point here. Yahweh rebuked and let his voice of thunder sound: then the waters fled and mountains and valleys appeared.[26] What is decisive, however, is the continuation in v. 9. The original chaotic sea can never return, for Yahweh excluded it from the world once and for all. He has set a boundary which the chaotic original waters can never again transgress. This corresponds with the statement that Yahweh gave the earth such a firm foundation that it can never be shaken again (v. 5). And this way of talking about a basic datum of the creator's activity that is altogether past, so that the "chaos" (in the form of those original floods) remains completely outside the world, seems to be a creation-concept typical of wisdom. In order to make this clear, it is necessary for us to cast a side glance at creation statements of a different kind, for in this respect one must not measure Psalm 104 against the very well known model of Genesis 1, but must compare it with texts which start from the confrontation of creation and chaos.

IV

These texts are first of all separate passages within larger complexes. A nice example may be found in the hymnic part of the royal lamentation, Psalm 89:

> Thou dost rule the raging of the sea;
> when its waves rise, thou stillest them.

Thou didst crush Rahab like a carcass,
  thou didst scatter thy enemies with thy mighty arm.
The heavens are thine, the earth also is thine;
  the world and all that is in it, thou hast founded them.
The north and the south, thou hast created them;
  Tabor and Hermon joyously praise thy name.
Thou hast a mighty arm;
  strong is thy hand, high thy right hand.

Ps. 89:10–14; Engl. 9–13

This form of the creation statement is already significant. Here, too, the chaos struggle is mentioned in connection with creation – in fact *also* as an event of the past – and here for good reason the stronger mythological image of the chaos dragon, "Rahab" (v. 11), is used. But the matter does not rest with this event of the past. It certainly is the *fundamental* happening in the strict sense of the word – at that time Yahweh made the foundation of the earth. But there remains the sea, and the necessity that the creator display his power against the raging of the sea (v. 9). Not without reason does the poet also praise Yahweh's mighty arm (v. 13): the created world needs it because of the resistance of the chaotic. This is still clearer in Psalm 93, as a few sentences from it may show:

The Lord has become king; he has put on majesty;
  ... he has girded himself with strength.
The world also is established;
  so it cannot be moved;
Thy throne is established from of old;
  thou art from everlasting.
The floods have lifted up, O Lord,
  the floods have lifted up their voice,
  (again) the floods lifted up their roaring.
Mightier than the thunders of many waters ...
  the Lord on high is mighty!

We find here traits already known. That deed of the past, the conquering of the chaotic original flood, is mentioned again. But in this psalm something else stands in the foreground, namely, Yahweh's present creative activity as experienced at the festival. Therefore, creation is perceived here not primarily as a distant past, but as an event which is presently repeating itself. For *now* the earth would be threatened, would be in danger of sinking back into chaos – if Yahweh had not become king, that is, if he had not proven

126

himself as the one he has been since primeval time, as the one he proved to be then, in the beginning, the sovereign king.[27]

Now someone may say that the chaos struggle in these texts is "nothing but" poetic imagery, and, besides, has lost its vividness more or less. That there is this tendency is certainly correct; only, what is gained by it? Hardly a particular superiority for Israel, for spiritualization and the use of myth as image were found also in the surrounding religions. Israel's peculiarity, Yahweh's superiority, consisted in the fact that Yahweh was *mēʿôlām*, eternal – he had not come into existence – and through this Israel was confronted with its own theological problems, which cannot be discussed here. However, one has to recognize the metaphorical importance of the sea insofar as it concerns not only the chaotic waters around the world but also the powers of chaos within the world. For the community assembled at Zion and singing this psalm is indeed threatened in different ways by the chaotic.

This ever-present evidence of the creative power, the *creatio continua* (or rather, *continuata*) through which the world has to become the world again and again, could be documented by a number of further texts.[28] Instead, we shall look at the other comparable motif. Psalm 104:5 reads:

> He has set the earth on its foundations,[29]
> so that it should never be shaken.

It is not shaken (*bal-timmôṭ*). The same thing seems to be said in Ps. 93:1, as well as in 96:10. But it is not the same, for there the certainty over the unshakable earth stands in the immediate context of the renewed proof of Yahweh's sovereign power; according to Psalm 104, however, the stabilizing occurred once for all time. Psalm 93 then can speak at best indirectly about the earth's being unshakable "forever," that is, only with regard to the unshakable throne of Yahweh, whose kingship guarantees the duration of the earth even now, as in the future. But this certainty by no means excludes for this community the experience – at a different time – of the earth's shaking. In distress from an enemy (Ps. 60:4), or when law and justice are lacking on earth, then the foundations of the earth shake (Ps. 82:5).

These remarks must suffice here. The difference between these creation statements and those in Psalm 104 should have become sufficiently clear, for the differences are especially visible in portions which are otherwise similar. These psalms of the Jerusalem cult reflect the experience of a world which time and again is kept away from chaos by Yahweh's superior creative power. In the creation hymn conceived by wisdom, on the other hand, there is the conviction that chaos was eliminated fundamentally from this world at one time. Chaos is located temporally at a great distance, before the beginning of the world, or, spatially, outside the boundaries of the world. As one can easily see, this is presupposed in the statements in Ps. 104:10–26, just as it is presupposed in wisdom's cognition of the world. One might argue the point whether this view of creation belongs specifically to wisdom, but this question may be left open until further texts have been studied.

V

Such a radiant view of the created world as is presented in Psalm 104 is certainly not without problems in the face of reality. But one must not scold the poet for being a dreamer, a hopeless advocate of a world intact. With all of ancient Israel he knew how to distinguish between a time to praise and a time to weep. And he composed his hymn with the modesty of a wisdom which, being well aware of its limits, knows how to enjoy within these limits the beauty of the world in its rationally transparent functioning. It is only at the edges of this world that the enigmas of existence, that which is unintelligible, appears. Among these enigmas is not that Yahweh hides his face, or that he makes all life return to dust (v. 29); for the rhythm of becoming and passing away belongs to the order of the created world. But it is different in v. 32, when Yahweh makes the earth tremble and the mountains smoke. And finally, the concluding pleas of the psalm reveal that in this well-ordered world there is still the disturbing element of the wicked, the sinner (Ps. 104:35). This is a dark tone in the otherwise bright picture. One can find here the first traces of a later quite evident fact: that wisdom found itself confronted by the problem of theodicy by having excluded chaos once and for all from creation. But, as has been said, this problem appears at the very periphery here; the boundaries of knowledge and existence are insignificant in comparison with the intelligibility of the world.

The picture becomes different already in our second major text, the speeches of God in the Book of Job (Job 38—41). To be sure, they, too, presuppose and describe a world well ordered in all of its parts; only here a basically different note is to be heard. A human being, Job, the suffering one, is unable to discern such a world. In the context of the Book of Job, this is not yet the utterly devastating insight it became later for Ecclesiastes, for the suffering person is taken up by a primal trust which is prior to all rational understanding.[30] For the good order which the creator gave to the world is not limited by man's not understanding it. What is hidden from him are the origins, the interrelations, the background; but there remains his amazement at that which lies before him as the result of the wise creator's activity.

That these speeches of God in the Book of Job are also a piece of wisdom literature is hardly to be disputed. Obviously, they stand in the vicinity of "catalogue science."[31] Moreover, the form of speech may be related to the standard questions of Egyptian wisdom teachers,[32] or it may be compared to the "disputation of the wise."[33] In composing these speeches the poet seems to have made use largely of the wisdom tradition. This tradition is functionally adapted to the present context, through the questioning, imperative address to Job, but it is conspicuous that Job's own problems appear only in the outer frame of God's speeches. This may be intentional, so we do not mean to imply that the author of Job did not compose God's speeches himself. However, he was not free in his composition, but was bound by tradition.

In this context of mostly wisdom thought, again we come across the motif of the sea, and here again – let us state our conclusion at the outset – in the beginning and once and for all the sea is confined to its limits by Yahweh's commanding word – he does not need to rebuke any more (38:11)!

> Thus far shall you come, and no farther,
> and here shall your proud waves be stayed.

Or, again, bars and doors have been set for the sea (38:8, 10).[34] There is no question any more of a struggle,[35] and the previously described foundation of the earth seems to be something independent of the limitation of the sea.[36] Giving precedence to the earth certainly accords with its importance within the whole of creation; but it is striking that the primeval ocean does not need to be removed first. The sea is "born" (v. 8), and it still has some traits of that primeval sea – above all the "pride" (*gāʾôn*) of its waves – but it no longer comes into play; it is shut out from birth on. Now apparently the description here is consciously kept ambiguous: as the chaotic sea it is locked out by gates and bars; but at the same time it appears as the infant for whom Yahweh provides swaddling clothes, and under this metaphor it is even less conceivable as an adversary.[37] On the other hand the sea appears visibly as part of the earth, and

129

is again limited concretely by the coastlines. But in such a context there is no longer anything threatening about the sea; therefore, it is not suitable as a metaphor of the chaotic powers of the world, as they were expressed in those very different creation texts referring to the primordial floods.

From this point we shall glance briefly at a third testimony to a strict limitation of the sea, namely Jer. 5:22. This text is found not in a Jeremian context, but in a context of wisdom (v.v. 20–25), as is shown by the didactic introduction of the speech (certainly adapted to prophetic forms of speech), the address to the audience (readers) as "stubborn people" (*'am sākāl*), and the comparison between the order of nature and the order of man. It is stated in a speech of Yahweh:

> Do you not fear me? says the Lord;
>   Do you not tremble before me?
> I placed the sand as the bound for the sea,
>   a perpetual barrier which it cannot pass;
> though the waves toss, they cannot prevail,
>   though they roar, they cannot pass over it.
>
> Jer. 5:22

This at first looks very much like a comparison in which the earthly sea is used as a motif of contrast. This is undoubtedly the case, but in the allusion to the fury of the waves and to the "eternal order" one can hear something of a double meaning in the barring of the chaotic sea from the world once and for all. What actually disturbs the order of the world is not an evil power, but rather human beings and their wicked actions. These are the addressees in Jer. 5:22. Similarly, in Job 38:13, 15, and in Ps. 104:35 the addressees are the wicked and sinners.

VI

The world well ordered, chaos excluded, the world therefore comprehmnsible within limits: this fits very well with the concepts of wisdom. We had raised the question whether the motif of the final limitation of the chaotic flood is a notion peculiar to wisdom. We may state now that in the OT at least it occurs only in wisdom contexts,[38] and that it fits them excellently. We are not dealing with a *quisquiliae* concerning the origin of the world, but with a basic statement which determines how man is to understand himself in his world. This became clear in connection with the hymnic statements of the festival cult, where the presence of the creator God is experienced in quite a different way, namely, as the creator's impulsive-dynamic penetration in his world, thus suppressing chaos in a constantly renewed proof of his sovereign power, and stabilizing the shaking earth. There Yahweh must be present to his world in the highest degree as the creator, while in the creation texts of wisdom the creator's activity is directed more toward continuation, toward perseverance, the maintenance of order and regularity. In this way, however, the creator God remained at a greater distance. Certainly this difference between cult and wisdom involved the difference between times of festivity and those of everyday life. Therefore, the two concepts do not have to be completely separated. Yet they lead to very different views of the world, each with its own theological problems. As far as the problems in wisdom's concept of the world are concerned, they have already been mentioned in reference to the wicked and to the real suffering in the world. Actually there is no room for either in this concept. Let us return to the Book of Job: Is the distant and unintelligible activity of the divine creator – beneficial as it is for the whole – an answer to Job's question? It is only part of the answer. The supplementary part, however, appears in a motif alien to wisdom and yet interestingly enough adopted by it, namely, the theophany of Yahweh, the unmediated turning of the distant creator God to the suffering person, who through this turning regains trust and finds healing in his suffering. But as Ecclesiastes, for example, might indicate, not all wisdom managed to resolve the perplexity over the good order and the incomprehensibility of the world and the aloofness of the creator God.

VII

We have attempted to comprehend something of the creation theology in selected wisdom texts and its fundamental significance for wisdom's perspective and its understanding of man and the world. The texts we have treated represent a small sample, which should be followed by a treatment of the comprehensive concepts of Proverbs 8 or Jesus ben Sira. What has been described here, of course, was never anything like a dogma of wisdom, which each sage had to recite when asked about creation. It was an attempt by wisdom to orient itself to the world, to give an explanation for that which one experienced in the world as wholesome order, and which could be recognized and named. In this the motif of the chaotic floods and their limitation was naturally not compulsory – it appears much too seldom and in too varied a form – but it was suitable, especially in a world which was able to understand itself in very different ways with the aid of mythical metaphors. For the important question is not whether Israel took over mythical material, but rather how in each case such adopted mythical elements were employed. On the basis of its traditions, wisdom incorporated the myth of the chaos struggle in thorough accordance with Yahwistic faith, that is, in such a way that every dualistic overtone was excluded.[39] But it then found itself confronted by problems which in the long run it could not solve by itself. This was connected finally with its universalism – the reverse side of that characteristic noted with W. Zimmerli at the outset, namely, that wisdom was unable to say anything about Israel and the "covenant" – nothing, that is, about the particular, unique relationship of God to his people. It is in such particularity – and still the particularity of the celebrating community gathered at Zion – that God's relationship to the world and to humanity could become concrete and be immediately experienced. The author of Job still knew this when he told of the creator God, who was present to the creation but scarcely to the individual, encountering the individual sufferer in a theophany. If on the other hand, in the scepticism of wisdom, the aloofness of the universal creator God became an unbearable problem, the identification of wisdom and Torah – most clearly in Jesus ben Sira – was one possible answer to the problem. The other answer – if in conclusion, with a great leap, the comprehensive theological context should at least be indicated – was the foolishness of the cross, as God's wisdom (1 Cor. 1:17–18), whereby God came to humanity. Not that the ancient creation theology of wisdom became invalid and obsolete; rather it was only in this way that it could be maintained.

NOTES

1   W. Zimmerli, "Ort und Grenze der Weisheit im Rahmen der alttestamentlichen Theologie," *Gottes Offenbarung. Gesammelte Aufsätze zum Alten Testament* (TBü 19, Munich: Kaiser, 1963) 302.

2   Prov. 14:31; 17:5; 22:2; 29:13; 20:12; 16:4; 16:11

3   E.g., Qoh. 3:11, 14; 7:14–15, 30; 8:17; 11:5.

4   Job 9:5–10; 26:5–14.

5   Sir. 16:26–30 + 17:1–13; 39:12–35; 42:15—43:33; cf. 18:1–6.

6   Cf., e.g., Sir. 36:7–15.

7   G. von Rad, *Wisdom in Israel* (Nashville: Abingdon Press, 1972) 153–55.

8   W. Zimmerli, "Ort und Grenze," 302.

9 Cf. H.-J. Hermisson, *Studien zur israelitischen Spruchweisheit* (WMANT 28; Neukirchen-Vluyn: Neukirchener, 1968) 140–41, 149–51.

10 When J. Crenshaw, in his useful discussion of creation theology of wisdom, begins with the problem of retribution and divine righteousness (*Studies in Ancient Israelite Wisdom* [New York: KTAV, 1976] 26), then this is rather a special case of the general question concerning the establishment of the orders of the world. [. . .]

11 Prov. 3:19; Ps. 104:24.

12 Cf. also Crenshaw, *Studies*, 34: "Creation . . . assures . . . that the universe is comprehensible."

13 For particulars, see, G. von Rad, *Wisdom*, 144–76.

14 The RSV is used for biblical quotations except for Ps. 104:5 (see n. 29) and Ps. 93:1, 3. [Ed.].

15 That this had already been done in old Israel is not inconceivable, but it remained in that case a misuse. To be sure, this proverbial wisdom developed no revolutionary pathos.

16 Cf. Ptahhotep 545–46 (pap. Prisse 16, 6–7) in Zybněk Žába, *Les Maximes de Ptaḥḥotep* (Prag: Editions de l'Académie Tchécoslovaque des Science, 1956).

17 Cf. Zimmerli's scepticism of 1933 concerning such a grounding of wisdom instructions, and further concerning the relation of the standard of human conduct to Yahweh's work as creator ("Zur Struktur der alttestamentlichen Weisheit," *ZAW* 51 [1933] 177–204). However, in his recent article (see n. 1, above), Zimmerli has revoked in part the more far-reaching conclusions.

18 The question may be answered briefly as to why this psalm appears to be an example of wisdom, even though R. Murphy, in his important and illuminating essay on the subject ("A Consideration of the Classification 'Wisdom Psalms,'" *Congress Volume, Bonn 1962*; VTSup 9 [1963] 156–67), does not place it among the wisdom psalms. [. . .]

19 On the structure and some details, see H.-J. Kraus, *Die Psalmen* (BKAT 15/2; Neukirchen-Vluyn: Neukirchener, 1960) 708–15.

20 On this, see, A. Alt, "Die Weisheit Salomos" (1951), in *Kleine Schriften* (3 vols.; Munich: Beck, 1953) 2: 90–99.

21 Surely the mythical prehistory of Leviathan stands in the background, but it is essentially superseded here, significant only insofar as the "giant's toy" indicates the superior greatness of its creator (!).

22 On this, see especially J. Assmann, *Ägyptische Hymnen und Gebete* (Die Bibliothek der alten Welt/Der alte Orient; Zurich/Munich: Artemis, 1975) esp. 209–25.

23 See also G. von Rad, "The Theological Problem of the Old Testament Doctrine of Creation" (1936), in *The Problem of the Hexateuch and Other Essays* (New York: McGraw-Hill, 1966) 131–43 [ch. 2 of this volume].

24 Cf. H.-J. Kraus, *Psalmen*, 712, and G. Fohrer, *Das Buch Hiob* (KAT 16; Gütersloh: Mohn, 1963) 497.

25 See, e.g., Kraus, *Psalmen*, 708.

26 I prefer this interpretation of v. 8 to the one defended mostly today (in which

the water is taken as subject to the verbs in v. 8a), because the verb *ysd* could hardly be construed as applying to the waters or to their "place" (*maqôm*). [...]

27 I shall not enter here into the debate over festival theories because it is irrelevant to our present question. [...]

28 See Ps. 65:6–8, esp. v. 8; also Hab. 3:8–11, or Nah. 1:4, in connection with depictions of theophany.

29 "He," following MT.

30 The questions to Job concern only partly his ability to imitate the divine work, but much more his insight into the coherences, the whence and whither of things.

31 Cf. G. von Rad, "Job XXXVIII and Ancient Egyptian Wisdom" (1955), in *The Problem of the Hexateuch* 281–91.

32 Cf. ibid.

33 Cf. Fohrer, *Hiob*, 496–98, and the further account of the characteristics of wisdom given there, e.g., in vocabulary.

34 On this, see S. Terrien, *Job* (CAT 13; Neuchâtel: Delachaux et Niestlé, 1963) 249, n. 2 (and p. 86 with n. 2). He indicates that the bounding of the sea is a motif borrowed from the creation epic, *enuma eliš*; "but it has been adapted to a theology of omnipotence"!

35 Terrien, *Job*, 249.

36 On this, see the important conclusions of Terrien (*Job*, 248–49). [...]

37 One should not press these shifting expressions so as to ask, for example, why a bar was necessary for a helpless infant.

38 Genesis 1, with its especially complex conception is being disregarded here. On this, see O. H. Steck, *Der Schöpfungsbericht der Priesterschrift* (FRLANT 115; Göttingen: Vandenhoeck & Ruprecht, 1975). For the Priestly writing creation concludes with the seven days, and one cannot speak at all of a continuing creation by Yahweh. Cf. also W. H. Schmidt, *Die Schöpfungsgeschichte der Priesterschrift* (3d ed.; WMANT 17; Neukirchen-Vluyn: Neukirchener, 1974).

39 See, S. Terrien, *Job*, 249.

8

*Creation And Liberation**

GEORGE M. LANDES

Though it is neither customary nor requisite for these opening convocation addresses to begin with, or even to have a text, this one does both. The text is the familiar words of the final verse of the 124th Psalm: "Our help is in the name of the Lord who made heaven and earth." Perhaps we have heard those words so often at the beginning of a worship service that we no longer pause to reflect on what they are saying. So it is their meaning and significance that I want to explore in this address.

In his concluding affirmation the Psalmist has succinctly brought together what very well may be the two most important themes in the entire biblical witness: liberation and creation—liberation, epitomized in the word "help," signifying the divine powerful assistance in deliverance from enemies and oppressors,[1] and creation, referred to in one of the chief identifying titles of the liberating Lord: He is the one who made heaven and earth.[2] Though on occasion one can find these two themes mentioned in the Bible quite independently and in isolation from one another,[3] more typically they appear inextricably linked, especially in the OT, but also in crucial NT contexts as well.[4] This raises at the outset at least two important questions: first, why were they joined together? Why did the biblical writers regularly feel compelled to unite their expressions of liberation- and creation-faith, and what does it mean that they did this? And secondly, how was the relation of the two elements in this conjunction conceived? Did liberation take precedence over creation, subordinating the latter to liberation's primary activity? Or did creation receive priority over liberation as its necessary ground and presupposition? Or is a hierarchical stratification of these themes really to misconceive their relationship altogether, to miss

---

*Inaugural address, Union Theological Seminary. First published in *USQR* 33/2 (Winter 1978) 79–89. In the interest of brevity the notes have been abridged.

the fact that they are crucial to each other, and that something is inevitably lost when either one is made secondary, to say nothing of being ignored or neglected?

The belief in divine creation of the cosmos is of course very old, attested literarily as early as the Sumerians in the third millennium B.C.[5] Moreover, to all the ancient Near Eastern peoples, there was no high god – that is, no deity of cosmic and widespread significance – who could qualify as such without possessing as a crucial attribute the power to create. For to these peoples there was no greater power conceivable than creation power, the power to bring the heaven and earth into existence and everything in them, and to order and maintain the cosmic structure free from all external threats, in particular the threat of uncreated watery chaos from whose defeat the universe was originally formed.[6] There was a sense, then, at least for the Mesopotamians, that the creation of the world was at the same time a liberation, a freeing of the ordered cosmos from the ever-present menace of primordial chaos, so that especially human social and political structures might be prevented from disintegration, the bonds of cohesion, cooperation, and stability maintained and strengthened, and continuity, social unity, and solidarity ensured.[7]

Though the early Hebrews did not buy into all the cosmological trappings associated with the views of world origin held by their ancient Near Eastern neighbors, there were nonetheless certain ideas which they could affirm. In using 'Elohim as the generic designation for their God – a plural of majesty and totality derived from the personal divine name 'El, whose common Semitic root meaning seems to refer to power, preeminently creation power[8] – the Hebrews would have linked creation activity with their deity from the beginning. Even when they came to venerate Yahweh, whom without hesitation or scruple they identified with 'El and 'Elohim, the function of divine creatorship was not lost. Indeed the very name Yahweh, which is probably to be derived from the initial verb form of a cultic epithet referring to 'El as the one who brings into existence all that exists,[9] must have been understood in connection with creation work.[10] And even though at the burning bush Moses is given to understand a unique broadening and extension of the meaning of the divine name to include creation work within history – indeed to identify this creation work with liberation work: Yahweh is the actively Present One in breaking the yokes of bondage – still the cosmic creativity of Yahweh is neither denigrated nor denied.

I therefore find it difficult to agree with the late Professor Gerhard von Rad; whose view on this issue continues to predominate within OT scholarship, when he argues that creation-faith within Israel was a comparatively late development, and even then was principally an ancillary and secondary belief supportive of, but subordinate to, Yahweh's primary redemptive deeds.[11] Yet when Israel told her story of the Exodus, the wilderness wandering, and the giving of the land, Yahweh's delivering actions were not depicted involving only historical human actors and political events, but also with the use of the forces and elements of nature – in the plagues against the Egyptian oppressors, in the parting of the waters of the Red Sea, in the sending of the manna, quails, and water, in separating the waters of the Jordan, in making the sun and moon stand still for Joshua. Only the Creator-God, the One who made the sea, the animals, the heavenly bodies, and all of nature, could employ these elements in His redemptive work. But out of all her experience in liberating events, Israel did not only at some distant later date infer that the Liberator-God must be the Creator-God, but rather, because she already knew Yahweh as the Creator of heaven and earth, she understood how it was that wind and sea, birds and insects, sun and moon could be used as instruments supporting the divine liberating activity.

From this she went on to affirm something new – something not shared by her ancient Near Eastern neighbors: the cosmic Creator was also the Liberating Creator, whose creative power was extended into history, not for the purpose of either continuing or redoing cosmic creation (these ideas receive no place in biblical thinking except in an eschatological framework beyond history), but for creating a people through liberating deeds and a covenant commitment, from which they would become enfranchised into a new service, the service of their creating and redeeming God. Like the original cosmic creation, Israel also was created out of nothing – "Once you were no people, but now you are God's people," as the author of the First Epistle to Peter puts it in addressing the early Christians (1 Pet. 2:10) – and the power that created her was just as strong and effective and awe-inspiring as that which formed the heavens and the earth. Thus for Israel, Yahweh's creation power in history was at the same time his liberation power, and they must be held together. One could not be properly understood without the other.

Why is it, then, despite the biblical canonical order, which, with Genesis, begins with an account of creation, that frequently when Israel told of Yahweh's liberating activity she not only did not begin with creation, but did not even mention it at all? How is to be explained this so-called reticence about world creation?

It seems to me that those who have made so much of the fact that references to cosmic creation are often missing in those places where Israel confessed God's mighty liberating acts have failed to pay sufficient attention to an important perception that Israel made with respect to God's creation of the world – a perception that sets her view apart from that of the other ancient Near Eastern peoples – viz., the creation of the cosmos by Yahweh was essentially *not* a liberating act.[12] Though it stands prior to and introduces God's salvific activity with His people, the creation of the heavens and the earth is not itself reckoned as the initiation of God's redemptive work.[13] Why? Because in Genesis 1 and other OT texts either describing or referring to Yahweh's cosmic creativity the heavens and the earth are not brought into existence from a situation requiring their liberation. The primordial waters, which have to be separated before the heavens and earth can be established as such, are not thought of as intrinsically evil or threatening, no more than are the waters from which all of us come from out of our mothers' wombs at birth. In Gen. 1:2 the earth is said to be *tohu wa-bohu*, a curious hendiadys rhyme formation in Hebrew that is best rendered in English as something like "darkened desolation or emptiness," not chaos.[14] At the beginning of its creation, the earth is empty, enclosed by waters in total darkness. But when God's Spirit moves over the waters to separate them, the earth can be born, so to speak, i.e., it can emerge from its primordial darkness into the light of time, its surrounding waters gathered and ordered into the seas, and its emptiness filled with plants, animals, and humanity. At the end of Genesis 1 the whole creation is declared to be very good, and this includes the darkness, the waters, along with everything else. To accomplish this creative work, Yahweh engages in no battle with the primeval waters, as did the Babylonian Marduk with Tiamat, or the Canaanite Baal with Yamm. In those psalmodic and prophetic texts where Yahweh is portrayed as in conflict with figures variously named Rahab or Leviathan, or *Tannîn*,[15] the background is probably not some early Israelite myth which described Yahweh's cosmic creation as the result of a theomachy,[16] no more than Baal's defeat of Yamm in the Ugaritic mythological texts devolved into an account of the origin of the world, but rather led to the affirmation of the kingly rule of the fertility-god over the sea in an already created cosmos.[17] So also Yahweh controls and orders the waters in history, viewed poetically either as a historical personification of

Israel's oppressors, as e.g., Rahab was identified with Pharaoh or Egypt,[18] or as an instrument of nature used by God in His activity of judgment and redemption.[19] Thus because in no place was Yahweh's cosmic creation seen as an act of liberation, it is understandable why the biblical writers did not regularly see fit to incorporate references to God's creation of the heaven and the earth as a part of the record of the divine salvatory events.

It might also be observed here that the literary form in which Israel mentioned Yahweh's cosmic creation, with its implied *Sitz im Leben*, is important, either by itself or in conjunction with His liberating deeds. For here we see it is principally the poetic texts, the hymns and liturgies, in which Israel celebrates the divine creativity in the setting of worship.[20] The purpose, then, in mentioning creation is not primarily to satisfy some idle curiosity about how the world may have come into existence, but to praise the Creator-God for His creation work with worshipful adoration in joy and thanksgiving. Though the same can be said for the poetic exaltation of Yahweh's liberating action, when the latter was expressed in prose (more in the service of a non liturgical function, i.e., to teach or inform), the references to creation drop out. For the biblical writers it was almost as if the most appropriate context for talking – or better, singing – about creation was the sanctuary, not the schoolroom or some other didactic setting.

So though there were sometimes plausible reasons for Israel's speaking about liberation-faith without any reference to cosmic creation-faith, the primary emphasis was upon their association, not their separation. Cosmic creation, though not itself an activity of liberation, was nonetheless the crucial supposition of God's liberating work in history, which was also a form of creation. Unless the Liberator-God is at the same time the cosmic Creator-God, responsible for the origin and ordering of the entire world in which He takes a constant and active interest as its Creator, the work of liberation is deprived of a critical authoritative and effective ground. It would seem then to be the task of any theology which finds its basic source in and has respect for the biblical witness, to include within its interpretive function this important conjunction between creation and liberation.

Now interestingly, when we turn to look at recent theology – quite in contrast to Barth, who, in his *Church Dogmatics*, devoted more space to the doctrine of creation (some 2,300 pages in the English rendering) than to any other[21] – there seems to be a tendency not simply to separate creation from liberation, but even to ignore or push out altogether its central theme. Within the 602 pages of the English translation of Hans Küng's massive theological tome on what contemporary Christian existence might mean,[22] very little explicit attention is given to the doctrine of creation, and none at all to its relation to liberation,[23] as if to say (which Küng very well might not, if pressed), that creation-faith has little or no significance for "being a Christian" today. Among the liberation theologians, especially those who want to take the Bible seriously, whether Black, Feminist, or Third World, my impression is that most tend to pass over the doctrine of creation, or if they deal with it at all, it is very briefly, and often inadequately from a biblical exegetical standpoint.[24] But perhaps none of this should really surprise us in the light of our knowledge of the history of Christian thought, in which the doctrine of creation has not infrequently been the source of difficulties.

In his 1971 presidential address before the American Theological Society, George S. Hendry, until his retirement last spring, Professor of Systematic Theology at Princeton Theological Seminary, while bemoaning what he called the "eclipse of creation" in current theology and its increasingly widespread loss of significance, traced its most recent decline in the American context to the influence of eighteenth-century deistic notions and to the fallout from the nineteenth-century science vs. religion controversies.[25] As a result, questions of origins were declared to be of no vital concern to faith and were either abandoned or turned over to the scientists for their investigation and speculation. The diminished role of creation-faith was also reflected in popular piety. As Hendry writes:

> ... when occasion calls for a brief, summary statement of faith, creation is often passed over. It is not mentioned, for example, in the membership formula of the World Council of Churches, or in the creedal statement that forms part of the service of ordination in the United Presbyterian Church. Even in the brief formula of faith composed by so circumspect a theologian as Karl Rahner, man is referred to God as the sacred mystery which constitutes the sustaining ground of his existence, but not (not expressly at any rate) as the Creator from whom he has derived his existence.[26]

I would imagine there are those who in no way share in Hendry's deploring of what has happened to the doctrine of creation in recent theology and piety, who indeed see a too strict adherence to a transcendent Creator Deity, who, to use John MacQuarrie's terminology,[27] is unfortunately conceived in a monarchial rather than organic relation to the world, implying a dependence and subservience that too much restricts the attainment to full humanity and the exercise of its potential. As it happens, I am more in sympathy with Hendry, and in my remaining remarks, I would like to focus first on what I see are some of the unhappy losses suffered when creation-faith is cut off from liberation-faith, and then in a more positive vein, look at some of the more vital contributions of creation-faith to liberation-faith.

First, the losses. To ignore or reject the linkage between creation and liberation is in the first place to remove an essential feature in the biblical view of the relationship between the Creator Deity and the created world which stands in need of His liberating creation work. As Creator, God functions in both an immanent and trans-cendent relationship to all types of his creativity. He creates not only authoritatively by His Word standing apart from all that which it calls into being, but also by working with that already created, to bring forth something entirely new, though still not a part of the Deity's own Being. To diminish or rule out the transcendent dimension to the Creator-God is to limit Him both spatially and temporally, to restrict His power principally to the terrestrial plane and hence court the danger of holding it as susceptible to human control and manipulation, broaching idolatry, and to refuse to acknowledge the cosmic dimensions of evil against which only the liberating power of a cosmic Creator-God can be effective.

In the second place, radically to divorce creation from liberation can also mean to lose the perspective of the total arena in which the Creator-God's liberation power is at work. Biblical faith affirms not only that it is effective with human instruments, their structures and relationships on the plane of history, but also, as we have noted earlier, in and through the forces of nature, which are under the control and direction of the Liberator-God as Creator of heaven and earth. We are rightly concerned today with what we do and have done to nature, how we can live in a more symbiotic, non-destructive relation to it. But biblical creation- and liberation-faith is also concerned about what God does to us in and through nature, both for our redemption and judgment. To the biblical writers, the forces of nature were not morally neutral,[28] and though this poses some difficult theological problems for us, that does not mean we should ignore or pass over in embarrassed silence the biblical witness to the divine use of nature in liberation activity, for in becoming more sensitive to this dimension, we are led to a great appreciation of the strength and magnitude of the divine power against

141

oppression, and of the lengths to which God is willing to go to assure the redemption of His people. Also, there is no realm of creation in which God's liberation power is excluded or without effect.

Finally, to separate creation from liberation runs the risk of losing a sense of the scope of the object of the divine saving work. One of the best examples of this in the OT is the case of the prophet Jonah. In the course of their desperate search for deliverance from the death-threatening storm, the sailors ask Jonah about his mission and identity (Jonah 1:8). In response, he confesses, "I am a Hebrew, and I fear Yahweh the God of heaven, who made the sea and the dry land" (1:9). It will be observed that Jonah's identification of himself with the Hebrew constituency is given as his answer to the sailor's question about his mission. For the Hebrews originally did not receive their total identity from their status as an oppressed people, but even more from the fact that they had been called by their God through Abram – who is called the first Hebrew in the Bible (Gen. 14:13) – to become a people with a mission, not simply to themselves, but to all the families of the earth (Gen. 12:3; 22:18). As a Hebrew prophet, Jonah had been commissioned by Yahweh to join in that mission – a mission to be the mediator of a potential blessing, not to Jonah's own Hebrew constituency, which he would doubtless have welcomed, but rather to the Ninevites, those cruel enemies and hated oppressors of his people. But Jonah cannot escape his mission even though he endeavors to run away from it. On the storm-tossed ship at sea, the upshot of his confrontation with the sailors, who clearly must be identified, like the Ninevites, with the non-Hebrew families of the earth, is that through his decision and action, he holds the key to their deliverance. His response to the sailor's questions thus underlines the deep irony of his position. On the one hand, his proud profession of a Hebrew identity suggests his divinely appointed mission to bring blessing and liberation to the nations, while on the other, his confession of faith that the God who has called him is also the one who has created the sea and the dry land implies the futility of his flight and rebellion. Jonah, of course, believes in both Yahweh's liberation and creation, but he refuses to hold them permanently together and accept the implications of that. When *he* is the sole beneficiary of the divine liberation, implemented by creation power, as he is when rescued from the sea by a great fish and delivered temporarily from his angry despair by the sudden growth of the *qiqayon*-plant, Jonah can sing Yahweh's praises and rejoice with great joy. But when the boundaries of this liberation are extended to the nations, including those who have terribly mistreated Israel, Jonah will have none of it. Yet it is because the Creator-God is the Liberator-God that liberation has universal dimensions. Yahweh's concluding words to Jonah emphasize this point: "You have had compassion for the plant, for which you did not labor, nor did you make it grow, which came into being in a night and perished in a night. But should not I have compassion on Nineveh that great city, in which there are more than a hundred and twenty thousand persons who do not know their right hand from left, and also much cattle?" (4:10–11). Jonah's compassion for the plant epitomizes his concern for his own liberation, which he has received as a gift of the divine grace; he has neither created nor nurtured it. By contrast, in addition to His compassion to Jonah through the plant, Yahweh also shows it to the populous Ninevites, because He *has* created and nurtured them, and therefore wills their liberation. By refusing to acknowledge the full implications of the fact that the Creator-God is the Liberator-God, Jonah, who himself is a rightful object of the divine deliverance, at the end remains undelivered, wishing only for death.

It has on occasion been observed – most recently by Professor Robert McAfee Brown in an article in *Christianity and Crisis*[29] – that "the Bible was written *out of* the experience of oppressed people, *by* oppressed people as a message for the liberation *of* oppressed people." This is certainly true, as far as it goes, but I do not think it goes far enough. Certainly, the Bible *was* written out of the experience of oppressed people, but not only that, as e.g., in the wisdom traditions, we encounter a broader base of experience than that coming solely from conditions of oppression. Some of the biblical traditions indeed probably did find their earliest expression from among the oppressed, but we must also keep in mind that much of the Bible, particularly the OT, was shaped, expanded, redacted, and edited by those associated with the royal court and the religious establishment, whom we would hardly identify with the oppressed.[30] And the message of the Bible is certainly for the liberation of the oppressed, but also for the liberation of the oppressors, in fact for everyone, regardless of their status or condition. The audience for which the author of Jonah primarily intended his message was hardly limited to the oppressed, just as in the NT, the parables that Jesus used as the chief vehicle of his teaching are frequently seen to be directed not first of all at the poor, the outcast, or mistreated, but rather to the Jewish religious leaders, whose beliefs and actions often contributed to oppressive conditions. My point is in no way intended to reduce the significance of the Bible's message for the oppressed –

indeed, it may be they who today will best hear and respond to it –
but to remind us that as the Bible was written and shaped and passed
on by all types of people from a variety of conditions and situations,
so its teaching is meant for all. Holding together creation- and
liberation-faith should prevent us from losing sight of this fact.

I have dealt with what I perceive to be, in light of the biblical
witness, some of the most important losses we incur when we
radically separate or isolate creation from liberation. Now in
conclusion, I would like briefly to turn to some of what I would
deem to be the more important of the particular features of biblical
creation-faith that especially should be held in mind when we reflect
upon and act for liberation.

First, the uniqueness of the divine creatorship. As is well known,
the Hebrews often employed a special verb when they wanted to
talk particularly of Yahweh's creating. Nowhere in the OT does this
verb (*bārā'*) ever occur with anyone but God as its subject. This
was not because of any peculiar nuance inherent to the verb as such,
or that its definition necessarily implied the unique modes of divine
creativity – *ex nihilo*, without effort, by the commanding Word –
but rather because of the types of objects which regularly receive
the incidence of this verb's action: preeminently the cosmos, the
heavens and the earth and their constituent creatures. It was also
this same verb which could be used with reference to the divine
creativity within history, now not primarily cosmic but salvatory.
Again in these contexts the subject of the verb continues to be only
Yahweh, because its objects are not the result of initiatory human
creativity: thus Israel (Isa. 43:15), various foreign persons or peoples
(Ezek. 21:30 [H, 35]; 28:13, 15), the new Jerusalem (Isa. 4:5), various
salvatory deeds (Exod. 34:10; Isa. 45:8; 48:7; 57:19) or the creation
of a "clean heart" within a human individual (Ps. 51:10[H, 12]),
or a unique form of divine punishment (Num. 16:30). All of these
are associated with *bārā'* as creative expressions of Yahweh's
liberating activity within history. Thus for Israel's creation-faith, a
clear demarcation was made between divine and human creativity.

With regard to cosmic and natural phenomena, there seems little
cause to dispute this distinction, for despite remarkable modern
scientific advances human creative enterprise has not been able (with
possibly only minor exceptions)[31] to produce creatures in the astral
or natural realms. But when it comes to the divine creativity
associated with liberation there has been a significant effort,
particularly among some of the liberation theologians, to treat this
in close conjunction with human creativity. Thus, for example in

Gustavo Gutierrez's *A Theology of Liberation*, we read, in the legitimate interest of correcting the neglect of markedly stressing the liberating and protagonistic role of humanity, that human creatures are the lords of creation and coparticipants in their own salvation, that salvation itself is the movement of human self-generation, humans assuming their destiny in history, forging and fulfilling themselves by continuing the work of creation through working to transform the work and build a just society by struggling against every form of human misery and exploitation.[32] Or in his *Theology of Human Hope* and *Tomorrow's Child*, Rubem Alves tells us that creation is a joint enterprise between God and humanity, particularly the future which is created by God and His human creatures in historical dialogical cooperation. Humanity helps God when they become involved through their actions in the task of transforming the world of today into the new earth of tomorrow.[33] Moreover, it is especially humanity that is the creator of the reality of the social system, and this creative act is the highest expression of human life.[34] Because God makes humanity free to create, creation is therefore unfinished; God remains open, and this openness implies unfinishedness.[35]

In these views of Gutierrez and Alves is affirmed a very high anthropology that clearly has some support from within the biblical tradition – in the creation of humanity as God's image, in the expectation that Israel was capable of obeying all of the covenant stipulations. As the Deuteronomist once put it: "But the word is very near you; it is in your mouth and in your heart, so that you can do it" (Deut. 30:14). To biblical liberation-faith, humanity was no mere passive observer to the activity of liberation, but was called to participate in it, to work for the betterment of human life and the destruction and transformation of all that frustrates this. Also in the NT, though Paul speaks of salvation as the gift of God's grace based upon faith rather than works (Eph. 2:8), he could also say to the Philippians, "work out your own salvation with fear and trembling, for God is at work in you, both to will and work for his good pleasure" (Phil. 2:12f). This is no contradiction, for grace stimulates moral exertions; because it is given, the recipient must work. Grace is exhibited in making humanity coworkers with God (cf. 1 Cor. 3:9).[36] But if all this is so, what is to be made of the biblical insistence on a distinction between divine and human creativity in redemption?

Here it is important not to isolate the high view of humanity found at the end of Genesis 1 from the somewhat different picture we get in Genesis 3 (and indeed elsewhere in the biblical story), and make the anthropology of Genesis 1 the only normative one for our understanding of human creativity. When we put Genesis 1 and 3 together, which of course is what the Bible has done, what we find is essentially a confrontation between two differing conceptions of the divine image. On the one hand, there is the image bestowed by God to humanity in His creating them; on the other, the image, as it were, taken by humanity from God in disobeying His command not to eat of the tree of the knowledge of good and evil. On the one side we have the endowment of humanity with the capacity to represent the divine rule and authority over the animals and natural world, and all the freedom and opportunities for creativity that that implies; on the other, we see the counting of equality with God as a thing to be grasped, in the exercise of human autonomy, decision making, and judgment without any reference to the Deity, because humanity has become like God, knowing good and evil. Thus not just one but two images are at work within human creativity, and because humanity does not simply represent the divine rule, but endeavors to usurp it, to play God on its own with overweening pride, self-confidence, hubris, this infects what humans do in their participation in God's liberating activity, so that the result is not clearly an unambiguous indication of a coincidence of the human with divine creativity. The conclusion to be drawn from this is not that human liberation work should be curtailed or become passive, but that in carrying it forward there must always be a frank acknowledgment that if too strong a stress is placed on the self-emancipation of humanity, then in the words of Norman Young in his recent book *Creator, Creation and Faith*, this "expects both too much and too little – too much of man who consistently turns his creative capacities to destructive ends; too little of God who comes from beyond man's own sphere of management to offer new directions and possibilities."[37]

I think there are also two other important factors in the divine creation activity for liberation that need to be brought into this picture. The first has to do with the motif of finishing, which within the Bible as a whole is applied to both creation and liberation. Just as at the end of the first creation story at the beginning of Genesis 2 God declares that all his cosmic creation work is brought to completion, so also in the NT the Fourth Evangelist records Jesus as proclaiming from his cross that his redemptive work is finished (John 19:30). At the end of the first creation story, the proclamation that the divine creation work is finished means that the fundamental structures and elements within the cosmos do not have to be redone, either annually on the New Year's Day, as in Babylonia, or in some other periodic cyclical rhythm, in order to insure the harmony and stability of nature and society from the constantly encroaching threat of chaos, and also that the problems of history are not to be resolved by cosmic re-creation prior to the final consummation, nor is their ground to be traced from the original creation work. In the NT, when Jesus says from his cross, "It is finished" (John 19:30), it means that the way of suffering love that leads through the valley of the shadow of death has reached its fulfillment, and Jesus has brought to completion what God had commissioned His Anointed to say and do. This is not to imply that either the OT or NT words about finishing are meant to reduce or preclude human creativity, or make human participation in liberating work both futile and without significance. But they do serve to remind us that even before we begin our redemptive tasks, something decisive has already been accomplished by God in relation to this work, and that what has been done provides the framework, sets the tone, and indicates certain characteristics and limits to our own activity. Thus Alves's assertion of the openness of creation, with its future and therefore its unfinishedness, is only partially correct. Obviously, there is a sense, acknowledged by the NT, in which all is not yet finished, neither with creation nor redemption. As Paul says in Romans (8:22f) "We know that the whole creation has been groaning in travail together until now; and not only the creation, but we ourselves, who have the first fruits of the Spirit, groan inwardly as we wait for adoption as children, the redemption of our bodies." We live in anticipation of yet another culmination, an even more all-embracing and climactic word about finishing.[38] But again, this is neither determined nor proclaimed as a result of the basis of human creative enterprise, but as John reveals in his final vision of the new heaven and the new earth in Revelation, it is the One sitting upon the throne who says: "It is done! I am the Alpha and the Omega, the beginning and the end. To the thirsty I will give water without price from the fountain of the water of life" (Rev. 21:6). At a point between the already and the not yet, we are privileged *now* to hear this divine word from the end, without which we are unable to undertake the unfinished task of bearing witness to God and His work with confidence and hope.

A second important factor that must be considered in the divine creativity for liberation relates to the problem which most frustrates and complicates our liberation work, viz., humanity's reaching out

147

for its own divine image, its propensity to play God, or in the biblical words, to be like God knowing good and evil. By the early sixth century B.C., with the fall of Jerusalem and its aftermath, several of Israel's prophetic voices were prepared to admit that the traditional solution to this problem – that is, through expressing loyalty to Yahweh alone and showing it through total obedience to the covenant stipulations – was a manifest failure. From among these voices, it was the prophets Ezekiel and Jeremiah who had the most radical proposal to make: the recreation of humanity, at the apparent sacrifice of human freedom. For Ezekiel, the new humanity would be constituted by the gift of a new heart and a new spirit, a heart not of stone but of flesh, and a spirit which would cause people to walk in God's statutes and carefully observe His ordinances (Ezek. 36:26–27). For Jeremiah, though using different imagery but with similar import, the new humanity required a new covenant, a covenant not like the one made with the ancestors at Sinai, but one which presupposes that the divine teaching has been placed within people from the beginning, written as it were, upon their hearts, so they will no longer have to be taught its precepts or be exhorted to know the Lord, for they will already know Him by nature. Neither Ezekiel's nor Jeremiah's vision of the new humanity was fulfilled until the coming of Jesus, for it was in his life and ministry that the Church saw the first living example of a human new creation, whose divine image was not in the form of grasping equality with God, but in representing the invisible God and manifesting His fullness by emptying himself, taking the form of a servant, being born in human likeness and found in human form, humbling himself and becoming obedient unto death, even death on a cross (Phil. 2:7–8). And so in this way, all things, whether on earth or in heaven, are reconciled to God through him, making peace by the blood of his cross (Col. 1:20), i.e., the new covenant is initiated, as Jesus indicated to his disciples at his last supper, when he gave them the cup, saying "This is my blood of the covenant, which is poured out for many" (Mark 14:24).

But how does Christ as the new humanity and the perfect divine image relate to our creative participation in liberation work? Obviously, we are not yet transformed or renewed after the image of our Creator, and we still wrestle with the double-image of on the one hand truly representing God's dominion, and on the other, acting as if only we were God. Yet Paul tells us that we can share in Christ's new humanity, we can become new creatures, to the extent that we become "in Christ," and this suggests that one of the most important things we do in relation to our liberation tasks is to learn what it means for them that we are in Christ. That, *in nuce*, may be what theological education is or should be about. Clearly there is no time left to explore this, but only to say that to be in Christ, far from indicating basically a mystical absorption or physical unification with Deity, suggests that we take seriously the model of Christ's liberation work for our own, that as we work for social justice and against all oppression, we be able to hear and respond to his call to repent, acknowledging our involvement in sin, receive his forgiveness and then extend it to others, that we be willing to risk being crucified, dying, and being buried for the sake of His kingdom that we might also be raised with him, and in the end sit with him in heaven and appear with him in glory.

I hope that in what I have been trying to say here, I have managed to escape the characteristics against which the author of the Epistle to the Colossians admonished his readers. In the translation of J. B. Phillips, it reads: "Be careful that nobody spoils your faith through intellectualism or high-sounding nonsense. Such stuff is at best founded on man's ideas of the nature of the world and disregards Christ!" (Col. 2:8) Of course, as you will doubtless experience, if you have not already done so, intellectualism, high-sounding nonsense, and the stuff best founded on men's ideas of the nature of the world disregarding Christ, are not foreign to the theological scene, and we should not only be aware of this, but expose them for what they are. However, if I have succeeded in challenging your thinking, stimulating your imagination, and making you even more eager to be about the work that your presence here entails, I shall be satisfied that your theological journey at Union has well begun, and it is my hope that while on that journey, you also may be emboldened to take a fresh and critical look, as I have tried to do here, at important points where biblical and theological issues intersect, and then assess what this might mean for our faith and action, both in the Church and in the world.

NOTES

1   For this usage of Hebr. *'ezer*, note esp. Exod. 18:4; Deut. 33:7, 29; Ps. 70:6 [Eng. v. 5]. God's *'ezer* can also refer to the divine sustaining support (cf. Ps. 20:3 [Eng. v. 2]) and protection (cf. Pss. 33:20; 121:2ff).

2   Cf. Gen. 1:1; 14:22; Exod. 20:11; 31:17; 2 Kings 19:15 (=Isa. 37:16); 2 Chron. 2:12 [Eng. v. 11]; Jer. 32:17; Jon. 1:9; Ps. 115:15; 121:2; 134:3; 146:6.

3   As, e.g., has often been pointed out for the OT where the tradition contains

a recital of Yahweh's mighty redemptive deeds, but no mention of creation. Cf. Deut. 26:5–9; Josh. 24:1–15; 2 Sam. 7:4–17; Pss. 78 and 105. For a possible explanation of this, see further below. Cf. n. 2 above for several references in which creation is mentioned, but not redemption.

4 Cf. John 1:1–18; 1 Cor. 8:6; Col. 1:15–20; Heb. 1:2–3.

5 See S. N. Kramer, *The Sumerians: Their History, Culture, and Character* (Chicago: Univ. of Chicago Press, 1963) esp. 112–13, 145, 292–93.

6 For discussion and illustrations, see S. G. F. Brandon, *Creation Legends of the Ancient Near East* (London: Hodder & Stoughton, 1963).

7 Cf. E. O. James, *Creation and Cosmology: A Historical and Comparative Inquiry* (Leiden: E. J. Brill, 1969) 3.

8 See the article on '*El* by F. M. Cross, Jr., *TDOT* 1 (1977) 242–61.

9 Cf. F. M. Cross, Jr., *Canaanite Myth and Hebrew Epic: Essays in the History of the Religion of Israel* (Cambridge: Harvard Univ. Press, 1973) 65f.

10 See J. Philip Hyatt, "Was Yahweh Originally a Creator Deity?" *JBL* 86 (1967) 369–77.

11 See G. von Rad, "Das theologische Problem des alttestamentlichen Schöpfungs-glaubens," in *Werden und Wesen des Alten Testaments* (BZAW 66; 1936) 138–47 [ET: *The Problem of the Hexateuch and Other Essays*, trans. E. W. T. Dicken (New York: McGraw-Hill, 1966) 131–43 [=ch. 2 of this volume]. For a recent criticism of von Rad's views on creation, see H. H. Schmid, "Schöpfung, Gerechtigkeit und Heil," *ZTK* 70 (1970) 1–19 [=ch. 6 of this volume].

12 Cf. P. Schoonenberg in his *Covenant and Creation* (London/Sydney: Sheed & Ward, 1968) 68. In *God and History in the Old Testament* (New York: Harper & Row, 1976), Denis Baly says, "... for the Israelites every act of creation is an act of salvation" (p. 116). This is patently hyperbolic, and not an accurate characterization of *all* creation traditions in the OT.

13 Cf. B. W. Anderson, "A Stylistic Study of the Priestly Creation Story," in *Canon and Authority: Essays in Old Testament Religion and Theology* (ed. G. W. Coats and B. O. Long Philadelphia; Fortress Press, 1977), 161.

14 [A note on "chaos" has been omitted here.]

15 For Rahab, cf. Pss. 87:4; 98:11 (Eng., v. 10); Isa. 30:7; 51:9; Job 9:13; 26:12; Leviathan: Pss. 74:14; 104:26; Isa. 27:1; Job 3:8; 40:25 (Eng. v. 41:1); Tannîn, variously rendered in English by "sea monster" (Gen. 1:21; Ps. 148:7; Job 7:12) and "dragon" or "monster" (Isa. 27:1; 51:9; Jer. 51:34; Ezek. 29:3; 32:2; Ps. 74:13), when depicting a creature whom Yahweh defeats in battle.

16 Though this is a widely accepted interpretation for these texts among many OT scholars. Cf. Mary K. Wakeman (*God's Battle With the Monster: A Study in Biblical Imagery* [Leiden: E. J. Brill, 1973]) and D. Baly (*God and History*, 111–12). For the view presented here, cf. S. L. Terrien, "Creation, Cultus, and Faith in the Psalter," *Theological Education* 2/4 (1966) 117–23; and D. J. McCarthy, "Creation Motifs in Ancient Hebrew Poetry," *CBQ* 29 (1967) 393–406 [=ch. 4 of this volume].

17 In his two studies, "Creation at Ugarit and in the Old Testament" (*VT* 15 [1965] 313–24) and "From Chaos to Cosmos" (*Encounter* 26 [1965] 183–97), Loren

R. Fisher has attempted to show how Baal's struggle with Yamm at Ugarit can rightly be interpreted as a cosmogonic activity, but he does this largely by broadening the traditional definition of creation to include the achievement of control over an already created order. For criticism of his effort, see McCarthy, "Creation Motifs," 393, n. 1.

18 Cf. Isa. 30:7; Ps. 87:4.

19 Cf. Isa. 51:9–10.

20 See B. W. Anderson, *Creation Versus Chaos* (New York: Association Press, 1967) 78–109.

21 Karl Barth, *Church Dogmatics* III, 1–4, focuses entirely on the doctrine of creation.

22 Hans Küng, *On Being a Christian* (Garden City, N.Y.: Doubleday & Co., 1976).

23 For Küng's reflections on liberation, see ibid., esp. 183–91, 554–602.

24 I must confess however, that I have not yet had sufficient time to work through all of the liberation theologians' writings, so there may be some notable exceptions that have escaped my attention.

25 G. S. Hendry "Eclipse of Creation," *TT* 28 (1970–71) 406–25.

26 Ibid., 419.

27 *Divinity at Oxford*, J. Macquarrie, "Creation and Environment," *Expository Times* 83/1 (1972) 4–9, note esp. p. 6.

28 See J. L. McKenzie, *A Theology of the Old Testament* (Garden City, N.Y.: Doubleday & Co., 1974) 195–202.

29 R. M. Brown, "Context Affects Content: The Rootedness of all Theology," *C & C* 37/12 (July 18, 1977) 172.

30 This obviously poses some difficult hermeneutical problems for the contemporary biblical interpreter, who may be tempted to resolve them too simplistically by opting for a "canon within the canon."

31 For instance, since 1940, scientific enterprise has been able to produce eleven new elements, to bring the total now known to one hundred and three, but these have been made from already existing elements, not *ex nihilo*.

32 Cf. G. Gutierrez, *A Theology of Liberation: History, Politics, and Salvation* (Maryknoll, N.Y.: Orbis Books, 1973) 159, 172–73.

33 Rubem Alves, *A Theology of Human Hope* (New York: Corpus Books, 1969) 144.

34 Rubem Alves, *Tomorrow's Child* (New York: Harper & Row, 1972) 71–72.

35 Alves, *Human Hope*, 144.

36 Cf. M. R. Vincent, *A Critical and Exegetical Commentary on the Epistles to the Philippians and to Philemon* (ICC; Edinburgh: T. & T. Clark, 1897) 65.

37 Young, *Creator*, 190. See also Roger Hazelton, *God's Way With Man: Variations on the Theme of Providence* (Nashville: Abingdon Press, 1956) 78.

38 See Jürgen Moltmann, *Theology of Hope* (New York: Harper & Row; London: SCM Press, 1967), esp. ch. 3, and, N. Young's critical assessment (*Creator, Creation, and Faith* [Philadelphia: Westminster Press, 1976]) (153–55). For an excellent study of the biblical background, see J. Reumann, *Creation and New Creation* (Minneapolis: Augsburg Pub. House, 1973).

9

Creation and Ecology*

BERNHARD W. ANDERSON

Not too many years ago the word *ecology* would have been a good candidate for the parlor game known as "fictionary," in which persons propose definitions – often humorously wild ones – of rare words. In recent decades, however, rapid social and scientific changes have brought this word into the active vocabulary of many people. Now it is commonly known that ecology, derived from Greek *oikos* (house), refers to the earthly habitation which human beings share with other living beings and specifically to "the mutual relations between organisms and their environment." The purpose of this essay is to explore in biblical perspective the relation between the human and the nonhuman creation.[1] As one whose specialization is OT theology, I approach the task with modesty, for the subject belongs to the interdisciplinary field of environmental ethics, a field that is much broader than the interrelated theological disciplines. Recently I have become aware of the fact that colleges and universities are beginning to establish graduate programs in environmental studies on an interdisciplinary basis.

Secular thinkers are just as aware as theologians, and sometimes more so, that the discussion takes place in a time of crisis – an eschatological situation. As I sit down to compose this essay, I have before me an article from the *Boston Globe* (Jan. 14, 1981) which announces that the "Doomsday Clock," created by the Educational Foundation for Nuclear Science in Chicago, has been moved up. Since 1947, we are told, this clock has been ticking ominously on the cover of *The Bulletin of the Atomic Scientists* and from time to time, depending on political developments, has been moved up or back slightly. The latest change of hands, which brought the clock to four minutes to midnight, was made because "as the year 1980 drew to a close, the world moved inexorably closer to nuclear

* First published in *AJTP* 1 (1983) 14–30.

disaster." At such a time it is appropriate to turn to the Bible if for no other reason than that many of its writings – for instance, the eschatological preaching of the prophets of Israel on the imminent Day of Yahweh (see Isa. 2:6–22) or the apocalyptic perspectives of the Gospel of Mark or the theology of Paul – speak to our contemporary sense of historical contingency and future foreboding. In the community of faith, of course, people also turn to the Bible in the conviction that it carries the weight of "Scripture" and hence is a primary source for theological understanding.

In this study our attention focuses not on the Bible as a whole (speaking in Christian terms) but on the so-called OT (Israel's Scriptures) and within that large body of literature our attention will be restricted for the most part to the Primeval History (Genesis 1—11). Admittedly, there are other portions of the OT that would claim our attention if the subject were to be treated adequately, such as certain creation Psalms (8, 104), the creation theology of the prophet of the Exile (Isaiah 40—55), or passages in Wisdom literature (e.g., Job). We turn to the Primeval History because often this is the scriptural ground that is chosen for discussion of environmental ethics or ecological theology, whether for criticism of the "dualism of man and nature" allegedly implied in the Creator's grant of dominion to 'ādăm (Gen. 1:26–28)[2] or to set forth a more balanced theological understanding of the relation between the human and the nonhuman creation.[3]

The Context of Interpretation

A problem that immediately confronts us is that of the context in which texts are interpreted. Too often, as we well know, biblical texts have been used as warrants or *dicta probantia* for ethical or theological positions arrived at on other grounds. Here it is appropriate to recall some wise words spoken by Eugene Borowitz during a discussion of environmental ethics (1980 meeting of the American Theological Society). He observed that while the mandate for human domination over the nonhuman creation is indisputably biblical, the imposition of modern views of domination on scriptural texts reflects the modern overthrow of religion and the emergence of secular perspectives based on the confidence that human beings can take the world into their own hands. The appeal to isolated texts, apart from the biblical context within which they function, has often led to the "use" of the Bible for particular purposes, whether in the religious community or in the modern technological world. One of the salutary results of the World Council of Churches (WCC) conference held at the Massachusetts Institute of Technology in 1979 was the chastened recognition that we read the Scriptures in our own "social location." A portion of the conference report merits repetition: "If we search the Scriptures, we find that the parts that move us most powerfully are those that address us where we are, that the concepts by which we interpret the Scriptures are those that we have developed in a given historical context."[4] Clearly, we read the Bible where we are: as people who are conditioned by the times in which we live and by the history which is part of us (including a philosophical heritage, capitalism and its Marxist counterpart, and the scientific movement). This sober realization of our "location" does not, in my estimation, mire us in interpretive relativism, as though the Scriptures and other literary works are "like a picnic to which the author brings the words and the reader the meaning," to invoke the celebrated words of Northrup Frye.[5] To be sure, we come to the Scriptures in our social location and, hopefully, with some creative imagination; but the words of Scripture, spoken or written in their own context, may criticize where we stand, limit our use of them, and challenge us with their strange social setting and theological horizon. Further, some of the ethical problems which are "burning issues" for us were not even anticipated in biblical times. I refer to such matters as overpopulation of the earth, potential exhaustion of natural resources, technology that changes the face of nature, science that can interfere with biological processes and present us with a startling new cosmology, and recent exploration of outer space.

The *dominium terrae*, then, or the whole creation story for that matter, must not be read by itself as a self-contained entity, isolated from its function within its larger literary context. Genesis 1 (creation) cannot be separated from Genesis 9 (flood) – two crucial passages from Priestly tradition – and that means that we must consider a given text in the context of the whole Primeval History. This contextual approach should restrain the reader from seizing a particular text – say the passage about the *imago Dei* or the passage about God's blessing upon humankind (Gen. 1:26–27 and 1:28) – and using it as a warrant for a theological or ethical position arrived at independently. Unfortunately, the matter is not so simple, however. The question arises as to what is the proper biblical context for understanding a given passage in the *Urgeschichte*. Here we find ourselves in the arena of hermeneutical debates that are not yet resolved. As I see it, there are three major hermeneutical possibilities. Let me summarize each briefly.

154

One possibility is to view a particular text in the context of a traditio-historical development which received its major impulse at an early stage, long before the final formulation of the book of Genesis. As Klaus Koch observes in his essay referred to above, "Genesis 1 is not the first word of the Old Testament nor the last." It is appropriate, he maintains, to begin, not with the Priestly account of creation, but with the older Yahwistic text (Genesis 2—3); for the Priestly account should not be removed from "its place in the history of Hebrew thought and literature." In other words, the proper context for understanding a text is a traditio-historical *process* which received its theological character at an early literary or pre-literary stage. This view is indebted to the OT theologian Gerhard von Rad, who capitalized on the traditio-historical approach which emerged from form criticism. Von Rad stressed the creative role of the Yahwist in shaping the Israelite epic and in particular in relating the Primeval History to the *Heilsgeschichte* of the Hexateuch. The Yahwist's work, according to von Rad, was decisive, even "canonical," for later stages in the literary development that led to the Hexateuch in its present form.[6]

Another hermeneutical possibility has been advocated by Claus Westermann in his massive commentary on Genesis. Westermann maintains that the *Urgeschichte* is a relatively self-contained totality. As such it was given to both the Yahwist and the Priestly Writer, not in the form of a literary prototype, but in an ontologically based mythical structure which can be traced by phenomenological analysis in the ancient Near East and, indeed, all over the world. To be sure, the Primeval History and the Ancestral History now serve as introductions to the *Volksgeschichte* that centers in the Exodus; but, he maintains, the relation of these separate "histories" to the center is that of concentric circles, the outer of which reaches out into the horizon of universal human experience of possibility and limitation, of harmony and conflict, of *Sein* and *In-der-Welt-Sein*.[7] Gerhard Liedke's stimulating paper, presented for discussion at the WCC conference referred to previously, seems to fall in this hermeneutical category in that it deals with Genesis 1 and 9 (the creation/flood polarity) as a mythic portrayal of the original harmony of creation and polar aspects of threat and conflict. His book on "ecological theology," with its intriguing title *Im Bauch des Fisches* (a reference to the Jonah story), moves fundamentally from the hermeneutical position of Westermann, under whom he wrote his dissertation and, as he tells us in the preface, from whom he learned "what biblical theology can be for the church."[8]

There is a third hermeneutical possibility – one that may take advantage of some of the insights provided by the traditio-historical and phenomenological approaches but emphasizes the given *scriptural* context. According to this view, the literary and theological context within which the various units of the Primeval History function is the final literary work (Torah, Pentateuch). Franz Rosenzweig once observed that the siglum R, which scholars have used for Redactor, should really signify *Rabbenu*, "our master," for it is from his hands that we have received the scriptures in their final form – the form in which we read them today and the form in which they have been read for centuries. This redactional approach does not necessarily commit one to a particular view of the prehistory of the final text of the Scripture. My own view, shared with many other scholars, is that the final form is that of the Priestly work (P), that this work has conservatively retained older traditions within its framework, and that the work, published during the exile, was substantially the Torah-Book that Ezra brought back with him from the Babylonian exile (see Nehemiah 9). It is sufficient for our purpose to say, however, that the basic context for interpreting the Primeval History is not a previous history of traditions, nor is it the context of a "prehistory" rooted in universal human experience; rather, the context is the literary framework of the final form of the Torah, into which older traditions have been incorporated for the sake of filling out and enrichment.

So much for hermeneutical review. One thing becomes clear especially if we read the scriptural tradition in its final, redacted form: it is necessary to look beyond the first chapters of Genesis, and indeed beyond the book of Genesis itself, to discover the literary and theological context in which the various parts function. In its received form, the Primeval History is part of a "history" or "story" which extends from Creation to Sinai – and beyond. Within this larger whole the book of Genesis is unified by a genealogical structure: five times the formula "these are the generations of" occurs in the Primeval History (2:4a; 5:1; 6:9 [cf. 5:32]; 10:1; 11:10); and five times in the Ancestral History (11:27; 25:12; 25:19; 36:1; 37:2). But even more significant is the fact that the entire history – Primeval History, Ancestral History, and Exodus-Sinai History – is "periodized" into a sequence of covenants, each of which is called a *běrîth ʿôlām*, a covenant in perpetuity.[9] This type of covenant, it should be noticed, stresses the unilateral initiative and sovereign grace of the covenant maker who "gives" or "establishes" the covenant, in comparison to the more bilateral covenant type in which the covenant initiator imposes conditions and sanctions on the other contracting party (Exod. 24:3–8).

According to the Priestly scheme, the first period extended from the creation to the end of the flood. The period was concluded with a *běrîth 'ôlām* between Elohim (God) and Noah, his family, and descendants (Genesis 9). This was a universal covenant in that it embraced all peoples (the offspring of Noah's sons) and an ecological covenant in that it included the animals and a solemn divine pledge regarding the constancy of "nature" (Gen. 8:21–22). The second period extended from Noah to Abraham with whom El Shaddai (God Almighty) made a *běrîth 'ôlām*, promising to "be God" to him and his descendants and granting the land as a "possession in perpetuity" (Genesis 17). The third period extended from Abraham to the sojourn at Sinai at which time and place God fulfilled his pledge to "be God" by giving his personal name and tabernacling cultically in the midst of the people. At this point the sabbath is regarded as the sign of the *běrîth 'ôlām* (Exod. 31:13, 16–17) between God and people. Thus the sabbath, which was "hidden in creation" (Gen. 2:2–3) and which became a cultic reality at Sinai, provides both a literary and theological *inclusio* that binds together the whole history with its system of covenants. As Frank Cross remarks: "While both the Noachic and Abrahamic covenants remained valid, each was provisional, a stage on the way to God's ultimate covenant and ultimate self-disclosure."[10] It is within this total literary and theological context that the Primeval History now functions to provide the cosmic and universal vista within which the human story, and particularly the story of Israel, unfolds.

From Creation to Chaos

Having established the interpretive context, we turn now to the *Urgeschichte* itself. This initial phase of the unfolding story has a dynamic of its own: a movement from creation toward chaos and finally to a new beginning, indeed, a kind of new creation. The story starts with the creation of the habitable earth out of chaos; it moves to a cosmic catastrophe in which the world was threatened with a return to pre-creation chaos; and it reaches a climax with the new beginning based on the Creator's sovereign covenant pledge which opens a future for human beings, animals and birds, and the whole earth. In this movement, the two crucial moments are the Priestly creation story and the Priestly edited version of the flood. Since these two passages, standing at the beginning and the climax, are decisive for understanding the story, let us consider each briefly.

In the carefully wrought and theologically reflective creation story (Gen. 1:1—2:3), several things claim our attention. First, in this account the opposite of creation is chaos, portrayed in terms of watery chaos and Stygian darkness. The creation drama begins when, at the command of the Creator, light bursts upon the chaotic scene like a cosmic nuclear flash. Order is created out of chaos, but chaos is not eliminated; it is only pushed back or given bounds as indicated by the placing of a firmament in the midst of the waters to separate the (lower) waters from the (upper) waters (Gen. 1:6–7). Chaos remains at the edge of creation, so to speak, as a threatening possibility. Psalm 104, which has many affinities with the Priestly creation account, portrays the contingency of creation in language that preserves more clearly the mythical view of the Creator pushing back or even subduing the powers of chaos, as in the psalmist's prayer in Ps. 104:5–9.

Second, the creation drama occurs in two movements, each of which concentrates on the *earth*, a motif introduced at the opening of v. 2 where "earth" stands in the emphatic position: "Now the earth was in a chaotic state...." In each three-day sequence (vv. 3–12 and 14–31) the movement is from heaven to earth, which increasingly becomes an orderly habitation. At the end of the first movement (third day), the narrative portrays the greening of the earth with vegetation: plants and trees according to their species (Hebrew: *mîn*). And at the conclusion of the second movement (sixth day), the narrative portrays the creation of animals "according to their species" and finally the supreme earth-creature, *'ādām*, to whom is given dominion over the earth. In view of the overall pattern of the account,[11] it is apparent that the emphasis falls not so much on anthropology, that is, the supremacy of humanity, as on ecology, that is, the earthly habitation which human beings share with other forms of "living being" (*nefesh ḥayyā*). To be sure, *'ādām* (human beings in the corporate sense) were made "in [as?] the image of God" and therefore were entitled and commissioned to have dominion over the earth as God's representatives;[12] but they share the earth and its resources with other land-creatures who, according to the dramatic sequence of the story, were created on the same climactic day. The earth-centered focus of the account is evident also in the way the cosmic regions are treated. There is no interest in the heavens (the number of heavens and God's celestial enthronement); and even the sun, moon, and stars are treated only in terms of their relation to the earthly sphere. These bodies are not living beings, as in other ancient religions, but only luminaries that function to regulate times and seasons.

Finally, an important feature of the creation story is the theme of fertility – procreation. In this connection, it is important to consider the place of the divine blessing. In the first movement of the story there is no mention of God's blessing. The greening of the earth occurs because God commands Earth to release her powers of fertility and "bring forth" (a maternal, childbearing verb, 1:12) vegetation of various species. In the second movement we find a major interruption in the formulaic pattern at the point of the appearance of "living being" (*nefesh ḥayyā*) or biological life. God commands the waters to "bring forth" (once again the maternal verb, 1:20) aquatic beings of various species and birds (apparently they were also to emerge from the waters; see LXX). To these creatures a special blessing is given. "Be fertile and multiply ..." (1:22). Strangely, this is not true in the case of the land animals. Once again the earth is commanded to "bring forth" (the maternal verb, 1:24) *nefesh ḥayyā* of various species: domestic animals, things that creep on the earth, and wild beasts; but no divine blessing is given them. Instead, the blessing is reserved for the supreme land-being, *'ādām*, and of this being it is said explicitly (for the first time in the account) that "they" consist of "male and female" (*zākār ûnĕqēbā*), an expression that is later emphasized in the Priestly recension of the flood story. To this earth-creature the Creator gives a blessing that exceeds the one given previously to fish and birds (Gen. 1:28).

How does this passage regarding God's conferral of the blessing relate to the previous passage concerning the creation of *'ādām* bisexually in [as] "the image of God"? Phyllis Trible is undoubtedly right in saying that the *imago Dei* in the aspect of sexuality does not pertain in a narrow sense to procreation: both sexes are equally created to image or represent God on earth and thus are to be co-responsible for maintaining the goodness of the earth.[13] However, it would be going too far, in my estimation, to say that the creation of *'ādām* as "male and female" is unrelated to procreation, either in the context of the creation account or in the larger context of the Primeval History. It is hardly accidental that the creation of human beings, sexually differentiated, is immediately followed by a special divine blessing. Apparently dominion over the earth means, at least in part, the human capacity to multiply and fill the earthly *oikos*, even as the fish multiply and fill their habitat (waters) and the birds theirs (sky). In some sense, dominion over the earth is connected with population growth and diffusion – a theme that is taken up later in the aftermath of the flood (see the "table of nations" in ch. 10; also the Babel story in 11:1–9).

In the Priestly narrative and Priestly genealogical structure which govern the Primeval History in its final form, creation and flood correspond. This is evident when one considers how the three features of the creation story that have been treated in the foregoing discussion are present in the flood story. Let me indicate the correspondences briefly. First, just as the habitable earth was created out of chaos, according to the creation story, so the flood is portrayed as a catastrophe that threatened to return the earth to watery chaos, the *tōhû wābōhû* of Gen. 1:2. Indeed, the flood, viewed in Priestly perspective, was a *cosmic* catastrophe, brought about when "the fountains of the great Deep [*tĕhôm rabbā*] burst forth, and the windows of the heavens were opened" (Gen. 7:11), allowing the "waters below" and the "waters above" (cf. 1:6–7) to come together. Second, the flood story portrays the renewal of the earth as a new creation out of watery chaos. Dramatically the narrative moves with crescendoing force toward a literary climax. The rising flood waters threaten the return of the earth to chaos. Yet there is a fragile ark tossing on the turbulent waters! Cassuto's commentary can hardly be surpassed.[14]

> We see water everywhere, as though the world had reverted to its primeval state at the dawn of Creation, when the waters of the deep submerged everything. Nothing remained of the teeming life that had burst forth upon the earth. Only a tiny point appears on the face of the terrible waters: the ark that preserves between its planks the seeds of life for the future. But it is a mere atom and is almost lost in the endless expanse of water that was spread over the face of the whole earth. A melancholy scene that is liable to fill the reader with despair. What will happen to this atom of life?

The turning point comes with the words: "However, God remembered Noah and all the wild and tame animals that were with him in the ark" (8:1). Then the narrative moves in decrescendo: God caused a wind to blow over the chaotic waters (8:2; compare the "wind of God" in 1:2); gradually the waters diminished until the dry land appeared again (8:5, 12–14; compare the gathering of the waters in 1:9–10); and the return of the dove to Noah with a freshly plucked olive twig was a tender sign of the greening of the earth once more (compare 1:11–12). The earth now becomes a permanent *oikos* for human and nonhuman creatures owing to God's pledge to maintain the constancy of the natural order (8:22). Finally, the ensuing divine address in chapter 9, which comes from Priestly tradition, highlights the divine blessing upon humankind. The blessing given to 'ādām at the time of creation is reiterated in the time of the new creation: "be fertile, multiply and fill the earth" (9:1 and 9:7).

The new creation, however, is not just a repetition of the first. There are profound differences which demand a different ordering of relations between the human and nonhuman creatures from that which prevailed in the time of creation. This is clearly evident in the passage in Gen. 9:2–6 which falls between the twofold reiteration of the divine blessing originally given at the creation (9:1 and 9:7). Animals who once lived in harmony with humans are now overcome with "fear and dread" of human dominion; and they are regarded as rivals and predators to be held responsible for the blood of 'ādām (9:2–5a). Furthermore, human beings, to whom the earth was given to manage as children inherit a parental estate, are now at such odds with one another that a strict, apodictic law, predicated on the *imago Dei*, has to be issued against murder (9:5b–6). Thus the movement from creation to flood and to a new beginning introduces a more tragic view of existence in comparison to the original state of creation. To appreciate this movement it is necessary to consider the theme which, in Priestly perspective, governs the interim between creation and flood; the disruption of the goodness and order of God's creation through violence.

Violence in God's Creation

In the preface to the flood story, which comes to us from the Priestly tradition, we hear the solemn announcement:

> Now, the earth was corrupt before God,
>> the earth was filled with violence.
> God saw how corrupt the earth was,
>> for all flesh had corrupted its way on the earth.
>
> Gen. 6:12

The theme of "violence" (*ḥāmās*) is picked up immediately in God's first address to Noah:

> The end of all flesh has come before me,
>> for through them the earth is filled with violence.
> I am about to destroy them and the earth.
>
> Gen. 6:13

161

In Priestly usage the expression "all flesh" may refer to all that is fleshy (including birds, fish, animals, humans), as in God's resolution "to exterminate all flesh under heaven that has the spirit of life" (6:17) or God's vow to "remember the everlasting covenant between God and every living being [*nefesh ḥayyā*] of all flesh that is upon the earth" (9:16). If this is the case in the passages quoted above (6:12 and 13), the text indicates a general corruption that permeates both the human and the nonhuman creation.

Here it is appropriate to consider a striking difference between our conception of "life" and that found in the Primeval History. We distinguish between inanimate things (stars, rocks, seas, etc.) and animate life (trees, flowers, birds, insects, etc.). In the Primeval History, however, the distinction is between those creatures that are *nefesh ḥayyā* (living being) and those that are not. Recall that in the creation story the vegetation that greens the earth (plants, trees) is not regarded as "living." Only during the second movement of the creation drama, on the fifth day, is *nefesh ḥayyā* created (fish, birds); and, as we have seen, this momentous development in the story is accompanied by a special divine blessing (1:20–23). Also the animals according to their various species are called *nefesh ḥayyā* (1:24). And, of course, it is self-evident that human beings fall in this category, even though this usage is superseded by the special status of "the image of God." Note: in the old Epic story of Paradise, which has been incorporated into the Priestly Work, *'ādām* is created as *nefesh ḥayyā* from the *'adāmā* or "soil" (Gen. 2:7), as are the birds and the animals (2:19).

Keeping this distinction in mind, the source of violence is not traceable to "nature" in a general sense. There is, as we well know, tremendous violence that breaks out in the natural realm: earthquakes, floods, disease, volcanic fire and brimstone, etc. Indeed, according to a modern view of nature, power to the extent of violence belongs essentially to the evolutionary process. This surly face of "nature" receives no attention at all in the Primeval History. The story of the deluge would seem to be an exception, especially if the biblical account is reminiscent of a natural calamity that attended the rampaging waters of the Tigris and Euphrates Rivers. But in the Primeval History, the flood story does not function to illustrate natural evil; rather, the story is told to show the severity of God's judgment upon "all flesh." The portrayal of a world on the verge of returning to pre-creation chaos is analogous to Jeremiah's poetic vision of the awesome wrath of Yahweh. "As if struck by a mighty nuclear bomb," so the annotator of the RSV text remarks, "the earth has been returned to its primeval state: waste and void" – the *tōhû wābōhû* of Gen. 1:2.[15]

> I looked upon the earth, and lo, *tōhû wābōhû*,
>   and unto the heavens, and their light was gone.
> I looked on the mountains, and lo, they were quaking,
>   and all the hills were trembling.
> I looked, and lo, there was no human being,
>   and all the birds of the sky had vanished.
> I looked, and lo, the orchard land was wilderness,
>   before Yahweh, before his burning wrath.
>
> Jer. 4:23–26

Moreover, while the animals were affected by the violence and corruption of the earth, there is no suggestion in the Primeval History that they were the source of the violence. It may be, as B. Jacob suggests, that the animals were denied the Creator's blessing (in contrast to the fish and birds) because they were potential threats to human beings on the land (earth);[16] but there is not the slightest hint anywhere in the narrative dealing with the period from creation to flood that their predatory instincts led them into conflict with human beings for living space or for survival. On the contrary, the picture presented in the creation story is that of a paradisaical peace in which human beings and animals live together in a peaceable kingdom. Those who have supposed that the *imago Dei* entitles human beings to exploit and destroy the animals overlook the fact that the *dominium terrae* is a call to responsibility. Made in the image of God, human beings are God's representatives, entitled to manage the Creator's earthly estate. The picture given in Psalm 8, which is somehow related to the Priestly creation story, is the same. The psalmist exclaims that humankind is elevated to a high rank, just a little less than God (or the angels), and hence is "crowned" to rule wisely and benevolently over the works of the Creator's hands. It is in this sense that "all things" are subjected to humankind. Notice that in the psalm, as in the Priestly creation story, the area of dominion is not explicitly all of "nature" but the nonhuman living creatures: the animals, birds, and fish (Ps. 8:5–8).

We come, then, to an uncomfortable point. In the Primeval History the "violence" that corrupted "all flesh" is traced to the Creator's noblest creatures. The Priestly Writer, who has given us the completed *Urgeschichte*, shows what violence means by including episodes from old Epic tradition (J), thereby "fleshing out" the Priestly historical and genealogical scheme that extends from

163

creation to flood. Violence is shown by the story of the Garden of Eden: a human couple who rebel against their Creator. Wishing to reach out for divine prerogatives of knowledge and eternal life, they disrupt their relationship with God and hence their relationship with each other and to the soil (*'adāmā*) to which they are intimately related and upon which they are dependent for existence. Violence is shown by the story of Cain who polluted the soil with the blood of the brother he murdered. Violence is shown by Lamech, the ancestor of those who originated the benefits of civilization (agriculture, music, metallurgy), whose lust for power prompted him to boast of measureless revenge. And violence is illustrated by that strange story in Gen. 6:1–4, which almost defies understanding, about the heavenly beings ("sons of God") who breached the Creator's distinction between heaven and earth and seized, and had sexual intercourse with, the beautiful human maidens that they fancied, and thus fathered abnormal offspring.

These episodes do not illustrate exhaustively the range of violence. The Priestly Writer has made use of an Epic tradition that undoubtedly was once fuller and has adapted it and worked it into his presentation, as can be seen from the blending of so-called P and J elements in the flood story itself. Enough illustrations are given, however, to indicate the character of violence. Notice, first of all, that violence (sin) is not essentially connected with sex, though it may become manifest in the relation between the sexes (Genesis 3) or even lead to illicit sexual union (Gen. 6:1–4). Second, the violence portrayed in the Primeval History is not directed against "nature" – that is, the natural environment or the animal world. The violence described occurs primarily in the human realm. Third, from the human realm violence spreads its corruption to the nonhuman sphere, so that it can be said of "all flesh" (human and nonhuman) that "through them the earth is filled with violence" (6:13). Notice that in the Epic tradition utilized by the Priestly Writer, God's curse on the soil (Gen. 3:17–19) is not intended as a direct curse on "nature." God's word of judgment to *'ādām* is: "cursed is the soil (*'adāmā*) on your account," because of what you have done. It is human actions that contaminate the soil. To be sure, the serpent, though demythologized into a natural creature (another "wild creature that Yahweh God had made," 3:1), still retains something of his mythical role as an uncanny, sinister power of chaos.[17]

In short, violence is a disease, as it were, that affects all those living in the same *oikos* (house). How is this widespread and deepseated corruption of the *earth* (notice again the ecological accent in Gen. 6:11) to be dealt with? In the perspective of Priestly tradition, which is dependent on old Epic tradition (see 6:5–7), the Creator resolved to tear down the house and start all over with a saved and saving remnant of humans and animals.

A New Creation

Translated into the terms of traditional theology, we are dealing here with the problem of power in a "fallen world" or, perhaps better, a marred creation. What is the source of the corruption? The narrator does not interrupt the flow of the narrative to raise this question or to reflect on the problem of evil (theodicy). We can only say that the creation story itself does not allow one to trace the source of the problem to the Creator. The marvelous order of creation, in which every creature, celestial and terrestrial, plays a role in a harmonious whole, receives the Cosmic Artist's imprimatur: "very good" (2:31). The supplementation of the story of Paradise Lost (Gen. 2:4b—3:24) to the creation story provided an opportunity for later generations to reflect on the serpent as the embodiment of the mysterious, uncanny powers of chaos, especially in apocalyptic contexts (e.g., Isa. 27:1; Revelation 12); but even this story did not allow a thoroughgoing dualism of co-eternal powers of good and evil. In the Primeval History the source of "violence" is traced to creaturely freedom. This freedom manifests itself as power: power to rebel against God ("You shall be as God, knowing good and evil," Gen. 3:4), power to crush a fellow human being under the illusion of impunity (4:8–10), power to exalt human revenge to a measureless degree (4:23–24). Notice that this creaturely power, as portrayed in the Primeval History, is ambivalent. It is not bad in itself. It leads to a new human independence, some would say even a new maturity (Genesis 3). It makes possible agriculture: the extraction of life-sustaining produce from the soil (4:1–16). It leads to the cultivation of esthetic sensitivities: music and the arts (4:21). It enables human beings to use natural resources, for instance, in forging instruments of bronze and iron (4:22). And, if we look beyond the flood story, it finds expression in technology of a sort: the revolutionary use of artificial stone (brick) for building a city (11:1–9). Yet for some strange reason, this power corrupts even the finest human achievements. In the preface to the flood, found in old Epic tradition (J), the problem is traced to a curious perversity in human nature (Gen. 6:5–6).

The Priestly Writer incorporates this older Epic view into his covenantal theology. Human beings, created to image or represent the rule of God in their exercise of dominion, have corrupted the earth with violence.

We have seen that the Primeval History moves from creation through ecological catastrophe into a new beginning. The nonhuman creation is involved in this movement too. Just as the animals are affected by the violence that corrupted "all flesh," so they are involved in the saving divine purpose expressed in God's favor toward Noah. With a fine touch the narrator describes the animals turning to Noah, as though led by their own impulse in the face of catastrophe.

> Two by two *they came to Noah* into the ark, male and female, just as God commanded Noah.
>
> Gen. 7:9

It is tempting to find in the story at this point an anticipation of Paul's testimony that the nonhuman creation (nature) is "groaning in travail" – sharing with human beings the bondage to decay and waiting with them for the promised deliverance (Rom. 8:19–23).

According to the Priestly account, the new creation is based on God's covenant with Noah, anticipated at the beginning of the flood story (6:18) and established at the end (9:8–17). Deserving of attention are several theological features of this ecological covenant that embraces all human beings, animals and birds, and the whole natural order. First, the Noachic covenant is a guarantee of the constancy of the natural order, upon which all *nefesh ḥayyā* are dependent. The Priestly Writer appropriately includes and emphasizes the motif of God's resolution found in the old Epic tradition (J): Gen. 8:21–22.

In the Priestly elaboration of this motif in Genesis 9, the constancy and regularity of nature are guaranteed by the Creator's "everlasting covenant," the sign of which is a natural phenomenon: the rainbow that appears after a storm. No human violence can be great enough to upset indefinitely the order and balance of "nature."

Second, the new creation involves the repopulation of the earth. We have seen that the motif of fertility and dispersion through the earth is dominant in the creation story, where it is emphasized by a special divine blessing. The purpose of Noah's taking the animals and birds into the ark in pairs, male and female (*zākār ûněqēbā*: 7:9), is to preserve the seed of *nefesh ḥayyā*. God's command to Noah, according to Priestly formulation, is emphatic (Gen. 6:19–20).

And clearly this is the purpose of the preservation of Noah and his wife, his sons and their wives. It is appropriate, then, that the new creation is inaugurated by a repetition of the divine blessing given to 'ādām, "male and female," at the time of the original creation: "Be fertile, multiply, and fill the earth" (9:1, 7). The remainder of the Primeval History (the table of the nations in Genesis 10 and the story of the Tower of Babel) deals with this theme. In a time of catastrophe, when the earth is on the verge of chaos, God preserves a remnant with which to make a new beginning.

Finally, the new creation opens up a new horizon: the future. It should be emphasized that this horizon is not the result of any change in the human condition. The old Epic tradition had affirmed that God's resolve never again to curse the soil or to destroy everything that lives was made despite the tendency of human thinking (8:21–22), the very tendency which had precipitated God's ominous judgment in the first place (6:5–8). The Priestly Writer restates this theme in terms of God's *bĕrîth 'ôlām*. As mentioned previously, this type of covenant (unlike the more reciprocal Mosaic covenant) is unilateral in character, resting solely on God's commitment, not on the human fulfillment of conditions. The verbs used are verbs of theocentric initiative: God "establishes" (6:18; 9:9, 11, 12, etc.) the covenant with Noah and his posterity, and with every *nefesh ḥayyā* with him. The future is open because of God's grace, not because of fragile, weak, creaturely "living being." Just as God "remembered" Noah and the remnant with him in the ark (8:1), so God will "remember" the covenant in perpetuity (*bĕrîth 'ôlām*) with "all flesh."

> Whenever the rainbow is in the clouds and I see it,
> I will remember the everlasting covenant between God
> and every living being of all flesh that is on the earth.
>
> Gen. 9:16

In the first and last analysis, the hope for the human and nonhuman creation is grounded in the *sola gratia* of God's universal, ecological covenant.

Human Responsibility within the Noachic Covenant

In conclusion it should be noticed once again that the new creation, according to the Priestly account, bears the marks of tragedy. This is evident, first of all, in the broken relation between human beings and animals. For the first time we hear that "fear and dread" falls upon the animals as though 'ādām were regarded as a predator who wages war against the animal kingdom, including wild animals, birds of the sky, everything that creeps on the soil, and the fish of the sea (9:2). A new word is spoken, which contrasts with the provision made for humans and animals at the time of creation (1:29–30): "Into your power they are given" (9:2, end of verse). However, human beings are reminded that their power is not absolute. These creatures may be killed for food, but not wantonly; indeed, there must be reverence for life as evidenced by the prohibition against eating flesh with blood, the vital element (9:4). Moreover, in the new era the broken relation between human beings persists as evident in the exercise of human power that results in the taking of another human life. With great force it is announced that human life is sacred to God: therefore both animals and human beings will be held accountable for the life of a human being. Precisely in this context, where the limitations on power are announced, the motif of the *imago Dei* is repeated in order to emphasize the God-given status and role of *'ādām* in the creation:

> Whoever sheds the blood of a human being,
>   by a human being his blood will be shed,
> for in the image of God God made humankind.
>
> Gen. 9:6

Even though the new creation has a tragic dimension, owing to the continuing problem of power, human beings do not cease to be who they are: creatures made in God's image who are called to represent God's rule on earth. And this "imaging" of God is to be manifest not only in reverence for human life, protected by apodictic law against murder, but in proper reverence for the nonhuman creation. It may well be, as Klaus Koch has suggested, that the ritual law concerning slaughter of animals, which also belongs essentially to the universal Noachic covenant, should not be disregarded without finding some way to express our reverence toward this part of God's creation. For animals too are *nefesh ḥayyā*, and "every *nefesh* has its direct connection to God and its own value which does not depend on human will or pleasure."[18]

As indicated at the beginning of this essay, many aspects of the ecological crisis are not specifically addressed in the biblical Primeval History. Indeed, many Americans, who believe that all problems are capable of solution ("After all, we are Americans," to quote a recent Inaugural), will be distressed by this part of Scripture which shows that the problem of power persists, not only in the time after the original creation but in the time after the new creation. (The story of the Tower of Babel comes shortly after the flood in the sequence of the Primeval History!) The biblical account, however, does not encourage a fatalistic view of history. To be sure, it portrays a world in which God is sovereign, a world in which people cannot escape divine judgment in consequence of their acts of violence. Yet human beings are called to responsibility: to exercise dominion within the rule of God. As we have seen, inherent in the image of God is the role of being God's representative on earth. Human beings, regardless of their ethnic identity or religious community, are called to an ecological task; to be faithful managers of God's estate, or as stated in Gen. 2:15, to till and keep God's garden. The dimension of chaos has not been erased from God's creation; indeed, human beings in their freedom can act to unleash the powers of chaos. Human responsibility, however, is grounded in God's covenant which is universal and ecological. Its sign is the rainbow after a storm: a phenomenon of the natural order known to all human beings.

Traditionally, hope for the human and nonhuman creation has been grounded in the so-called *protoevangelium* of Gen. 3:15 which allegedly anticipates the ultimate messianic victory over the evil that mars God's creation. This is a precarious textual foundation on which to base hope, and few there are today who would build on it. Since, however, the opening chapters of Genesis are to be interpreted in the literary context that embraces a movement from creation to flood and to the new beginning that lies beyond, hope is grounded more securely in the Noachic covenant which the Creator has established, not only with Noah and his descendants, but with *the earth*.

> Then God said [to Noah]:
> This is the sign of the covenant that I am making between me and you [pl.],
> as well as every living being that is with you, for endless generations.
> My bow I have set in the clouds, and it shall be a covenant sign between me and the earth.
>
> Gen. 9:12–13

This Noachic covenant opens up the horizon of the future by predicating the hope of the human and nonhuman creation on the unconditional commitment of the Creator to humankind, to nonhuman creatures, and to the order and regularity of "nature."[19]

NOTES

1   A version of this paper was presented to the 1981 annual meeting of the American Theological Society.

2   The controversy over this "man/nature dualism" thesis was stirred up by Lynn White, Jr., in his famous essay, "The Historical Roots of our Ecological Crisis," reprinted in *The Environmental Handbook* (ed. G. De Bell; New York: Ballantine Books, 1970) 12–26. See my response, "Human Dominion over Nature," in *Biblical Studies in Contemporary Thought* (ed. Miriam Ward; Somerville, Mass.: Greeno, Hadden & Co., 1975) 27–45.

3   See the essays in the January 1979 issue of the World Council of Churches journal *Anticipation* entitled "Burning Issues," especially those by Klaus Koch on "The Old Testament View of Nature" and by Gerhard Liedke, "Solidarity in Conflict." These essays were prepared for the WCC "Conference on Faith, Science, and the Future" held at the Massachusetts Institute of Technology, Cambridge, Massachusetts, July 1979.

4   Quoted by Roger Shinn in a paper presented to the American Theological Society (1980) 28.

5   See David C. Steinmetz in "The Superiority of Pre-Critical Exegesis," *TT* 37/1 (1980) 37, who in turn refers to E. D. Hirsch, Jr., *Validity in Interpretation* (New Haven, Conn.: Yale Univ. Press, 1967) 1.

6   See von Rad's now classic essay of 1938, "The Form-Critical Problem of the Hexateuch," in *The Problem of the Hexateuch and Other Essays* (New York: McGraw-Hill; London: Oliver & Boyd, 1965) 1–78; also the preface to his commentary, *Genesis* (OTL; Philadelphia: Westminster Press, rev. ed., 1972).

7   See the introduction to Claus Westermann's *Creation* (ET, J. J. Scullion; Philadelphia: Fortress Press; London: SPCK, 1974) 1–15 [ch. 5 of this volume]. His view is set forth fully in the treatment of the primeval history in his *Genesis 1–11* (BKAT I/1; Neukirchen-Vluyn: Neukirchener, 1976).

8   Gerhard Liedke, *Im Bauch des Fisches: Oekologische Theologie* (Stuttgart: Kreuz, 1979).

9   On the genealogical structure and the periodization of history, see Frank M. Cross, "The Priestly Work," *Canaanite Myth and Hebrew Epic* (Cambridge: Harvard Univ. Press, 1973) 293–325; also my essay, "From Analysis to Synthesis: The Interpretation of Gen. 1—11," *JBL* 97/1 (1978) 23–39.

10 Cross, "The Priestly Work," 297.

11 This pattern is worked out in detail in my essay, "A Stylistic Study of the Priestly Creation Story," in *Canon and Authority* (ed. G. W. Coats and B. O. Long; Philadelphia: Fortress Press, 1977) 148–62.

12 For a discussion of the functional or representative significance of *imago Dei* (a title also applied to kings in Near Eastern texts), see my essay on "Human Dominion," esp. 40–43; also von Rad, *Genesis*, at Gen. 1:26–27.

13 I refer to Phyllis Trible's unpublished paper presented to the William Rainey Harper Conference on Biblical Studies (University of Chicago, October 1979). See also her illuminating discussion in *God and the Rhetoric of Sexuality* (OBT 2;

Philadelphia: Fortress Press, 1978) 1–30. For an opposing view, see Phyllis Bird, "Male and Female He Created Them: Gen. 1:17b in the Context of the P Account of Creation," *HTR* 74 (1981) 129–59.

14 Umberto Cassuto, *Commentary on Genesis* (Jerusalem: Magnes Press, 1964) II: 97.

15 See *The New Oxford Annotated Bible* (1973) on Jer. 4:23ff.

16 Benno Jacob, *Das Erste Buch der Torah* (Berlin: Shocken, 1934) on Gen. 1:24–25.

17 For further discussion of the symbolic significance of the serpent, see my *Creation versus Chaos* (New York: Association Press, 1967), ch. 5, esp. 155–59; also "Sin and the Powers of Chaos" in *Sin, Salvation, and the Spirit* (ed. D. Durken; Collegeville, Minn.: Liturgical Press, 1979) 71–84.

18 Koch, "The Old Testament View of Nature," 50.

19 In this essay I have put the word "nature" in quotation marks in recognition of the fact that the OT has no word for our term which is laden with a philosophical history of its own.

Bibliography

Albertz, Reiner, *Weltschöpfung und Menschenschöpfung*. Calwer Theologische Monographien 3. Stuttgart: Calwer, 1974.

Anderson, Bernhard W. s.v. "Creation." *IDB.* (Revised edition forthcoming. In *The Cry of the Environment and the Rebuilding of Christian Creation Tradition*, ed. P. Joranson and K. Butigan. Bear & Co., 1984.)

—"Creation and the Noachic Covenant," ibid.

—"Creation and Ecology." *AJTP* 1 (1983) 14–30. Included in this volume as ch. 9.

—*Creation versus Chaos: The Reinterpretation of Mythical Symbolism in the Bible*. New York: Association Press, 1967.

—"The Earth is the Lord's." In *Is God a Creationist?* ed. Roland Frye, 176–96 [= Revised edition of *Int* 9 (1955) 3–20].

—"From Analysis to Synthesis: The Interpretation of Genesis 1—11." *JBL* 97/1 (1978) 23–39.

—"Human Dominion over Nature." In *Biblical Studies in Contemporary Thought*, ed. Miriam Ward, 27–45. Somerville, Mass.: Greeno, Hadden Co., 1975.

—"'The Lord has Created Something New.' A Stylistic Study of Jer. 31:15–20." *CBQ* 40 (1978) 463–78.

—"Myth and the Biblical Tradition." *TT* 27 (1970) 44–62.

—"A Stylistic Study of the Priestly Creation Story." In *Canon and Authority*, ed. G. W. Coats and B. O. Long, 148–62. Philadelphia: Fortress Press, 1977.

—"The Wonder of God's Creation." In *Out of the Depths: The Psalms Speak for Us Today*. Philadelphia: Westminster Press, 1983.

Barr, James. "Man and Nature – The Ecological Controversy and the Old Testament." *BJRL* 55 (1972) 9–32.

—"The Meaning of 'Mythology' in Relation to the Old Testament." *VT* 9 (1959) 1–10.

Barth, Karl. "The Doctrine of Creation." In *Church Dogmatics* III: 1–4. Edinburgh: T. & T. Clark, 1958.

Berry, Richard W. "The Beginning." *TT* 39 (1982) 249–59 [= *Is God a Creationist?* ed. Roland Frye, 43–55].

Bird, Phyllis. "Male and Female He Created Them: Gen. 1:27b in the Context of the P Account of Creation." *HTR* 74 (1981) 129–59.

Boman, Thorlief. "The Biblical Doctrine of Creation," *CQR* 165 (1964) 140–51.

Brandon, G. F. *Creation Legends of the Ancient Near East.* London: Hodder & Stoughton, 1963.

Brueggemann, Walter. *Genesis.* Interpretation. Atlanta: John Knox Press, 1982.

Bultmann, Rudolf. "Faith in God the Creator." *In Existence and Faith: Shorter Writings of Rudolf Bultmann,* ed. Schubert M. Ogden, 171–82. New York: World Pub. Co., Meridian Books, 1960. See also "The New Testament and Mythology." In *Kerygma and Myth,* ed. H. W. Bartsch, 1–44. New York: Harper & Row, Torchbooks, 1961; London: SPCK, 1953.

Childs, Brevard. *Myth and Reality in the Old Testament.* SBT. London: SCM Press, 1960.

Clifford, Richard J. "Creation in the Old Testament." Address at the annual meeting of the Catholic Biblical Association of America, St. Paul, Minn., 1983.

Crenshaw, James L. "Prolegomenon." In *Studies in Ancient Israelite Wisdom,* 1–60. New York: KTAV, 1974.

Cross, Frank M. *Canaanite Myth and Hebrew Epic,* esp. "Yahweh and El," 44–75; "The Song of the Sea and Canaanite Myth," 112–44. Cambridge: Harvard Univ. Press, 1973.

—"The Divine Warrior in Israel's Early Cult." In *Biblical Motifs,* ed. Alexander Altmann, 11–30. Cambridge: Harvard Univ. Press, 1966 [= *Canaanite Myth and Hebrew Epic,* 91–111].

—"Yahweh and the God of the Patriarchs." *HTR* 55 (1962) 225–59.

Curtiss, A. H. W. "The Subjugation of the Waters Motif in the Psalms: Imagery or Polemic?" *JSS* 23 (1976) 245–56.

Eichrodt, Walther. "Cosmology and Creation." In *Theology of the Old Testament* I: 93–117; see also II: 50–55. ET, J. A. Baker. OTL. Philadelphia: Westminster Press, 1961.

—"In the Beginning: A Contribution to the Interpretation of the First Word of the Bible." In *Israel's Prophetic Heritage: Essays in Honor of James Muilenburg,* ed. Bernhard W. Anderson and Walter Harrelson, 1–10. New York: Harper & Row 1962. Included in this volume as ch. 3.

Eissfeldt, Otto. "Das Chaos in der biblischen und in der phönizischen Kosmogonie." *Forschungen und Fortschritte* 16 (1940) 1–3 [= *Kleine Schriften* II: 258–62. Tübingen: Mohr/Siebeck, 1963].

—"Gott und das Meer in der Bibel." In *Studia Orientalia Ioanni Pedersen,* 76–84. Copenhagen: Munksgaard, 1953 [= *Kleine Schriften* III: 256–64. Tübingen: Mohr/Siebeck, 1966].

Eliade, Mircea. *Cosmos and History: The Myth of the Eternal Return.* ET, Willard Trask. New York: Harper & Row, Torchbooks, 1954.

—*Die Schöpfungsmythen: Aegypter, Sumerer, Hurriter, Hethiter, Kanaaniter und Israeliten. Quellen des alten Orients I*, Preface. La naissance du monde. Sources orientales I. Paris: Edition du Seuil, 1959.

Fisher, Loren R. "Creation at Ugarit and in the Old Testament." *VT* 15 (1965) 313–24.

—"From Chaos to Cosmos." *Encounter* 26 (1965) 183–97.

Foerster, Werner. "Ktizo." *TDNT* 3 (1965) 1000–35.

Frankfort, H. and H. A., John A. Wilson, and Thorkild Jacobsen. *The Intellectual Adventure of Ancient Man: An Essay on Speculative Thought in the Ancient Near East*. Chicago: Univ. of Chicago Press, 1946, 1977 [= *Before Philosophy*. Baltimore/Harmondsworth: Penguin Books, 1949].

Froehlich, Karlfried, "The Ecology of Creation." *TT* (1971) 263–76.

Frye, Roland, ed. *Is God a Creationist? The Religious Case Against Creation-Science*. New York: Charles Scribner's Sons, 1983.

Gaster, T. H. S. "Cosmogony." *IDB*.

Gilkey, Langdon. "Creationism: The Roots of the Conflict." *C&C* 42 (1982) 108–15 [= *Is God a Creationist?* ed. Roland Frye, 56–67].

—*Maker of Heaven and Earth*. New York: Doubleday & Co., 1959.

Gunkel, Hermann. *Schöpfung und Chaos in Urzeit und Endzeit: Eine religionsgeschichtliche Untersuchung über Gen 2 und Ap Joh 12*. Göttingen: Vandenhoeck & Ruprecht, 1895. Included, in part, in this volume as ch. 1.

Habel, Norman. "Yahweh, Maker of Heaven and Earth." *JBL* 91 (1972) 321–37.

Harner, P. B. "Creation Faith in Deutero-Isaiah." *VT* 17 (1967) 298–306.

Harrelson, Walter. "The Significance of Cosmology in the Ancient Near East." In *Translating and Understanding the Old Testament: Essays in Honor of Herbert Gordon May*, ed. H. T. Frank and W. L. Reed, 237–52. Nashville: Abingdon Press, 1970.

Heidel, Alexander. *The Babylonian Genesis*. Chicago: Univ. of Chicago Press, 1963.

Hendry, George S. "The Eclipse of Creation." *TT* 28 (1972) 406–25.

—*Theology of Nature*. Philadelphia: Westminster Press, 1980.

Hermisson, Hans-Jürgen, "Observations on the Creation Theology in Wisdom." In *Israelite Wisdom: Theological and Literary Essays in Honor of Samuel Terrien*, ed. J. G. Gammie, W. A. Brueggemann, W. L. Humphreys, J. M. Ward, 43–57. Missoula, Mont.: Scholars Press, 1978. Included in this volume as ch. 7.

Horowitz, Mary Anne Cline. "The Image of God in Man: Is Woman Included?" *HTR* 72 (1979) 175–206.

Houston, James M. *I Believe in the Creator*. Rev. ed. Grand Rapids: Wm. B. Eerdmans, 1983.

Humbert, Paul. "La relation de Genèse 1 et du Psaume 104 avec la liturgie du Novel-An israélite." In *Opuscules d'un hebraïsant, 60–83*. Neuchâtel: Université de Neuchâtel, 1958.

Hyatt, J. P. "Was Yahweh Originally a Creator Deity?" *JBL* 86 (1967) 369–77.

Jacob, Edmund. *"God the Creator of the World."* In *Theology of the Old Testament*, 136–50. ET, A. W. Heathcote and P. J. Allcock. New York: Harper & Row 1958. See the bibliography, 149–50.

Jacobsen, Thorkild. "The Battle Between Marduk and Tiamat." *JAOS* 88 (1968) 104–8.

—"Mesopotamia." In *The Intellectual Adventure*, H. Frankfort et al., chs. 5–7 [= *Before Philosophy*, 137–234].

James, E. O. *Creation and Cosmology: A Historical and Comparative Inquiry*. Leiden: E. J. Brill, 1969.

Kaiser, Otto. *Die mythische Bedeutung des Meeres in Aegypten, Ugarit und Israel*. BZAW 78. Berlin: Walter De Gruyter, 1959.

Kapelrud, Arvid. "The Relationship between El and Baal in the Ras Shamra Texts." In *The Bible World: Essays in Honor of Cyrus H. Gordon*, ed. G. Rendsburg et al., 79–85. New York: KTAV, 1981.

Knight, Douglas. "Cosmogony and Order in the Hebrew Tradition." Forthcoming publication.

Koch, Klaus. "The Old Testament View of Nature." *Anticipation* (January 1979) 50.

—"Wort und Einheit des Schöpfergottes in Memphis und Jerusalem." *ZTK* 62 (1965) 251–93.

Landes, George M. "Creation and Liberation." *USQR* (1978) 78–99. Included in this volume as ch. 8.

—"Creation Tradition in Proverbs 8:22–32 and Genesis 1." In *A Light Unto My Path: Old Testament Studies in Honor of Jacob M. Myers*, ed. Howard N. Bream et al, 279–94. Gettysburg Theological Studies 4. Philadelphia: Temple Univ. Press, 1974.

Lane, W. R. "The Initiation of Creation." *VT* 13 (1963) 63–73.

Liedke, Gerhard. *Im Bauch des Fisches: Oekologische Theologie*. Stuttgart: Kreuz, 1979.

—"Solidarity in Conflict." In *Faith and Science in an Unjust World I*, ed. R. L. Shinn, 73–80. Report of the World Council of Churches' Conference on "Faith, Science, and the Future." Philadelphia: Fortress Press, 1980.

Lindeskog, G. "The Theology of Creation in the Old and New Testaments." In *The Root of the Vine: Festschrift for Anton Fridrichsen*, 1–22. London: Dacre Press, 1953.

Loretz, O. *Schöpfung und Mythos: Mensch und Welt nach den anfangskapiteln der Genesis*. Stuttgarter Bibel Studien 32. Stuttgart: Katholisches Bibelwerk, 1968.

Ludwig, Theodore M. "The Traditions of the Establishing of the Earth in Deutero-Isaiah." *JBL* 92 (1973) 345–57.

Luyster, Robert. "Wind and Water: Cosmogenic Symbolism in the Old Testament." *ZAW* 93 (1981) 1–10.

May, H. G. "Some Cosmic Connotations of *Mayim Rabbîm*, 'Many Waters'." *JBL* 74 (1945) 9–21.

McCarthy, Dennis J. "Creation Motifs in Ancient Hebrew Poetry." *CBQ* 29 (1967) 393–406. Revised and included in this volume as ch. 4.

McCurley, Foster. *Ancient Myths and Biblical Faith: Scriptural Transformations.* Philadelphia: Fortress Press, 1983.

Miller, J. Maxwell. "In the 'Image' and 'Likeness' of God." *JBL* 91 (1972) 289–304.

Miller, Patrick D., Jr. *The Divine Warrior in Early Israel.* Cambridge: Harvard Univ. Press, 1973.

—"El, the Creator of Earth." *BASOR* 239 (1980) 43–46.

Mowinckel, Sigmund. *The Psalms in Israel's Worship.* 2 vols. ET, D. R. Ap-Thomas. Nashville: Abingdon Press; Oxford: Basil Blackwell, 1962.

Napier, B. Davie. "On Creation-Faith in the Old Testament." *Int* 10 (1956) 21–42.

Oakley, Francis, and Daniel O'Connor. *Creation: The Impact of an Idea.* New York: Charles Scribner's Sons, 1969.

Oden, Robert, "*Ba'al Sāmēm* and *'El.*" *CBQ* 39 (1977) 457–73.

Olson, Edwin A. "Hidden Agenda Behind the Evolutionist/Creationist Debate." *Christianity Today* 26 (April 1982) 26–30 [= *Is God a Creationist?* ed. Roland Frye, 31–42].

Otzen, Benedict, Hans Gottlieb, and Knud Jeppesen. *Myths in the Old Testament.* ET, F. Cryer. London: SCM Press, 1980.

Pettazzoni, Raffaele. *Myths of the Beginning and Creation Myths* (Mythes des origines et mythes de la création). *Proceedings of the Seventh Congress for the History of Religions,* 67–78. Amsterdam, 1951.

Rad, Gerhard von. *Genesis.* ET, J. H. Marks. OTL. Rev. ed. Philadelphia: Westminster Press; London: SCM Press, 1972.

—*Old Testament Theology* I: 136–53. ET, D. M. G. Stalker. New York: Harper & Row; Edinburgh: Oliver & Boyd, 1962.

—"The Theological Problem of the Old Testament Doctrine of Creation." In *The Problem of the Hexateuch and Other Essays,* 131–43. ET, E. W. T. Dicken. New York: McGraw-Hill; Edinburgh: Oliver & Boyd, 1966. Included in this volume as ch. 2.

—*Wisdom in Israel,* 287–319. ET, J. D. Martin. Nashville: Abingdon Press; London: SCM Press, 1972.

Rendtorff, Rolf. "Die theologische Stellung des Schöpfungsglaubens bei

Deuterojesaja" *ZTK* 51 (1954) 3–13. [= *Gesammelte Studien zum AT*, 209–19 (TBü 57; Munich: Chr. Kaiser, 1975)].

Reumann, John. *Creation and New Creation*. Minneapolis: Augsburg Pub. House, 1973.

Reymond, P. *L'eau, sa vie et sa signification dans l'Ancien Testament*. VTSup 6. Leiden: E. J. Brill, 1958.

Richardson, Alan. "The Parables of Genesis." In *Genesis I–XI*, 27–40. Torch Commentary. London: SCM Press, 1953.

Ricoeur, Paul. *The Symbolism of Evil*. Boston: Beacon Press, 1969.

Sarna, Nahum. *Understanding Genesis*, esp. 1–23. New York: Schocken Books, 1970 [= *Is God a Creationist?* ed. Roland Frye, 155–75].

Schmid, H. H. "Schöpfung, Gerechtigkeit und Heil." *ZTK* 70 (1973) 1–19. Included in this volume as ch. 6.

Schmidt, Werner H. *Die Schöpfungsgeschichte der Priesterschrift*. WMANT 17. Neukirchen-Vluyn: Neukirchener, 1974³.

Schoonenberg, P. *Covenant and Creation*. London: Sheed & Ward, 1968.

Soggin, J. A. "God the Creator in the First Chapter of Genesis." In *Old Testament and Oriental Studies*, 120–29. BibOr 29. Rome: Biblical Institute Press, 1975.

Steck, O. H. *Der Schöpfungsbericht der Priesterschrift*. FRLANT 115. Göttingen: Vandenhoeck & Ruprecht, 1975.

Stuhlmueller, Carroll. *Creative Redemption in Deutero-Isaiah*. Analecta Biblica 4. Rome: Biblical Institute Press, 1970.

—"'First and Last' and 'Yahweh-Creator' in Deutero-Isaiah." *CBQ* 29 (1967) 495–511.

—"The Theology of Creation in Second Isaiah." *CBQ* 21 (1959) 429–67.

—"Yahweh King and Deutero-Isaiah." *BR* 15 (1970) 32–45.

Terrien, Samuel. "Creation, Cultus, and Faith in the Psalter." In *Horizons of Theological Education: Essays in Honor of Charles L. Taylor* [= *Theological Education* 2/4 (1966) 116–28].

Trible, Phyllis. *God and the Rhetoric of Sexuality*, esp. "The Topical Clue," 12–23; "A Love Story Gone Awry," 72–143. OBT 2. Philadelphia: Fortress Press, 1978.

Vawter, Bruce. "Creative Misuse of the Bible." In *Is God a Creationist?* ed. Roland Frye, 71–82.

—"Prov. 8:22: Wisdom and Creation." *JBL* 99 (1980) 206–16.

Wakeman, Mary K. "The Biblical Earth Monster in the Cosmogonic Combat Myth." *JBL* 88 (1969) 313–20.

Waltke, Bruce. "The Creation Account in Genesis 1:1–3." *Bibliotheca Sacra* 132/525, 526, 527, 528 (1975) 25–36, 136–44, 216–28, 327–42, and ibid. 133/529 (1976) 28–41.

Westermann, Claus. *Beginning and End in the Bible*. ET, K. Crim. Facet Books. Philadelphia: Fortress Press, 1972.

—*Creation*. ET, J. J. Scullion. Philadelphia: Fortress Press; London: SPCK, 1974. Included, in part, in this volume as ch. 5.

—*The Genesis Accounts of Creation*. ET, N. E. Wagner. Facet Books. Philadelphia: Fortress Press, 1964.

—*Genesis I*. Biblischer Kommentar. Neukirchen-Vluyn: Neukirchener, 1976. ET of Genesis 1—11 forthcoming, London: SPCK, 1984.

—"God and His Creation." *USQR* (1963) 197–209.

Wensinck, A. J. *The Ocean in the Literature of the Western Semites*. Amsterdam: Müller, 1918.

White, Lynn, Jr. "The Historical Roots of Our Ecologic Crisis." *Science* 155 (March 10, 1967) 1203–7, and ibid. 156 (May 12, 1967) 737–38. [= *The Environmental Handbook*, ed. G. de Bell, 12–26. New York: Ballantine, 1970].

Young, Norman. *Creator, Creation, and Faith*. Philadelphia: Westminster Press, 1976.

Zimmerli, Walther. "Ort und Grenze der Weisheit im Rahmen der alttestamentlichen Theologie." In *Gottes Offenbarung: Gesammelte Aufsätze zum Alten Testament*, 300–15. TBü 19. Munich: Chr. Kaiser, 1963.

—"The World as God's Creation." In *The Old Testament and the World*, 14–26. ET, J. J. Scullion. Atlanta: John Knox Press; London: SPCK, 1976.